SANCTI STONES
PARISH MEMORIALS
OF
WIVELISCOMBE, SOMERSET

'The first notice we find of the church is a confirmation of the
ownership of the church and town of Wiveliscombe ...
and all things belonging thereunto, as possessions of the Church of Bath,
by Pope Alexander III, on March 4, 1179.'

Wifela's Combe : A History of the Parish of Wiveliscombe
F. Hancock, MA, SCL, FSA (The Wessex Press, 1911)

for
Mother and Dad

SANCTI STONES
PARISH MEMORIALS
OF
WIVELISCOMBE, SOMERSET

A Millennium Survey of Surviving Inscriptions
in the Churches and Churchyards of
Wiveliscombe, Somerset

Susan Maria Farrington

Illustrations
Diana Farrington

Published by
Colden Publications
P O Box 22
Wiveliscombe
Somerset
TA4 2ZH

ISBN 0-9540992-0-6

Printed by
Antony Rowe Limited
Chippenham, Wiltshire

CONTENTS

Acknowledgements

When Dixon Luxton, Churchwarden of St. Andrew's, first suggested a survey of the Wiveliscombe churchyard, I was overwhelmed. My experience was in recording cemeteries in the Indian Sub-Continent, and at the time I was working on a publication about British graves in pre-Independence Bangladesh. As a family we moved to the town in 1960, so we are but newcomers. However, with the help, advice and input of many long-standing local residents, if unnamed none the less appreciated, I hope that between us the shortcomings have been kept to the minimum. Any errors in the many dates are much regretted but, in the nature of such an undertaking, are unavoidable.

I am grateful to Michael Austin, David Bond, Jonathan Bright, David Bromwich, Michael Burge, Richard Cornish, Mary Crabtree, Bob Dalgleish, Lt Col David Elliott, Hugh Flatt, Charles and John Farrington, William Hancock, Paul Hopkins, Dick Moody, Julia Robb, Graham Sacker, Eric Smith, Valdis Valuks, Captain James Wilson, RM, Colin Winchester and Wesley Wyatt. Also my thanks to the Archivists of the Old Cliftonian Society, Haileybury and Imperial Service College, and the Royal Engineers Museum, together with the staff at the Somerset Record Office and Somerset Studies Library. Mrs. Nesta Shopland, David Bailey and Anthony James' in-depth and professional knowledge of the churchyard has been invaluable. Two pupils from Wiveliscombe Community School, Michael Whitman and Harry Smith, assisted in the survey - the "grubbing in churchyardes" - to quote the English antiquarian John Aubrey 1626-1697 – in addition to Frances Dransfield and Susan and Robin Harward. The latter three alone know how much time they have contributed to this project: it is not inconsiderable and without their efforts and encouragement, this publication would never have been completed. Robin also prepared the heraldic blazoning of the arms in the Church. I owe much appreciation to my sister-in-law Diana Farrington for her enchanting drawings and artistic input. A special thanks, too, to Roger Perkins for his informed guidance, in particular the researching of the War Memorials.

Finally, I am especially grateful for the direction and support of Dixon Luxton, who has cheerfully answered my endless queries, and contributed much of his local knowledge to the work.

July 2001   *Susan Farrington*

Preface

The original concept for this publication was to carry out a survey of the churchyard surrounding St. Andrew's Church, Wiveliscombe at the time of the transition into the third Millennium. Such a site is constantly changing, not only with the installation of headstones and memorials following interments, but also with the natural evolution of the plants and trees. Although there has been a church here since at least the 12th Century, the churchyard as seen today dates from the first quarter of the 19th Century. This survey, therefore, runs from the 1820s to 31st December 2000 (although inscriptions have been included in the New Year up to the time of going to print). Detailed mapping is important in order to fix accurately the position of individual graves, but the preparation of these lists has also identified further avenues of study; these have not been pursued fully here as they are outside the original remit.

As well as being a place of remembrance and respect, the churchyard provides a unique record of the community, and is an excellent source of genealogical information. It is evident from an examination of the alphabetical *Index of Inscriptions [page 199]* how headstones and tablets may be the starting point for family research. From this beginning, it is possible to examine the old Burial Registers in the Somerset Record Office; indeed the Wiveliscombe registers are extant from 1558 (with the exception of the years 1687-1695). Research can then be continued at the Family Records Centre in London, the Public Record Office at Kew and appropriate sites on the Internet – but all perhaps based upon a small detail gleaned from a headstone.

With this wider perspective in mind, the survey has been extended to include the tablets in the church and the names of those buried in the catacombs below, as they complement the inscriptions in the churchyard. In addition, all other known memorials in the parish of Wiveliscombe have been included. Populations nowadays are increasingly transitory, and in future there will be less continuity of families within communities, so it seems pertinent to put on record our West Country parish at this time.

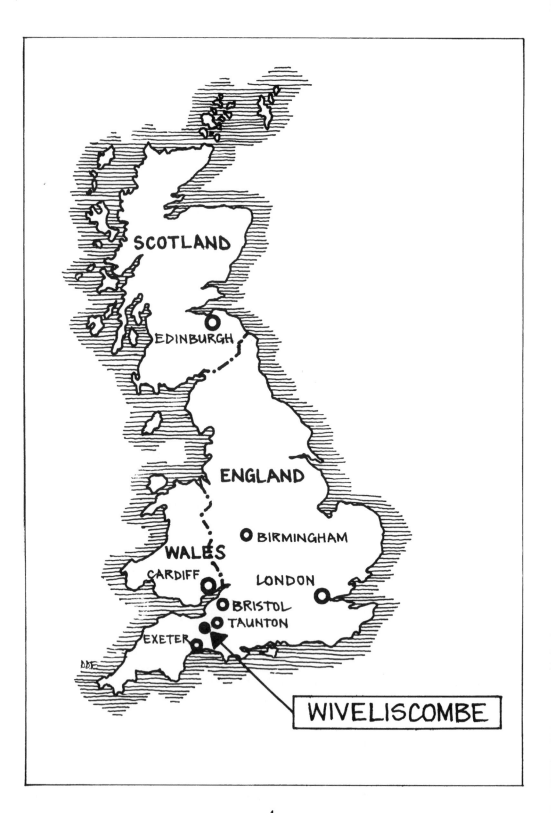

SCOTLAND

EDINBURGH

ENGLAND

BIRMINGHAM

WALES

CARDIFF

LONDON

BRISTOL
TAUNTON

EXETER

WIVELISCOMBE

Historical Introduction to the Parish

For the most comprehensive and modern (although 'modern' is something of a misnomer as it was published nearly 100 years ago) history of Wiveliscombe, reference should be made to *Wifela's Combe: A History of the Parish of Wiveliscombe,* by the Reverend F. Hancock, MA, SCL, FSA (The Wessex Press, 1911). This publication was reprinted in 1998 on the initiative of his great-grandson William Hancock, and is a fine definitive history of the town to the beginning of the 20th Century. It includes much information based on the Manoral Rolls and other hitherto unpublished material, as well as recounting some of the local legends, such as the murder in Grant's Lane (23rd December 1856). Earlier sources are *The History and Antiquities of Somerset* by John Collinson (1791), and *A Popular History of West Somerset* by Edward Jeboult (1893). More recent anecdotal information is contained in Ivor Burston's *Wiveliscombe 'Bits and Pieces' 1920's-1980's,* published in 1983.

Situated at an altitude of 400ft in a hollow on the edge of the once much wooded Brendon Hills, Wiveliscombe stands at a strategic crossroads between the hills and the Vale of Taunton and has, therefore, long been the site of human habitation. There are claims of Ancient British, Celtic, Roman, Saxon and, eventually, Norman occupation of the area. The only confirmed archaeological evidence, however, of such early settlements has been of the Romans at Nunnington Park, and at Castle, a hill just to the east of the town, where there was an Iron Age camp later taken over by the Romans. During the Second World War a large cache of Roman coins dating from AD 270 to AD 338 was found at this latter site, and they are on display in the Taunton Museum.

The supposed origins of the name are numerous and unclear. They range from Weevils-combe, Weaselscombe and Wife-less-combe, to Wifela or Wyfel, an old English chief who, being in possession of the valley (or combe), gave his name to it. In the first two pages alone of *Wifela's Combe,* no less than eight different spellings are given, but by the 17th Century, it seems that 'Wiveliscombe' had become the standard.

The history of Wiveliscombe is entwined inextricably with that of the Church. It held properties here until early in the 19th Century. Wyvelscombe appears as 'ecclesiastical property' in the Domesday Survey of 1086, the third largest landholding of the Bishop of Wells. Originally part of the royal estate, Bishop Giso was given the Manor of Wiveliscombe and Fitzhead by Edward the Confessor (1042-1066). The Bishop's rights to Wiveliscombe were first recorded in the Papal Bull of 1179, and in 1208 it became a Prebend of Wells. The Prebendary received the revenues and tithes from the parish but, not always being resident, appointed a deputy (a Vicar) to carry out the religious duties, this latter appointment first taking place in 1262. On page 35 is a reproduction of the roll of incumbents of the 'Vicarage of Wiveliscombe' that hangs in the Church. The

Chapelry of St James' at Fitzhead was separated from Wiveliscombe in 1755, and a Rector was appointed in 1867, the incumbent of Wiveliscombe remaining a co-Patron.

By the time of Bishop John Drockensford (1309-1329), there were no less than sixteen official residences in the county for the use of the Bishop. The building beside the Cathedral at Wells, however, was his only dwelling that could be called a Palace. It was therefore a Manor that Bishop Drockensford built at Wiveliscombe using the site of an earlier house. With subsequent improvements this Manor became quite substantial and a popular destination for the Bishops and their households. Virtually nothing remains of it today except the archway to the east of the churchyard and a few windows in the old school building overlooking the north-western corner of the churchyard. At its height, there were stables, a court, a mill-pond and a chapel at the Manor, and a park to the south. In 1551 this covered 271 acres and provided excellent sporting recreation for the Bishop. By 1791 the Manor House had deteriorated badly and, when sold to Lord Ashburton in 1838, little remained apart from the Poor House that had been built on part of the site in 1735. Lord Ashburton sold the property in 1894. Another property with connections to the Church was built by Bishop Bourne. After his expulsion from the Church in 1559 at the accession of Queen Elizabeth I, he retired to Wiveliscombe and the house he built still stands in Church Street and bears his name *[see page 50]*.

[JOHN BUCKLER, FSA, 1770-1851]

Remains of the Bishop's Manor - 1837

Other substantial houses came later: Oakhampton House built in 1734 but since pulled down, Abbotsfield 1872, and Castle, Victorian but on much older foundations. Many buildings and locations in the area retain the names of the families from earlier days; for example, Jews (originally D'Ewe) and later, in a 1642 list of Wiveliscombe taxpayers, can be found Chorley, Washer, Hellinge and Fleed, among others.

The town has grown over the centuries, from the early Saxon settlement in the area south of the main road between the church, Rotton Row, and Gullet (South Street), across to Plain Pond, once the fishponds supplying the Bishop's Manor. In its time Wiveliscombe has had its own mint; by 1559 a market was operational in the same area as the modern day Square; in 1791 there was a racecourse on the 500 acres of common land at Maundown; in 1804 the Infirmary and Dispensary was established [see page 68] and, because of the town's geographical location and commercial importance, there were many inns, reputedly as many as thirty-three at one time. The fluctuating fortunes of the local industries are reflected in the population figures. There were 1,533 inhabitants in the parish in 1777, with 359 houses. In 1840 the parish acreage was recorded as 5,441.

POPULATION OF WIVELISCOMBE							
1791	-	1,900	1871	-	3,172	1931	-	2,006
1821	-	2,791	1881	-	1,624	1951	-	2,168
1841	-	3,407	1901	-	2,214	1961	-	2,093
1851	-	2,861	1911	-	2,080	1971	-	2,145
1861	-	2,735	1921	-	1,970	1981	-	2,120

Agriculture was the predominant industry, and in 1798 the Wiveliscombe Agricultural Society was formed. Farming and cider orchards were important, but the most significant activity until the mid 19th Century was the wool trade. Surrounded by hills providing excellent grazing and water, for nearly three hundred years a considerable proportion of the parish earned their living from sheep. A wide variety of woollen goods were produced, including blankets, coatings, baize, collars and shrouds (a 1678 Act of Parliament ordered that bodies should be wrapped in wool for burial). Goods went as far as Newfoundland for use by fishermen, and a particular coarse indigo-dyed material called 'pennystone' was made into clothing for slaves in the West Indies. The 1833 Act of Emancipation and the greater capacity of the woollen industries in the north of England resulted in the demise of the trade. A paper read to the Somerset Archaeological Society in 1883 describes how 'fifty years ago the sound of the shuttle and the rattle of the loom might be heard in nearly every street of the town'. Another anecdote relates how, during festivities on 29th June 1814 to celebrate the defeat of Napoleon Bonaparte, a sheep was shorn during the morning procession. By 2pm its wool had become a coat, which was worn by Mr W Hancock at the dinner that same evening.

As the wool trade declined, brewing became the major employer. At this time of commercial change the Diocese also disposed of its remaining properties. The first Hancock brewery was built in 1807 and, by 1861, it was reputed to be 'the largest brewery in the West of England', owning over two hundred public houses. In 1829 wine and spirit vaults were also established, by Messrs Bond and Son. As the parish includes the hamlets of Croford, Ford, Langley and Whitefield, there were several other industries in the area. The Oakhampton quarry produced attractive but unfortunately friable slates and ceased major commercial operation in 1883. Bricks were made at Slape Moor from local clay [see page 170] and, until 1901, top quality agricultural lime was produced in kilns at Tipnoller and Castle. An important support for these industries was the Taunton to Barnstaple railway, opened on 8th June 1871.

7

The first piped water system within Wiveliscombe came from springs in the hills to street hydrants installed in the 1840s, followed by the establishment of a gas company to light the town in 1857. The Town Hall was built by Lord Ashburton in 1841, employing the same architect Richard Carver who had designed the new church in 1829. The Police Station was built in 1858; in 1873 it was manned by a superintendent and eight men. A Council Chamber, free Library and reading rooms were erected in Silver Street to commemorate the Jubilee of Queen Victoria in 1887.

There was a sporting milestone with the inauguration, in 1872, of the Wiveliscombe Rugby Club. From the early days the high calibre team was supported by the Hancock family. At one stage, seven of ten Hancock brothers played rugby for Somerset. One captained England, another Wales, and in 1885 F E Hancock introduced the four three-quarter game, later adopted by all Rugby Union Clubs. Another sporting credit was the pack of Wiveliscombe Harriers, kennelled in the mid 19th Century at Castle.

The wool trade has gone, the brewery closed in 1960, the railway ceased operation on 3rd October 1966, the weekly cattle market ended in 1985 and the current outbreaks of disease are having an adverse effect on agriculture, but as we move into the new Millennium, Wiveliscombe is still developing. New industries are starting up (including two breweries and a meat processing plant), the population is on the increase as new houses are built, and although Bishop Drockensford might not recognise the town were he to return seven hundred years later, there are still vestiges of the past to be cherished for the future.

[JOHN BUCKLER, FSA, 1770-1851]

East View, St. Andrew's Church - 1842

St. Andrew's Church and Crypt

St. Andrew's Church

The origins of the current St. Andrew's church are comparatively recent. During the time of the vicar John Sunderland (1813 - 1837), a significant crack was discovered in the tower, so much so that the structure oscillated when the bells were rung. When the pillars in the church were also found to be out of perpendicular, a parish meeting was called in June 1826, as a result of which the architect Richard Carver, from Bridgwater, was engaged to survey the building. He concluded that all the necessary repairs would cost £3,109. A further meeting, in March 1827, agreed to his alternative; a new building, with catacombs, costing £4,185.4s. In the event, the cost of the new church was charged to the rates, to be paid off by the parish over twenty years. The newly designed building provided an additional 558 seats, bringing the capacity to 1,250, of which 457 were to be 'free and unappropriated for ever' *[see T60 – page 31].*

As already noted, the first formal confirmation of a church in Wiveliscombe dates from 1179. The Bishop of Wells had been Lord of the Manor prior to that date, so it is likely there had been an earlier place of worship, albeit humble. Certainly, Bishop Ralph (1329-1363) built a new church on the site of a more ancient building. This was subsequently enlarged and, in 1705, a choristers gallery was added. A Sunday School had been established in 1787 but, otherwise, little is known of the church from that period, except that there was a step down into the old building. The following contemporary drawing hangs in the church and the crack that prompted the reconstruction can be clearly seen, as can the entrance in the South aspect.

11

The last service held in the old church was the marriage in 1827 of Mary Ann Hancock with John Prestwood Bellew. When leaving the church, she is recorded as having removed a stone from the porch just prior to the start of demolition. Very few memorials were retained for the new edifice but these include the Windham effigies *[T45, T46]*, the alabaster for which is believed to have come from the cliffs between Blue Anchor and Watchet. The Norman font was not included in the rebuilding, but was returned to the church a hundred years later, in 1924, after being retrieved from use as an ornament in a garden in the town. The octagonal bowl now stands on a more modern base; the Edwardian oak cover was installed in memory of Paul Tudball, in 1982 *[T56]*. Likewise, by good fortune, the wooden panel *[page 33]* was spotted in an antique shop by a former Vicar who brought it back to Wiveliscombe, and whose widow later presented it to the church. It is believed to have come from a chimneypiece in the Bishop's Manor House. Panels from the 'beautifully carved oak screen' of the pre-demolition church are incorporated into the pulpit, erected in memory of W S Capper (1914-1943) *[T34]*.

[JOHN BUCKLER, FSA, 1770-1851]

North Aspect of St. Andrew's

Reconstruction began very soon after the demolition had been agreed, and the foundation stone for the new church was laid on 6th June 1827. Dismantling the old structure proved more difficult than anticipated and dynamite was required; it was much stronger than it had appeared. Built in Gothic style of Devonian sandstone, with ham stone dressings and pitched slate roof, the new building was consecrated in 1829. One design for it shows four wooden pinnacles on each corner of the tower (see illustration above). After a trial period these were deemed inappropriate and were never installed in cast iron as planned. Also designed by Richard Carver were the entrance gates and railings, which were built at the same time as the new church. *[see page 13]*

The current configuration of the Choir and Sanctuary dates from 1872 when there was a re-ordering of the interior *[see page 28]*. In 1897 a new cage had to be supplied for the bells in the tower, of which there are eight, the earliest dating from 1751. In the later part of 1914 it was decided to re-model the Sanctuary again, the architect for this work being Mr F Bligh Bond. The large oil painting of Jesus now hanging in the north aisle was by a West Country artist William Brockedon (1787-1854). It was replaced above the altar by a 'rose' window designed by Miss Alice Erskine in memory of a most accomplished young all-rounder, Lieutenant Ralph E Hancock, DSO, killed in action at Festubert in 1914 *[page 181 and T27]*. In 1916, the Lutley and Chorley stained glass memorial windows in the Sanctuary were reinstated in the south wall of the Church *[T42]*. The Lady Chapel was created 1924-1926, at which time the Choir Vestry screen was erected in the south aisle, an area previously used by the Sunday School Scholars. The screen was dedicated to two members of the choir who together completed 123 years of service to the church *[T52]*.

At the instigation of Clementi Collard, builder of Abbotsfield House, a small organ from a London church was installed in the musicians' gallery in 1845. In 1892 it was moved to the east end of the south aisle where it was enlarged in 1900 by E J Minns, in Taunton, before being rebuilt and returned to the gallery in 1929. It has since undergone several enlargements, producing what is now a magnificent organ. A mark on the floor under the gallery shows where the Victorian font once stood. Originally installed in 1829, it was given to a church in Essex in the 1970s. The 17th Century altar rails came from a church in Flanders, virtually destroyed during the 1st World War, and were presented by Mrs Froude Hancock in memory of her husband Philip Froude Hancock *[T39]*.

On the outside of the north-west entrance to the church is an Ordnance Survey Bench Mark (111.61 m – 366 ft). Although not within the purview of the church, the old vicarage in South Street was rebuilt in 1845, when Richard Beadon was the Vicar. This building was given up in favour of a further new vicarage, built in 1966.

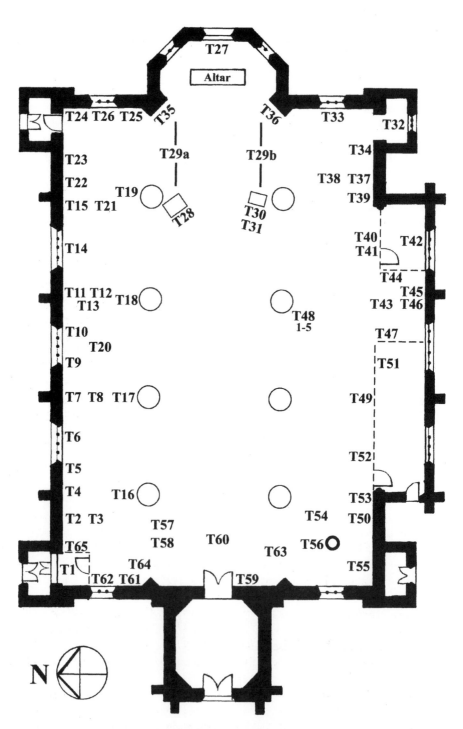

Location Plan of Tablets
St. Andrew's Church

14

St. Andrew's Church - Tablets

The location of tablets *[T = TABLET]* in the church can be found in the Plan on page 14

T1 ***[White Marble]***   Sacred to the memory of / Elizabeth relict of / William WALKER Esqr / of Everley Lodge in the county of Herts / who died at Castle in this parish / January 14th 1832 aged 80 years / also / to the memory of her son / Charles Augustus WALKER / of Wheatleigh House in the parish of Wilton / in this county / Major General in the Honorable East India / Company's Service Madras Establishment / who likewise died at Castle / October 2nd 1842 Aged 59 years

T2 ***[White Marble]***   In memory of / Elizabeth Christina ROWLES / widow of the late / Thomas ROWLES Esqre / for many years in the Civil Service / at the Cape of Good Hope / who died at Wiveliscombe / on the 21 day of July 1862 / Aged 72 years / This tablet is erected to the memory / of their mother / by her affectionate daughters.

T3 ***[Metal]***   Sacred to the memory of Andrew Francis EDWARDS, MD who / practised in this town for forty years and met his death by an / accident whilst in the exercise of his profession Aug 18, 1876 / In affectionate remembrance of him as a man and / in grateful recollection of his professional skill / his many friends erect this tablet. *[Hart, Son Peard & Co, London]*

T4 *[White Marble]* Sacred / to the memory of / Thomas BOUCHER / who died Augt 28th 1811 / Aged 81 years / also / Mary his wife / who died Decr 22nd 1777 / Aged 42 years.

T5 *[White Marble]* In / memory of / John LUTLEY / of the parsonage, in this parish / who died Feb^{ry} 2nd 1860 / Aged 70 years / Also of Mary, his wife / who died Octr 25th 1862 / Aged 68 years. / This tablet was erected / by their daughter / Mary Pugsley LUTLEY / who died August 11th 1863 / Aged 38 years.

T6 *[White Marble]* As a token of dutiful affection / This window was erected / to the loving memory of / Thomas and Jane POCOCK / by their daughter Caroline / March 1887. *[Stained glass by CLAYTON & BELL]*

T7 *[White Marble]* Sacred to the memory / of / Edward BOUCHER who died July 4th 1823 aged 64 / Betty his wife who died Feb^{ry} 29th 1812 aged 46 / Edward their son who died Decr 20th 1805 aged 17 / George Green another son who died July 13th 1818 aged 20 / Elizabeth Ann who died Novr 27th 1824 aged 10 months / and / twin children / of / Benjamin and Catherine Mary BOUCHER / and / grand-children of Edward and Betty BOUCHER / Catherine Mary who died Octr 23rd 1824 aged 9 months. / This marble was erected / by Catherine Mary and Elizabeth Green BOUCHER / the affectionate daughters of the above / Edward and Betty BOUCHER.

T8 *[White Marble]* In / memory of / Benjamin BOUCHER / who died on the 26th day of August / 1838 aged 41 yrs / and / Catherine Mary his wife / who died on the 9th day of October / 1858 aged 58 yrs / of / Edward their son / who died on the 23rd day of October / 1835 aged 10 years / and / Adelaide their daughter / who died on the 7th day of April 1838 / aged 6 mths / and of / Elizabeth Green BOUCHER / who died on the 7th day of January / 1860 aged 57 years. *[For illustration see page 20]*

T9 *[Brass]* This window is dedicated to the glory / of God and in most loving memory of / Benjamin BOUCHER. Born July 10th 1831 Died / Dec^{ember} 9th 1874 Aged 43 years by Ada his widow / "He will swallow up Death in Victory and the Lord / God will wipe away tears from off all faces"

T10 *[Brass]* In loving memory of / Benjamin Hamilton BOUCHER DSO / Lieut-Colonel The Hampshire Regiment / son of Benjamin and Sophia BOUCHER / Born at the Croft in this Parish 20 Feb 1864 / Died at Minehead 8 Jan 1928. Aged 63 / Also of Helen his wife who died 27 Nov 1904 / Aged 28. Buried at Wolverton, in Hampshire / Erected by their three sons.

T11 *[White Marble]* In memory of / Sir William YEA / of Pyrland House, Somersetshire, Bar^t / who died the 18th Novr 1806 / Aged 79 years / And of / Lacy YEA Esqre / of Oakhampton House in this Parish / his son / who died the 15th Jan^{ry} 1811 / Aged

/cont.....................

T11 cont.
52 years / "Verily there is a reward for the righteous" / "Verily there is a God" / And of / George YEA Esqre / of this parish / son of Sir William YEA / who died the 2nd Octr 1811 / aged 51 years. {Esto Semper Fidelis} *[R Shout, London fecit]*

T12   [White Marble]   In memory of / James WALDRON / of Hartswell in this Parish / who died 16th May 1862 in the 76th year / of his age / and of Edith his wife / who died 19th January 1861 / Aged 70 / "Inter spem curamque, timores inter et iras, / Omnem crede diem tibi diluxisse supremum".

T13   [Brass]   In loving memory of / Charles BOUCHER / of Greenway in this parish who died 16th Augt 1886 / Aged 78 years / Also of Ann BOUCHER his wife / who died Jany 5th 1925 Aged 90 yrs / Sorrow and sighing shall flee away. Is.LI.II.

T14   [Stained Glass Window]   In loving memory of Eliza CHORLEY widow of the late Edward CHORLEY formerly of Leeds who died 23rd February 1891 aged 95. This window was erected by her grandsons Arthur and Clayton WOODHOUSE and by her esteemed friend Eleanor SHARP of Cheltenham.

T15   [White Marble]

*Shield impaled.   Dexter: **1 & 4** Sable, a lion rampant gules, augmented with a crescent mark of cadency (second son)*
*Sinister: **2 & 3** Gules, three Stirrups {?} This coat of arms is impaled with the Field (tinctures lost), a Chevron between 3 birds {partridges?}*
MOTTO: DIFFICIALI QUE PULCHIA

Sacred to the memory of / Jonathan ELFORD / of Oakhampton House in this Parish / and of Crapiton in the County of Devon Esqr / second son of the Rev^d. Launcelot ELFORD / of Bickham in Devonshire. He was a magistrate / for the Counties of Devon and Somerset and / Colonel of the 1st Reg^t of Devon Local Militia / died 27th March 1832 / In the 81st year of his age / He was highly respected and eminently / useful in the various stations which he filled / during a long course of years / Also in memory of Mary his wife / daughter of Henry LUXMOORE of Okehampton / in Devonshire Esqr died September 3rd 1822 / in the 71st year of her age / Beloved and lamented by her friends and deeply / regretted by the Poor.

In December 1811 Mr Elford took the lease of Oakhampton Manor from
Mr George Scott, although the landlord was the Dean and Chapter of Wells.
For many years a Churchwarden, he owned one of the vaults in the catacombs.
According to <u>Wifela's Combe</u>,
"Mr Elford, who was a bachelor, resided at Oakhampton until his death in 1830,
when his interest in the property passed to his nieces."
There is an anomaly, however, as the tablet indicates he was married and died in 1832.

T16   *[Wood]*   In 1648 Henry STORY Gent. Gave to David STORY and others of this Parish A Messuage containing two Burgages, situate in Golden Hill, for one thousand years upon trust that they should yearly pay all the rents and profits thereof unto the churchwardens and overseers of the poor to be distributed amongst the indigent persons for their better relief, on the feast day of S^t. Thomas, in every year during the said Term.

T17   *[Wood]*   In 1647 Thomas HOLWAY Gent. Gave until several inhabitants in this Parish the inheritance of those six Burgages situated in Golden Hill, part whereof is a certain parcel of ground now called the Parish close, in trust that they should yearly for ever at the feast of Easter pay all the rents and Profits thereof unto the churchwardens and overseers of the poor to be by them yearly for ever apply'd towards repairing the Church and maintaining the Poor.

Burgage = *A tenure in socage for a yearly rent.* *Tenure*= *Holding, occupation*
Socage = *Feudal tenure of lands by service fixed and determinate in quality*
Messuage = *A dwelling and offices with the adjoining lands appropriated to the household.*   *[CHAMBERS DICTIONARY]*

The original burgage plots were located to the north of Church Street and in the area of Golden Hill and date from the period 1309-1329.
At this time the annual rent was paid to the Church, as landowner.
From these tablets it can be seen that at a later date additional burgage plots were donated, again with the Church receiving the rents, but with the poor of the parish as the beneficiary.   Until the mid 19th Century, all charity monies were managed by the Vicar and church-wardens.   At the end of the 1890s, all the remaining disposable assets were consolidated, and Charity Trustees still hold limited funds to be distributed annually within the Parish.
Almshouses dating from the 15th Century no longer exist.
These wooden tablets were re-installed in the church c. 1900.

T18   *[Wood]*   In 1589 John HUTCHINS, Gen. Gave to Robert STORY, John YEA and their Heirs one close of Land containing three acres lying at Croford Hill-head upon trust that they should yearly for ever distribute the profits thereof among the poor of the parish fourteen days before Easter.

T19   *[Wood]*   In 1647 Samuel BIRD of London Gent. Gave two hundred pounds to be laid out in lands for the use of the poor of this Parish with which money certain lands at Poleshill in the Parish of Milverton were purchased.

T20 *[Metal Plate on Cope Chest]*   Georgio Wyndham / Bathone et Wellen / Episcopo / ad Regis britt omn consecrationam / Edwardi Septimi / necnon / futuris hujusce sedis episcopis / cum hae cista cappam sericam auratam / D.D. / Testimonium amicitiae / viri feminaeque fidelis Somersetenses / vikal Jul. / MCMII.

> Loaned to the Churchwardens by the Bishop of Bath and Wells, this cope chest was made for the Bishop to store the cope he wore at Edward VII's coronation in Westminster Abbey.

T21 *[White Marble]*   *No colours. A Fret.*
Crest: On a wreath an arm Enbowed holding a jug and pouring into a bowl.
MOTTO: TOUT D'EN HAUT.

In memory of / Henry BELLEW of Oakhampton Manor / in this parish / Born August 31st 1808 Died April 19th 1894 / and of / Mary Froude BELLEW his wife / Born Sep 9th 1819 Died April 12th 1902 / Also of / Ada Mary BELLEW their daughter / Born April 6th 1851 / Died February 16th 1882.

T22 *[Brass]*   To the glory of God / and / in sacred & loving memory of / our dearly loved parents / Edward John FEATHERSTONE died March 17th 1871 / Aged 75 / Elizabeth his wife died Feby 2nd 1897 Aged 87 / Also to the children of the above / Elizabeth Ann died July 4th 1849 / Edwin died January 19th 1852 / Frederic died July 17th 1853 / John Tyler died Feby 27th 1866 / Louisa Abigail died Novr 30th 1879 / Florence wife of Wm BRIGGS died Sepr 15th 1899 / Frances Mary died Dec 6th 1916 / Adelaide Died June 30th 1918 / Emily Died Nov 29th 1920 / Lucy Edith BRIGGS Died Nov 20th 1928 / Lillie FEATHERSTONE Died May 8th 1934 / Requiescant in pace.

T23 *[White Marble]* Sacred / to the memory of / Thomas BOUCHER / of Jews, and Lambrook / in this Parish / who died on the 23rd day / of September 1858, aged 67 / Also of Mary Ann his wife / who died on the 24th day / of December 1858; aged 65.

T24 *[White Marble]* In memory / of / Edward BOUCHER / of Jews and Prospect House / in this parish / died March 31st 1881 / aged 80 / also of Mary Timewell / his wife / who died at Prospect House / December 27th 1888 / Aged 77 / Erected by the widow Mary Timewell BOUCHER.

T25 *[White Marble]* In memory / of / four daughters of / Edward BOUCHER and Mary Timewell / his wife. / Ann died at Jews Jan. 14th 1873 / Emma died at Prospect House Feb. 20th 1877 / Elizabeth wife of Joshua KEEVIL / died at Clinch Wilts, May 19th 1880 / Laura wife of Rev. C. H. COTES, M.A. / Died at Musselburgh Midlothian / June 24th 1883. / Also Edward their son / who died at Jews March 9th 1885 / Erected by the mother Mary Timewell BOUCHER

T26 *[Stained Glass Window]* This window is erected to the Glory of God and to the sacred memory of / Emmanuel BOWDAGE late churchwarden of this parish by his widow Mary BOWDAGE 1893.

T38   *T8*

T27 *[Engraved Wood Behind Altar]*   To the Glory of God & in loving memory of Ralph Escott HANCOCK, D.S.O. Lieutenant in the Devonshire Reg^t who was killed in action at Festubert Oct. 29th 1914, Aged 26 years.

T28 *[Pulpit]*   William Stewart / CAPPER / 1914 – 1943.

T29 *[Choir Stalls]* a) In loving memory of Alfred Stewart CAPPER 1871-1966.
                           b) and his wife Nora Janet CAPPER 1879-1971.

T30 *[Engraved on Brass Lectern]*   To the Glory of God. In memory of Lavinia. Daughter of Henry SULLY, M.D. of Wiveliscombe / Born July 1804 Departed this life September 1880. Requiescant in pace.

T31 *[Inscribed in Bible on Lectern]*   Presented to St Andrew's, Wiveliscombe / January 2000 / by Miss Dorothy FLOOD / as a legacy.

T32 *[Inscribed in Holy Communion Book in Lady Chapel]*
In memoriam / Alfred / Thomas / MORANT / 1907 – 1987 / Sometime / Churchwarden / Treasurer / & / faithful servant / of / St Andrew's / Wiveliscombe.

T33 *[Stained Glass Window]*

[Stained glass by
Towers Kemp]

Shield:
Argent (diapered) charged
with three wolfs' heads gules

In honour of the Holy Incarnation of our / Lord Jesus Christ and in thankfulness to God / for the life and work of the Rev. Howard McCRIRICK / thirty years Vicar of this Parish, who died / 26th May 1922 to whose memory this window / is dedicated by his parishioners and friends.

T34   *[Wood]*

Quartered 1 & 4 Sable, a Chevron engrailed or, in chief or, two deer's head caboshed sable, two bees Volant or,   in base,   a beehive or. 2 & 3 Checky sable and argent, a Bend pean charged with three billets sable. CREST: On a wreath sable and or, an arm sable embowed cuffed in pean holding a banner sable fringed or charged with bee Volant or.
MOTTO: QUI POTEST CAPERE CAPIAT

[Royal Artillery Badge]   In proud and loving memory of / William Stewart CAPPER / Major, Royal Artillery / only child of / Colonel Stewart CAPPER, DSO and Nora his wife / Died at sea whilst on active service / and buried off Tobruk / Born 20 November 1914, died 3 November 1943.

T35

For God, For King, And Country
To the Glory of God
and in remembrance of the men
connected with Wiveliscombe
who gave their lives
in the Great War 1914-1919

Lieut	R E HANCOCK, DSO	Devon R.
2nd Lieut	A E PARSONS	R. Fus
2nd Lieut	R M D HARVEY	N. Staff R.
2nd Lieut	A G WALKER	N. Staff R.
Fl Sgt	F RICHARDS	R.A.F.
Lance Corpl	W E BALMAN	R. Westm'rs
Lance Corpl	W L VICKERY	Sea. High'rs
Sapper	T BAKER	R.E.
Sapper	F HOWELL	R.E.
Sapper	W GREEDY	R.E.
Private	S KELLAND	Som. L.I.
Private	W KING	Som. L.I.
Private	C RICHARDS	Som. L.I.
Private	J STONE	Som. L.I.
Private	C VALLANCE	Som. L.I.
Private	W VALLANCE	Som. L.I.
Private	E WEBBER	Som. L.I.
Private	W J WEBBER	Som. L.I.
Private	E LEWIS	Lon. R
Private	S RICHARDS	Wilts R
Private	E R NATION	Midd'x R
Private	S KNIGHT	Cold'st. G.
Private	W F STEVENS	R.A.
Private	P BULL	R.A.S.C.
Private	J BURSTON	R.A.S.C.
Private	W STRICKLAND	R.A.S.C.
Private	A VICKERY	R.A.S.C.

"Lest we Forget"

T36

For God, For King, And Country
To the Glory of God
and in remembrance of the men
connected with Wiveliscombe
who gave their lives
in the Great War 1914-1919

Captain	W F B EDWARDS	24 Punjaubis
Lieut	C B BOUCHER	York & Lancs. R.
2nd Lieut	E COX	Som. L.I.
Sergt	W GAMLIN	Som. L.I.
Lance Corpl	A HARRISON	Som. L.I.
Private	H J BURNETT	Som. L.I.
Private	R CHURCHILL	Som. L.I.
Private	P CRUMP	Som. L.I.
Private	W GREEDY	Som. L.I.
Private	W FURZE	W. Som. Yeo.
1st Class P.O.	T KELLOW	R.N.
Stoker	F ARTHUR	R.N.
Lance Corpl	F W PARSONS	R.M.L.I
Private	H SHOPLAND	R.M.L.I
Private	G KELLOW	Ches. R.
Private	E GUY	D. of Corn. L.I.
Private	C COLLARD	Worcs. R
Private	J MULLINS	Worcs. R
Private	J K DINHAM	Welsh R.
Private	S BARWICK	R. War. R
Private	J FURZE	N. Lancs R
Private	V A WARREN	Yorks R
Private	F GREEDY	Can. Forces
Private	W J HYETT	Can. Forces
Private	A J ADAMS	Devon R
Private	W KING	Devon R.
Private	J TROAKE	Devon R.
Private	W G TUCKER	Devon R.

"Lest we Forget"

T37   [White Marble]   Sacred / to the memory / of Philip HANCOCK / of Ford, in this Parish / who died / on the 19th day of April A.D. 1838 / Aged 72 years / and of / Frances his wife / (daughter of the Rev^D John MOGRIDGE / Vicar of Holne in the County of Devon) / who died / on the 17th day of May 1858 / Aged 84 years

T38   [White Marble]   In / memory of / William HANCOCK / who died on the 19TH day of Jan^{RY} 1849 / in the 80TH year of his age / His public life was full of useful deeds, / and his private life was a pattern of / simplicity and goodness / His benevolent character   endeared / him to all around, and his many virtues / were honoured by universal esteem / His body was taken to its resting place / in this church amidst every mark of / respect that the living can bestow / upon the dead, and this monument has / been erected by a public subscription / in testimony of his deeds of usefulness / and his acts of charity.   *[For illustration see page 20]*

T39   [Stone]   The high altar rails were / made in the seventeenth / century. They were given by / his wife in memory of Philip / Froude HANCOCK who died / on 16th October 1933.

T40   [White Marble]   This window is dedicated by his mother / to the dear memory of / Hugh Llewellyn BOUCHER / Born at the Croft in this parish / Feb: 16th 1870 / killed in the Argentine Republic / May 5th 1891

T41   [Brass]   Harold George ELLIOTT / 1892 – 1973 / 48 years Lay Reader / of this Parish / The Lenten Array was given / as his memorial / R.I.P.

T42   [Stained Glass Window in Vestry]   To the glory of God and in mem. of John and Elizabeth LUTLEY / by their loving and dutiful children. mdccclxiv
To the glory of God and in the beloved mem. of Edward CHORLEY / of Williton by his affectionate widow. mdccccliv.

        [Brass tablet] records that the Lutley and Chorley Memorial Windows
        were removed from the Sanctuary in the year 1916.

T43   [White Marble]   Here rest / in hope of the Resurrection to eternal life / through our Lord Jesus Christ / the mortal remains of / John HARVEY who died July 17th 1792 aged 62 years, Father / Elizabeth HARVEY who died April 14th 1819 aged 46 years, Wife / Elizabeth HARVEY who died Feby 23rd 1797 aged 2 years, Daughter /And Elizabeth Dawbney HARVEY who died / January 16th 1816 aged 18 years, Daughters of / John HARVEY of this parish, Gent / by whom / this stone is / with all duty and affection / of a son, husband and Father / made sacred to the Memory / of their Virtues and his Sorrow / 1819 / With the same Christian hope, filial piety and brotherly love are inscribed the names of John HARVEY their father who died April 4th 1821 aged 36 years and / John Dawbney HARVEY their brother who died March 23rd 1823 Aged 27 years / by the dutiful and affectionate / surviving members of their family.

T44

[Left column] During the War of 1939-45 the Vicar and Churchwardens of Wiveliscombe gave the use of the crypt beneath this church as a place of safety for ancient and valuable goods from all parts of England: Here was stored priceless stained glass from the cathedral churches of Exeter and Salisbury, from Sherborne Alms Houses, from the parish churches of Tickenham, Weston in Gordano and Walton near Clevedon in Somerset, the great 15th Century east window of S. Peter Mancroft, Norwich, and important new glass prepared for Sheffield Cathedral, Toddington, Bedfordshire, Morecambe, Lancashire, Heckington, Lincolnshire & the church of the Ascension, Bitterne Park, Southampton. Plate from Lambeth parish church, and from several Bristol churches, namely S. Stephen, S. George, Brandon Hill, All Saints Clifton and Aust: from Paglesham in Essex; from Rowner in Hampshire; Chiddingstone and Sandwich in Kent, and Charmouth in Dorset; from Great Yarmouth, North Walsham, Bacton and Edingthorpe in Norfolk. Records and documents from the Guildhall of the City of London, the diocese of Bath and Wells, the cathedrals of Salisbury, Exeter and Lichfield, and from Sherborne School. From Lichfield also came the 8th Century Gospel Book of S. Chad, while the French Protestant Church in London sent their entire library, dating from the time of the Huguenot persecution. Among larger objects were the 17th Century pulpit of Odiham in Hampshire, and an Altar table from Sandwich in Kent.

[Right column] The pictures included the 13th Century painted reredos from Thornham Parva in Suffolk and the 15th Century reredos from Sherborne Alms Houses. There were many relics of maritime history from Portsmouth Cathedral, including the Tangier Plate and the model of the "Mary Rose". In addition to all these things, hospitality was gladly given to liturgical furniture, Scrolls of the Law and records, from the Spanish and Portugese Synagogue, the Great, the Central, the United, the Bevis Marks, the South East London, and Sandys Row Synagogues. From the following churches in the city of London came: Woodwork from S. Martin Ludgate, S. Mary Abchurch, and other churches including the reredoses of S. Mary Woolnoth, S. Stephen Walbrook, with candle branch, altar rails, font, and bust of Peter le Maire from Saint Margaret, Lothbury. From London outside the city came the reredoses of S. James Piccadilly and All Hallows, East India Dock. Some of these buildings were subsequently severely damaged:

This storage scheme was organised by the Central Council for the Care of Churches:

Let us give thanks to God for the preservation of all these treasures and of this Church of Saint Andrew And pray that wars may Cease in all the world:

Written out for the church of S.Andrew Wiveliscombe by Ruth Mary Wood 1952. Laus Deo.

Stained Glass Window in the Lady Chapel

Only a fragment remains of the mediaeval glass that used to grace the door of what was previously the Vicar's Vestry in the north aisle. The glass, originally a gift to the Parish in 1860, was installed in the Lady Chapel by the Rev Frank Bentley (Rector 1966-1976). The Vicar's Vestry moved to its current location in the South Aisle in the 1920s when the Sunday School pews were removed. A cast iron access door to the old heating system still remains in the north aisle vestry with the following embossed details:

'Inspection Door / John Grundy Ltd / Heating / & / Ventilating / Engineers /
893A City Road / London EC1 / & Ironworks / Tyldesley, Lancs'

****

T45 [Black Slate]

Nine quarterings: 1. Azure, a Chevron or. 2.Azure, a Bend or. 3. Argent, a Saltire engrailed 4. Argent, a fess double cotised 5. Argent, a Chevron sable between three deer passant sable. 6.Argent, a Fess sable between three legs sable. 7. Gules, a Saltire engrailed argent between 3 molets or. 8. Argent. 3 undecipherable charges, gules and cendree. 9. Sable, per chevron pean charged in chief two wolf's heads or

26

T45

To Posteritey / Heere rest in asured hope of a joyful resurection / through Christ Jesus ye Bodies of Humphrey WINDHAM of / Goulder Hill, in ye Parish of Wivelscombe in ye contey / of Somerset Esqr. Third sonne of Sr John WINDHAM of / Orchard in the same County Knight (long since deceased) / and Margerey his wife eldest daught^{er} / and coheire of John STEPHENSON of Hodson in / ye Countie of Hertford Esqr who lived together / above 43 yeares having issue a sonne and one daughter / wch sonne dying young, Elizabeth their sole daughter / and heire married John COLLES of Barton in ye Countey of Somerset Esqr by whom hee hath had issue at y^e / erecting of this monument 6 children, a sonne & / 5 daughters, wch sonne died an infant, and lieth in / this vault ye said Humphrey WINDHAM departed this / mortall life the 29 Day of May in the yeare of / our Lord God 1622 beeing aged 84 yeare^s and / upward Margerie his wife died the first of / September in the yeare of ouer Lord God 1620 / in the 72 yeare of hir age or somewhat above / Habete Pares incomparabilis / Festinantes Sequimur

T46

To the eternall memorie / of Humphrey WINDHAM Esqr / and Margery his wife / Heere lies a paire, whome for their equall love^s / Let after ages terme, the turtle doves / A Hee and Shee, whose like This Western Soil / Shall hardl^y match, nay scarce againe our ile: / that fame, her self adores the memorie / of Humphrey WINDHAM, and his Margerie / His matchles wife, whose Heave^n blest skill and cost / curd sundry, (whome the surgeon held for lost) of dangerous wounds, dym eies, and festerd sores / sent maimed criples crutchles from her dore / To fower score fower of yeares hee did aspire, / a counceller a Justicer, and a Squire / Hence was hee wise to judge and just to doe, / religious, good and nobly minded too. / The orphanes father, and the widowes frend / learned, wise, sincere, and constant to the end / yet from this none, such couple, did proceed / but one sole daughter faire and heire indeed / both of their virtues and estates who lives / and in her life, their second being gives / Here only doth their earthly pawne remaine / which at Chrises coming must be fetcht again

T47   *[Framed Photograph hanging on Choir Vestry Wall]*
The details given on a label below the photograph provide
much interesting information about the earlier internal church layout

St Andrew's Church – Wiveliscombe
Architect – Richard CARVER
This photograph shows the alterations
to the Sanctuary and the construction
of the Chancel by Giles and Gane 1872.
Their scheme for the east end was
modified by R. BLACKING over the
period 1929-1938.
The present pulpit, priests stall &
choir stalls by Michael TORRENS 1967

T48   *[Brass Tablets on Small Side Pews]*
1. In loving memory of our father W.B.   4. In loving memory of my aunt G.A.
2. In loving memory of our mother S.E.B. 5. In loving memory of my mother
3. In loving memory of our brother E.B.B.   M.E.H.F.

28

T49 *[White Marble]* Sacred to the beloved memory of / Henry NAZER Esq[r] / late a Commander in the Royal Navy / who departed this life / the 10 November 1810 Aged 52 / This tablet is erected / as a tribute of affection and respect, / by those who are left deeply to regret / the loss of an affectionate and kind / husband and father / Blessed are the dead which die in the Lord / Rev. Chap XIV. V.15 (?13)

T50 *[White Marble]* In loving memory of / Ronald Marmaduke Dawnay HARVEY / 2nd Lieut. 4th North Staffs Light Infantry / attached to 1st Beds Reg[t] / killed in action on Hill 60 near Ypres, April 20th 1915 , / in his 28th year. / Also of / Archdale Gillam WALKER / 2nd Lieut. 4th North Staffs Light Infantry / Attached 2nd Royal Scots Fusiliers. / Killed in action near Festubert, May 17th 1915, / in his 26th year. *[see page 182 and 184]*

T51 *[Brass Plaque on Box in Choir Vestry]* Presented to / St Andrew's Church / in 1994 / for the Choristers / by Mr M O PARNELL / in memory of Nikki PARNELL / 1965-1989.

T52 *[Brass Plaque on Choir Vestry Door]* To the Glory of God / in memory of / the long faithful service / of / George DAVIS. Aged 78 years / died Dec. 26, 1923 / and / Thomas BELLEW Aged 79 years / died Feb 3, 1924 / For 58 and 65 years respectively / members of the choir / of this church / this choir vestry screen / was erected August 1924.

T53 *[Metal]*

Shield: Gules, a Bend wavy counter vair sable and or. *Crest:* On a wreath gules and sable an Heraldic tyger passant

Here lyeth Will⁻m CROWTER / Master of Artes & Viccar of / Wiveliscombe who died the / XXIIIth day of June A⁻no 1617
  *[This tablet, together with **T55** and **V/F** [page 45] and the effigies **T45** and **T46**, appear to be the only memorials remaining from the pre-1829 church]*

T54 *[White Marble]* To the / beloved memory / of / the Reverend / John LLEWELLIN, M.A. / late of / the Vicarage, in this parish, / obiit December 28th 1869 / aetat 61 / also of / Elizabeth Winifred LLEWELLIN / widow of the above John LLEWELLIN / and eldest daughter of George OVERTON Esq[r] / of Llanthetty Hall Brecknockshire, / obiit March 31st 1872, / aetat 64 / also in tender and loving memory of / Eliza Winifred Mary TAYLOUR / of Kensington in the County of London / youngest daughter of the above and widow of / Major General Lord John Henry TAYLOUR / who entered into rest on October 22nd 1928, / Aetat 82 / He shall cover thee with his feathers, and under his wings / shalt thou trust; his truth shall be thy shield and buckler. / Psm. XCI.4.

T55 *[White Marble]* Reliquiue / Viri Reverendi Benj: HANCOCK, A.B. / Hujus parochiae Fidelis Vicarii. / Subtus deponuntur / Qui sanctis officiis per triginta annos / Placide et sedulo peractis / Primo die Septembris 1784 Aetat 58 / Omnino amatus et / Flebilis Occidit / Hoc monumentum sacrae amicitiae / Jussu divino paululum disjunctae / Haud insinceris lacrymis erexit / Vidua plorans. *[See T53]*

T56 *[Font Cover]*

The octagonal Font, on a restored base, is dated between 1154-1189.

The Font Cover, originally in St. James' church, Taunton, has the following inscription:

Given to the church of St. Andrew, Wiveliscombe in memory of Paul TUDBALL 1967 – 1982.
[Died 15th January 1982]

[Processional Cross]

Made for the Parish by Leslie Thurlow, ARCA, *des et fecit* 1981, in memory of Clifford George Tudball (1911-1980)
[Died 29th February 1980]

T57 *[Brass]* The sound / reinforcement system / was installed / in memory of / Yvonne FELLOWES / 1923 – 1993.

T58 *[Brass]* 1979 / To mark the 150th Anniversary / of the rebuilding of this church / the interior was redecorated / in white with rose coloured panels / in the nave roof / C J B MARSHALL / Vicar / Dixon H LUXTON. C S ROBINSON Church-wardens.

T59 *[Brass]* In memory of / Lucy and Elizabeth Sarah / daughters of James LEAN Esq / of Clifton Bristol and of / Lucy (late STUCKEY) his wife / who were for some years / residents of this parish / and who are interred in the / adjoining churchyard / The memory of the just is blessed.

T60   [Organ Loft]

> The Royal Arms of George IV and William IV
> on the front of the Organ loft
> were erected in this Church between 1820 and 1837.

John SUNDERLAND, Vicar. Richard KEATS, Curate.   This church was rebuilt and enlarged in the year 1829, by which means 558 additional / sittings were obtained and in consequence of a grant from the Society for Promoting the / Enlargement and Building of Churches, and Chapels, 457 of that number are hereby / declared to be free and unappropriated for ever, in addition to the 158 formerly provided. Richard CARVER, 1829, Architect. John TYLER & John C TIMEWELL, Churchwardens.

T61   [Brass]   To the glory of God / and in loving memory of / William HANCOCK / of Court House in this Parish / Born August 20th 1810 / Died December 2nd 1896 / This tablet is erected by / public subscription / in testimony of the esteem & regard / in which he was held by all classes

T62
[Stained Glass
Window]

Two Badges
1. A greyhound sejant, gorged and chained with a crown all surrounded with an argent garland on a wreath or and sable.
MOTTO: LE BON TEMPS VIENDRA (enscrolled round charge)

[Stained glass by Towers & Kemp - the company's "logo" of wheatsheaf and tower can be seen in the bottom left hand corner of the window.]

2. A Bengal tiger passant all garlanded by laurel wreath with tudor rose in base, argent and gules, all over crowned with a crown of the sons of a sovereign.

To the glory of God / and in loving memory of / Lieut: Charles Bailey BOUCHER / 2nd York and Lancaster Regiment / killed in action at Hooge, Flanders / 9th August 1915, aged 24 years / This window is dedicated / "Dulce et decorum est pro patria mori".

T63   [Brass Tablet on Table]   Presented by Mr & Mrs H G Derwent MOGER / on the occasion of the Marriage / of their Daughter / Alison Mary Derwent / to Robert Patrick CAMPBELL / on the 29th January 1947.

T64   [Brass Tablet on Bookcase] In memory of / Eric William STEVENS / 1913-1981

T65   [Brass Tablet on Notice Board]   In loving memory of / Victoria May BOWERING / nee GREENWAY / 1897 – 1991.

[Box Pews]

Another unusual feature of St. Andrew's are the Box Pews, dating from the rebuilding of the church in 1829. At that time they were a source of revenue for the Churchwardens. Families could rent their own pew, and the Pew Rent Books are deposited in the Somerset Record Office in Taunton. To differentiate, the pews without doors were free for anyone's use. About half of the original total of these now quite rare pews have been removed, in particular from the North and South aisles. The illustration below looks west from the pulpit.

19th Century Graffiti in one of the Pews

FORTITVD OMEÆ:ET
LÄVS:ME   Æ:DVS

W   K

WILLIAM KNIGHT
Bishop of Bath and Wells 1541-1547

Arms granted by Emperor Maximillian
(Letters Patent July 14, 1541)

*Per Fess or and gules double-headed displayed eagle sable
having on the breast a semie rose and a demi sun conjoined in
one and counter changed of the field*
Motto: *FORTITUDO MEA ET LAUS MEA DOMINUS*

Ps. 118. v. 14
He left £4 to the poor of Wiveliscombe and was
Prothnonotary to the Apostolic See and Ambassador to the
Emperor from Henry VIII of England

---

*A wooden panel hanging in the back of the church is believed to have come from the
Bishop's Manor [see page 12].   During his tenure as Bishop (1541-1547),
William Knight used the Wiveliscombe Manor as his main residence.*

Mothers' Union
R.I.P.
To the Glory of God and in memory of members of the Wiveliscombe Branch of the Mothers Union.

Laura BAKER	
Charlotte BARWICK	*2nd panel*
Catharine BARRINGTON	
Mary Ann BARRINGTON	*2nd panel*
Ada BELLE	
Elizabeth J BERRY	*2nd panel*
Emily I BERRY	
Elizabeth BOND	
Elizabeth BOUCHER	
Emma Jane BROOM	
Mary BURTON	
Emily Ann CHEDZEY	
Charlotte CHIDGEY	*2nd panel*
Bessie CHIPLIN	
Sarah Elizbth COGGINS	
Sophie COLES	*2nd panel*
Sarah CONNIBERE	
Annie CORNISH	
Cordelia CROSS	*2nd panel*
Elizbth A CUMMINS	
Mary EASTMENT	
Jane EVANS	
Sarah Jane FERRIS	*2nd panel*
Emily GOSS	*2nd panel*
Ann GREEDY	*2nd panel*
Emma GREEDY	*2nd panel*
Mary GREEDY	
Amelia GUY	*2nd panel*
Alice Amelia HALL	
Anna Claire HANCOCK	*2nd panel*
Ann HEMBURROW	

Salome HILL	
Lois HOOPER	*2nd panel*
Catherina A HURLEY	
Louisa M HUTCHINGS	*2nd panel*
Emma IRISH	
Mary Hannah JONES	
Mary Ann KING	*2nd panel*
Mary Anne LUTLEY	
Elizabeth MILLETT	
Georgina MOGFORD	
Ruth NATION	*2nd panel*
Anne PAYNE	
Emma PAYNE	
Sybella Symons PYNE	
Mary PROUT	
Clara QUICK	
Jane RAWLE	
Sarah RICHARDS	
Nellie E SAFFIN	*2nd panel*
Annie SALTER	
Sarah SEDGBEER	
Sarah A SELLICK	
Alice SMITH	*2nd panel*
Sarah Anne SMITH	
Lucy Ellen STEWART	
(founded this Branch 1910)	
Lucy Mary UPHAM	*2nd panel*
Frances Sarah WARMAN	*2nd panel*
Verena WHITE	*2nd panel*
Jane WILLIAMS	
Lucy WINDSOR	

****

The names on the above tablet have been put into alphabetical order for easier reference

THE VICARAGE OF WIVELISCOMBE
Memorial Board drawn up by the Revd. Howard McCririck, Vicar from 1891 until his death and burial in the Parish in 1922

VICARAGE OF WIVELISCOMBE
(WITH THE CHAPELRY OF FITZHEAD ANNEXED)

"We beseech you to know them which labour among you,
and are over you in the Lord, and admonish you:
and to esteem them very highly in love
for their work's sake."   II. Thess. V, Ver. 12.

Settlement of the Vicarial Endowment copied from
original in Bishop's Registry, Wells, dated 1262./
"Ordination or settlement of Vicarial Endowment at
Wiveliscombe, by Bishop William BYTTON
(dated Banwell 1262), Cannon Thomas de BYTTON,
as the Prebendary of Wiveliscombe, and / the Vicar,
Robert de Bosco, assenting. Vicar to have alterage
at Wiveliscombe and Fitzhead Chapel, all small Tithes,
and of grain in cartilages, of venison in Bishop's Park,
of / hay at Fitzhead, and of Mills: also the Mortuaries
and 'principale legatum', with Vicar's houses at
Wiveliscombe and at Fitzhead." /

Prior to the year 1208 the incumbents of Wiveliscombe
were Rectors; in that year a Prebend was formed,
endowed with the tithes and glebe of the Parish.
The Prebendary / became the Patron of the Vicarage,
the endowment of which was settled as above in 1262.

35

Date of Institution	Names of Vicars	How Vacated	Patrons
1262 A.D.	**ROBERTUS DE BOSCO**		Thos. de Bytton, Prebendary
	The family of De Bosco or Boyse were for a long succession of years tenants in the Manor of South Cadbury under the Courtney and Pauncefoot families. This Robert De Bosco was also Vicar of South Cadbury, in 1265		
1317	**ROBERT IKELYNTON**		The Prebendary
1330	**THOMAS ....**		The Prebendary
1344	**WALTER DE WYNDLESORE**		The Prebendary
....	**.........GRIFFIN**		The Prebendary
31 May 1402	**RICHARD GODELEY**	By death of Griffin	John Bath, Prebendary
15 March 1438	**WILLIAM TREBELLE**	By death of Rich.Godeley	Peter Stucley
3 August 1474	**NICOLAS DYSSUM (or DISSUM)**		Richard Worthington Prebendary
	He was a Public Notary, Vicar of Seaburrow, Somerset 1466-1480. Vicar of St Mary's Taunton, 1460 till his death in 1502.		
1 July 1490	**JOHN BOREMAN, M.A.**	By resignation of Nicolas Dyssum	Edward Willoughby Prebendary
9 February 1509	**WILLIAM BOWERMAN (or BOURMAN)**	By resignation of John Boreman	John Chambers, Prebendary
	LL.B. B.C.L. 12th March, 1506-7. B. Canon L. 15th Dec. 1523. D Canon Law, 26th Jan 1523-4. Vicar of Dulverton, 1510-1530. Rector of Little Ley, Essex 1513. Vicar of Bishop's Lydiard. Rector of Croscombe 1520. Vicar of Doulting 1530-1571. Sub-Dean of Wells 1531. Prebendary of Taunton 1537. He gave to the poor of Wiveliscombe twenty pounds, to be lent by the Church-wardens to four honest Clothiers, for two years gratis, that should employ the poor people in spinning and weaving.		

23 February 1571   PHILIP BYSSE (OR BISSE) S.T.B

B.A., 28th June, 1560. Fellow of Brasenose College, Oxford, 1561. M.A.1564. Fellow of Magdalen College, Oxford, B.D. 14th July 1569. D.D. 8 July, 1580. Incorporated at Cambridge, 1581. Son of Richard Bisse, of Stockland, Somerset. Rector of Batcombe, 1564-1613. Sub. Dean of Wells and Canon of Wells, 1571. Archdeacon of Taunton, 1584, till his death 28th October, 1613, aged 72. Buried at Batcombe, Somerset. He gave two thousand books to Wadham College, Oxford, a benefaction so highly esteemed that the Foundress caused his portrait, drawn in his formalities, to be hung in the Library; she also named him co-founder.

By death of William Bowerman

Ex Coll Episcopi

26 June 1577   WILLIAM CROWTHER, M.A. Oxford

B.A. 10th October, 1566. M.A. 8th July, 1570. Buried in Wiveliscombe Church, June 16, 1617. Brass erected to his memory in south aisle of Parish Church.

By resignation of Philip Bysse

Philip Bysse Sub.Dean for this time, per John Yonge, Kt. of Abbotsbury, Dorset.

15 September 1617 RICHARD WOOD

Buried in Wiveliscombe Parish Church, in the chancel, April 2nd 1645.

By death of William Crowther

Brian Crowther of Knighton, County of Radnor, Wales Executor of the Will of William Crowther aforesaid

3 July 1645   NICHOLAS HOW, M.A., Wadham College Oxford

Matriculated at Wadham College, 9th Nov. 1621, aged 17. B.A. 7th February 1623-4. Married in Wiveliscombe church, the 5th of October 1626, to Margaret Woode, probably daughter of the last Vicar. Vicar of Timberscombe, 1625. *Ejected from the livings of Wiveliscombe and Timberscombe by the Puritans, 1653.* Died at Wiveliscombe and was buried here, January 21st, 1660.

By death of Richard Wood

John Barlow, Prebendary.

24 January 1660   GEORGE DAY, M.A., Hart Hall, Oxford

Matriculated 28th March, 1655. B.A. 13th October 1657. M.A. 3rd July, 1660. Resigned the living of Wiveliscombe in 1662, on being required to sign the Act of Uniformity. Became Pastor of a non-conforming congregation at Radcliff, London, where he died in 1697.

Thomas Westley, Prebendary

30 December 1662   THOMAS KERSWELL, M.A, Corpus Christi College Oxford

Son of William Kerswell, of Croscombe, Somerset. Matriculated at Brasenose College, Oxford 10th Oct., 1634, aged 19. B.A. from Corpus Christi Coll., 25 June, 1636. M.A. 15th June, 1639, Canon of Wells, 1679.

By resignation of George Day

Charles Thirby, Prebendary.

12 April 1688   WILLIAM PRITCHARD,
M.A. Trinity College, Cambridge

Son of Walter Pritchard, of Whitelackington, Somerset Clergyman. Matriculated at Wadham College, Oxford 9th March 1666-7, aged 16. B.A. 1680. M.A. from Trinity College, Cambridge, 1709. Vicar of East Lambrook 1685-88. Brother of John Pritchard, Vicar of Whitelackington.

By death of Thomas Kerswell — James Aston, Prebendary

7 January 1701   EDWARD BURTON, B.A. University College, Oxford

Son of John Burton, of Highly, Shropshire, clergyman. Matriculated at University College, Oxford, 5th Oct. 1693, aged 18. B.A. 1697. Vicar of St Mary, Taunton 1728. Married the second time in Wiveliscombe Parish Church, to Elizabeth Taylor, Oct. 28th 1724. Buried in the Parish Church here, October 16th, 1754.

By resignation of William Pritchard — John Wells, Prebendary

9 October 1754   BENJAMIN HANCOCK,
B.A. St John's College, Cambridge

B.A. St John's College, Cambridge, 1747. Buried in the Parish Church, Wiveliscombe, September 15th, 1784. Tablet to his memory in the south aisle.

By death of Edward Burton — Elias Rebotier, Prebendary

31 January 1785   HARRY DOWNING, Magdalen Hall, Oxford.

Son of Henry Bowles Downing, of Envill, County Stafford, clergyman. Magdalen Hall, Oxford. Matriculated Nov. 22nd, 1770, aged 20.

By death of Benjamin Hancock — Paul George Snow, Prebendary

19 November 1813   JOHN SUNDERLAND,
M.A., Trinity College, Cambridge

B.A. Trinity College, Cambridge, 1792. M.A. 1795. Resigned 1837. During his incumbency the Parish Church was rebuilt, the foundation stone of which was laid on 6th June, 1827.

By death of Harry Downing — Walker King, Bishop of Rochester, Prebendary

20 September 1837   RICHARD À COURT BEADON,
MA. St John's College, Cambridge.

B.A. St. John's College, Cambridge, 1832. M.A. 1835. Ordained Deacon, 1832. Priest 1833, by the Bishop of Winchester, for the Bishop of Bristol. Prebendary of Wiveliscombe, 1833-1891. Vicar of Cheddar, Somerset 1836-1883. During his incumbency the Vicarage was rebuilt.

By resignation of John Sunderland — Richard à Court Beadon, Prebendary

8 November 1881   JOHN THOMAS TROTT
M.A., St Mary's Hall, Oxford.

B.A. St Mary's Hall, Oxford 1874. M.A. 1881. Ordained Deacon 1874. Priest 1875 by the Bishop of Bath and Wells. Curate of Leigh-on-Mendip, 1874-1876. Curate of East and West Cranmore 1876-1878. Curate of Cheddar 1878-1881, all in Somersetshire. Vicar of Newborough, County of Northampton 1891.

By resignation of Richard à Court Beadon — Richard à Court Beadon, Prebendary

12 October 1891   HOWARD MCCRIRICK,
B.A., St John's College, Cambridge

Ordained Deacon 1883. Priest 1885 by the Bishop of Manchester. Curate of St. Matthew's, Burnley, Lancashire, 1883-1885. Vicar of Hempnall, Norfolk 1885-1886. Vicar of Newborough, Northamptonshire 1886-1891. During his incumbency Iron Mission Churches built in hamlets of Langley and Croford. The first incumbent presented by the Bishop of the Diocese, the patronage having been transferred from the Prebendary to the Bishop, with whom it is for the future rested. Died 26th May 1922.	By resignation of John Thomas Trott	The Bishop of Bath and Wells. (Lord Arthur Hervey)

12 August 1922   RICHARD YERBURGH BONSEY
M.A. St John's College, Cambridge

Ordained Deacon 1898. Priest 1900 by the Bishop of Bath and Wells. Curate of Crewkerne, 1898-1901. Curate of Pitminster and Angersleigh, 1901-1906. Vicar of Trull. 1906-1914. Vicar of Evercreech 1914-22.	By death of Howard McCririck	The Bishop of Bath & Wells (St John Basil Wynn Wilson)

1931   KENNETH WILLIAM PRIDGIN TEALE
M.A. Emmanuel College, Cambridge

Hon: C.F. Deacon 1903. Priest 1904. Ox. C. of Stoke Poges, 1903-05. Havant 1905-08. Miss. P. Dio. Aukld 1908-10. Vicar of Warkworth 1910-12. Curate of Aulk Hucknall 1912-13. St Mary Magdalene, Taunton 1913-14. Vicar of All Saints Trull 1914-19. T.C.F. 1917-19. Rector of Thurloxton with Durston 1919-31.	By resignation of Richard Yerburgh Bonsey	The Bishop of Bath & Wells (St John Basil Wynn Wilson)

November 1938   EDGAR ALBERT AUST

Kelham Theo College,1905.Deacon, 1911. Priest 1915; Dio. of Bath and Wells. Curate of St. Michael and Old Angels, Yeovil 1911-1912. Curate of St George, Nottingham 1912-1913. Curate of Holy Trinity, Frome 1914-1915; Curate in Charge of St Thomas, Wells 1915-1917; Temp. Chaplain to Forces 1917-1919. Curate of Brislington 1919-1920. Curate of St. Aidans, Bristol 1920-1925. Rector of Writhlington 1925-1935. Curate of Crewkerne 1935-1938. Vicar of Wiveliscombe 1938.	By resignation Kenneth William Pridgin Teale	Francis Underhill, Bishop of Bath and Wells

May 1942   CHARLES WILLIAM BISHOP.

Durham, L.TH. 1922. St Boniface Theo. College, Warminster. Deacon 1922. Priest Dio. of Southwark 1923. Curate of Benhilton, 1922-25. Curate of St Marks, Jarrow 1925-27. Priest in charge, Corrigin, Western Australia 1927-1930. Curate of Holy Trinity, Hounslow 1930-35. Vicar of Holy Trinity, Tottenham 1935-42. Vicar of Wiveliscombe 1942.	By exchange	Francis Underhill Bishop of Bath and Wells.

May 1948   VICTOR AUGUSTUS CHARLES ALLEN

King's College, London. B.A. 1907. Deacon 1937. Priest 1938. Southwark. Curate of St Mildred, Lee, 1937-39, Woolwich; and in charge of St. Anne, 1939-41. Rector of St Thomas, Old Charlton 1941-48. Curate in charge of Holy Trinity, New Charlton 1942-48. Vicar of Wiveliscombe 1948-56. Rector of Fitzhead 1950-56.

By exchange

Harold William Bradfield, Bishop of Bath and Wells

June 1957   JOHN CAMPBELL SEYMOUR CHAMBERLAIN

Emmanuel College Cambridge, 1921. R.N. 1917-33, Wells Theological College 1934-35. Deacon 1935. Priest 1936, Southwark. Curate of St. Mark, Plumstead 1935-38. Findon and in Charge of All Saints, Findon Valley 1938-39. Vicar of Christ Church, Shooters Hill, 1939-57. Wiveliscombe 1957. Curate in Charge and Rector of Fitzhead 1957.

By resignation of Victor Augustus Charles Allen

Harold William Bradfield, Bishop of Bath and Wells

1966   FRANK WILLIAM HENRY BENTLEY

King's College, London. A.K.C. 1957. Deacon 1958, Priest 1959; Dio. of Bath and Wells. Curate of SS Peter and Paul, Shepton Mallet 1958-62. Rector of All Saints, Kingsdon with St Peter, Podymore Milton 1962-66; Curate in Charge of St. Bartholomew, Yeovilton 1962-66; also Rector of Holy Cross, Babcary 1964-66. Vicar of Wiveliscombe 1966.

By resignation of John Campbell Seymour Chamberlain

Edward Barry Henderson Bishop of Bath and Wells

July 1976   CHRISTOPHER JOHN BICKFORD MARSHALL

King's College, London. AKC 1956. TD 1979. Deacon 1957. Priest 1958. Curate Leatherhead 1957-1960 and Crewkerne 1960-1963, Vicar of Long Sutton 1963-1976 (With Long Load 1972-1976). CF (TA) 1965-1979, Vicar of Wiveliscombe 1976. Rural Dean of Tone 1978-1987. Rector of Wiveliscombe with Chipstable, Huish Champflower and Clatworthy 1993. Prebendary of Worminster in Wells Cathedral 1988.

By resignation of Frank William Henry Bentley

John Monier Bickersteth, Bishop of Bath and Wells

July 1997   PETER ALAN EAST

Southampton University LLB 1982, ACIB 1989. Cranmer Hall, Durham 1990. Deacon 1993, Priest 1994. Curate Combe Down with Monkton Combe and South Stoke 1993-1997. Rector of Wiveliscombe with Chipstable, Huish Champflower and Clatworthy 1997.

By resignation of C J B Marshall

James Lawton Thompson, Bishop of Bath and Wells.

January 1998   GRAHAM ANTHONY OWEN

R.N. 1973-1992. Birmingham University BA (Comb. Hons) 1977. Dip. HE 1994. Trinity College Bristol 1992. Deacon 1994, Priest 1995. Curate Wiveliscombe with Chipstable, Huish Champflower and Clatworthy 1994-1997. Rector of this Benefice 1998.

By resignation P A East

James Lawton Thompson, Bishop of Bath and Wells.

St. Andrew's Church - Crypt

In the crypt beneath the church, and behind iron gates, are the now no-longer used catacombs. At the time of the church rebuilding, in 1827, it was becoming common practice to introduce vaults under new churches and thirty-six were included under St. Andrew's. Families could apply for the use of a vault and, initially, eighteen were allocated on payment, for a minimum fee of £20. These eighteen vaults have been used to a greater or lesser degree but only two are full and bricked up. Wooden coffins, with lead liners and a third outer box, were laid across the width of the vault, to a maximum of about thirty per vault. On occasion, elsewhere, coffins can still be seen in catacombs but at St. Andrew's all the coffins have been bricked in.

On a few of the vaults there are memorial tablets, the inscriptions from which appear on the following pages. Interesting details can be gleaned from these tablets. With so many names on a particular plaque, for example *V/C* and *V/D*, it is possible to piece together family pedigrees, especially if looked at in conjunction with the memorials in the church or later burials in the churchyard.

No entombments have taken place since 1926 and the vaults are now mainly used for storage, with an allocation at one end for the Bath & Wells Diocese Redundant Churches

Furnishings Store. Two vaults at the east end, being unused, have been incorporated into the new crypt development and now contain the children's play area and the lavatory. The oil-fired church heating system, which replaced the old coke boiler, is located in two further unused vaults on the north wall.   The area used as a kitchen is believed to have been intended as a vault for clergy but was never used.   The most recent vicar to have died in office and to have been buried in the parish is the Reverend Howard McCririck, whose grave *[B22]*, dating from 1922, can be found outside the west door of the church. A curate, Reverend John Llewellin, is also buried in the churchyard *[T54* and *C40]*.

Tablets *V/G, V/H* and *V/I* do not belong to St. Andrew's. When worship ceased in the Wesleyan Chapel in South Street in June 1986, the tablets were removed to St. Andrew's for safekeeping. For further information on the Wesleyan Chapel see page 167; for the Evangelical Congregational Church, with its own dedicated cemetery, see page 163.

Prior to their current function as St. Andrew's Parish Rooms, the catacombs played a special role during the Second World War. From all over England came a wide variety of valuable and irreplaceable items to be stored in the vaults for safekeeping: a fortuitous move as some of the original buildings sustained heavy damage.   Pictures, woodwork, documents, silver, altar rails and stained glass windows were among the items given refuge. A document commemorating this act of preservation hangs in the church *[T44]*.

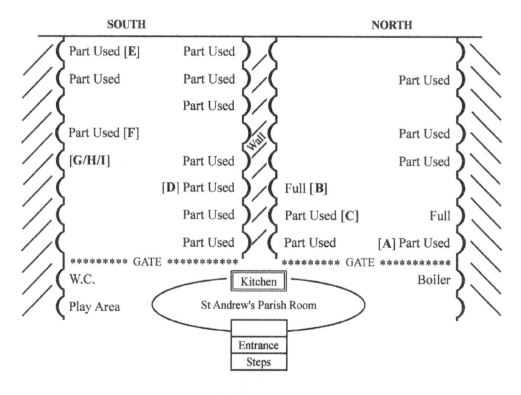

Plan of the Vaults in the Catacombs

VAULT TABLETS

The location of tablets *[V = VAULT]* in the vaults can be found in the Plan on page 42

V/A *[Black lettering on Oak Door]*   No 34 / Mr Jonathan ELFORD
*Mr Elford served as Churchwarden for many years, including the period of the church rebuilding 1827-1829.   He resided at Oakhampton Manor. [see **T15**]*

V/B *[Black Slate]*

Sacred / to the memory of / Elizabeth Dorothy NORMAN / Died March 12th 1822 / Aged two years / Also of / James Tudball NORMAN / Died March 20th 1825   Aged 6 months / Also of   William TUDBALL / Died April 18th 1829   Aged 12 years / Also of/ Mary Jane NORMAN / Died August 6th 1831. Aged 6 months

V/C   *[White Marble]*

Sacred to the memory of

Robert John LUTLEY	Elizabeth LUTLEY JUNR.1864
Dr Edward CHORLEY 1833	Maria Hurley LUTLEY. 1872.
INFANTS	Samuel Baker LUTLEY. 1872.
William Chorley LUTLEY)	Abraham Christopher LUTLEY 1889.
John LUTLEY)	Eliza CHORLEY 1891
Maria ")	Emma LUTLEY March 10, 1906. 92 yrs.
Lucy ")	Helen Hurley LUTLEY. 1926.
Jane Moore ")	Susannah Eliza EVELYN. 1926.
John LUTLEY SENR. 1852.	
Elizabeth LUTLEY SENR. 1853.	

"Make them to be numbered with Thy Saints in Glory Everlasting"

V/D   *[Black Stone]*

THE FOLLOWING ARE INTERRED IN N°. 16 CATACOMBE			
PHILIP HANCOCK		DIED 1838	AGED 72
FRANCES HANCOCK	HIS WIDOW	" 1858	AGED 84
PHILIP HANCOCK	THEIR SON	" 1870	AGED 61
ANNE BLAKE HANCOCK	HIS WIDOW	" 1883	AGED 70
CHILDREN OF PHILIP AND ANNE HANCOCK			
PHILIP KARSLAKE		" 1832	INFANT
FRANCES JANE		" 1844	AGED 7
WALTER MOGRIDGE		" 1838	INFANT
MARGARET FROUDE		" 1917	AGED 77
MARY GRACE		" 1844	INFANT
GEORGE		" 1864	AGED 20
SPEED		" 1861	AGED 14
ARTHUR		" 1851	INFANT
FRANCES MARY		" 1864	AGED 10
BROTHERS OF THE ABOVE			
PHILIP KARSLAKE		" 1868	AGED 34
BURIED AT SEA			
ROBERT IVESON		" 1908	AGED 73
BURIED AT CAPE TOWN			
EDWARD BELLEW		" 1874	AGED 35
BURIED AT SEATON, DEVON			
FREDERICK		" 1920	AGED 71
BURIED AT DUNSTER, SOM			
ELIZABETH		DIED 1925	AGED 79

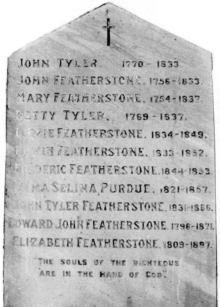 

V/E [Grey Stone]

JOHN TYLER	1770 – 1833
JOHN FEATHERSTONE	1756 – 1833
MARY FEATHERSTONE	1754 – 1837
BETTY TYLER	1769 – 1837
LIZZIE FEATHERSTONE	1834 – 1849
EDWIN FEATHERSTONE	1833 – 1852
FREDERIC FEATHERSTONE	1844 – 1853
EMMA SELINA PURDUE	1821 – 1857
JOHN TYLER FEATHERSTONE	1831 – 1866
EDWARD JOHN FEATHERSTONE	1796 – 1871
ELIZABETH FEATHERSTONE	1809 – 1897

"The Souls of the Righteous are in the Hand of God"

[Millers and landowners, the Featherstones were a leading family in the town]

V/F [Black Slate]

In memory of / Sarah wife of Edward / ROGERS who died / September y. 6th 1814 / Aged 62 [yrs] / Edward ROGERS, died / November 22, 1824 / Aged 74 years

[As it pre-dates the 1829 rebuilding, this tablet may have been located originally in either the churchyard or the previous church.]

V/G *[White marble]* Sacred to the memory of / George DULEY / who died July 6, 1849. Aged 28 years / Resting with unshaken confidence on the / Atonement, Death for him had lost its sting, / and the Grave its Victory. / Beloved by all who knew him, he was early / summoned from a life of arduous and / self sacrificing labour on earth to the rest / and unfolding reward of Heaven / Also to / Georgiana Esther, infant daughter / of the above George DULEY / and Mary his wife / who died at the age of 5 months Oct. 31, 1849.

V/H *[White Marble on Black Slate]* In Memoriam / 1889 – 1895 / To the glory of God / and in remembrance of / John Peter COCK / and Louisa his wife / formerly of this Parish / they were for several / years actively associated / with this church and / were beloved by all / who knew them.

V/I *[Brass]* The Electric Heating System / is the gift of / James Gore TUDBALL / In memory of his wife Ellen / A faithful member of this church / December 1957.
[This small tablet used to be on a seat-end in the old Wesleyan Chapel]

St. Andrew's Church – circa 1840

St. Andrew's Churchyard

St. Andrew's Churchyard
An Historical Look

St. Andrew's churchyard has grown over the years. The original churchyard, up to 1826, was confined by cottages on the northern side. These were demolished soon after the 1829 church was finished, and part of the site, where parking currently takes place north of the railings, was ceded for use by the civil authorities. The remaining ground was taken into the churchyard. It is worth noting that the small cobbled area on the western side of this ground was not transferred to the civil authorities and remains the property of St. Andrew's church; recently bollards have been put in place here to protect the amenity area outside the church gates.

It is evident that the original churchyard has been used over and over again for burials. However, no visible signs of such burials remain, as the whole yard was cleared of headstones when the new church was built in 1829 and it is regrettable that so few pre-1829 memorials were preserved.

The church authorities realised that there was a need for more ground and there followed the first of the extensions in 1840. This plot went south into Cater Close, with the southern boundary running roughly east to west in line with the gatehouse to the Bishop's Manor house. In 1895 a further extension southward was necessary into land owned by the church and in the 1950s the 'New Extension' was taken from the gardens between Rotton Row and the existing west wall. Even this proved insufficient, and a small plot of Charity land called 'Sancti' (extending north from the 'New Extension') was purchased from the Wiveliscombe Consolidated Charity Trustees and consecrated in 1985.

The frequent need for churchyard extensions is caused by our modern reluctance to re-use land already used for burials. It is worth noting, however, that the yard north of the church and the first part to the south have been used for more than a thousand years and this could preclude reburial unless the Parish considers setting up a charnel house.

Dixon Luxton, Churchwarden

*Approaching the Church from the East with
a corner of Bourne's House on the right*

Today's churchyard therefore dates from 1829. The new church was built on the same
site as its predecessor, but at a higher elevation, as material was brought in to cover over
the previous burial ground. As late as 1841 in the south-east corner there still existed a
Poor House, which had once been within the boundary of the Bishop's Manor. The
'Wiveliscombe National School' in the building in the north-west corner, near the main
churchyard entrance, was erected on the site of old cottages in 1842. The Primary School
in North Street was opened in 1876, but some teaching continued in the old building until
the construction of Kingsmead School in 1953 (with the exception of the 2nd World War
when it was used as a billet for American soldiers). It is now in private ownership after a
period of use as a Parish Room. Of historical interest are some windows from the old
Bishop's Manor House.

By 1829, a change in burial practices was taking place nationally. The population was
increasing and, as people moved to the cities for employment, the urban parish churches
could no longer cope with all the burials. The development of the independently located
cemeteries began. Joint-stock companies created almost garden-like burial grounds, with
a wide range of substantial monuments and mausolea and elaborate epitaphs. Rural parish

churchyards, by contrast, may not have such spectacular funereal architecture as some of these well-known 19th Century cemeteries (for example, Arnos Vale in Bristol, Highgate, Kensal Green and Nunhead in London, and Brookwood in Surrey) but, as is the case with Wiveliscombe, they are no less important especially as they complement the formal historical record of the local area.

The inscriptions that appear on the following pages have been recorded from the head-stones in the churchyard.   In many instances only tantalising fragments remain and these are noted as such.   Additionally, over the generations, many more burials have taken place than have surviving headstones. With the exception of the New Extension (which has its own explanatory introduction - page 132), no attempt has been made to research archival sources to include the names of those who may have been interred here but who have no lasting memorial.   As already mentioned in the *PREFACE,* burial registers are stored in the County Archives and are available for individual study.

Unlike the more formal urban cemeteries, churchyard memorials tend to be smaller and more simple, possibly a pragmatic choice whenever space was limited.   Fashions change for both the shape and material of the headstones and the design of the lettering, en-graving and motifs inscribed upon them *[see page 191].*   For example, there are very few box tombs in Wiveliscombe. This was partly because, by the time burials began after the church building in 1829, the more popular style of memorial was round-topped and upright. They gave way to a more gothic-pointed style, followed by the introduction, around the turn of the century, of the cross.   In the 1920s gravestones became smaller, a feature which continues to the present day.   The use of kerbs as memorials, rather than solely for marking the outline of a grave, was in vogue for a short while but, subsequent to the 2nd World War and, as with the use of crosses, this practice has declined. Examples of all these designs can be seen in the churchyard.

Originally headstones were made from whatever was available locally - wood, sandstone, slate, granite, Portland stone. The slates from the nearby Oakhampton quarry, for example, were regarded as ideal for tombstones.   Increasingly these gave way to imported materials, most conspicuous of which was the introduction of Italian marble at the beginning of the 20th Century. The materials weather at different rates, and the old slate memorials now seem particularly vulnerable to climatic factors. The lone oak 'lily cross' *[C46]* is unique, and was copied from a similarly designed memorial which stood to the north of the church until just after the 2nd World War. In the same area is planted a cutting from an ancient yew tree, presented by the Diocese in the Millennium Year.

All denominations at present in the Parish are free to use St. Andrew's churchyard for burials. A variety of walks of life are represented and these, where recorded, have been listed on page 196. The earliest surviving legible inscription is one of the few memorials from the pre-1829 church rebuilding period - *D24* Ester and David North.   *D174* John Bale, who died in 1861, is a link back to earlier times, being described as having fought in the Battle of Waterloo;   *D25* tells of the tragic loss of eight Luff children;   and *F166* records that Muriel Tester lived to an age of 108.   Latvian and Polish residents of Wiveliscombe are recorded on *F37, F39, N147* and *N260.*

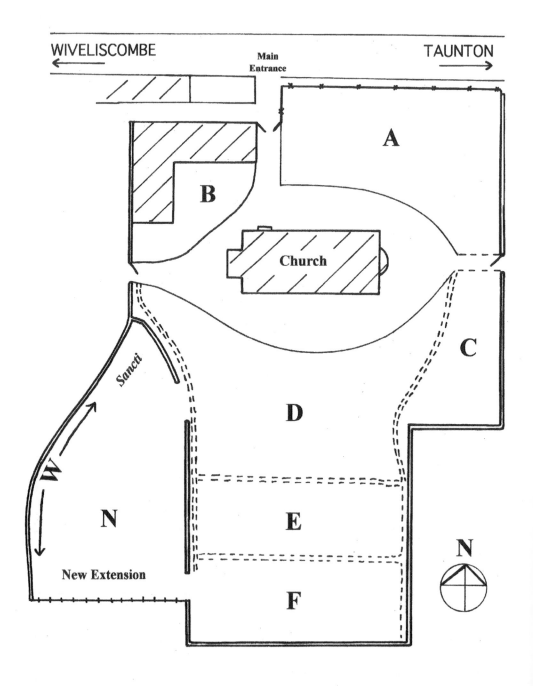

WIVELISCOMBE

TAUNTON

Main
Entrance

A

B

Church

C

Sancti

W

D

N

E

New Extension

F

N

St. Andrew's Churchyard – General Plan

St. Andrew's Churchyard Inscriptions

KEY to Inscriptions

The churchyard has been surveyed section by section, as indicated on the Plan on page 52. Within a Section, each headstone has its own identifying Plot Number. To locate a grave, find the name in the *INDEX OF INSCRIPTIONS* on page 199 and ascertain its Plot Number. This can then be located in the relevant Section list, and on the appropriate Section Plan.

Italic script = No headstone but the person is known to have been buried in that particular grave

F/H = Flower Holder

(Wall) = Tablet set in wall

mb = Metal Railings or Box

[Name in Italics] after an inscription = the stonemason's name

(E) East = The geographical direction towards which the stone faces

/ = Indicates the end of a line of inscribed text

(Surround) = Also known as 'kerbs' or 'bodystones', these ground level markers are described as 'surrounds' to cover any anomalies.

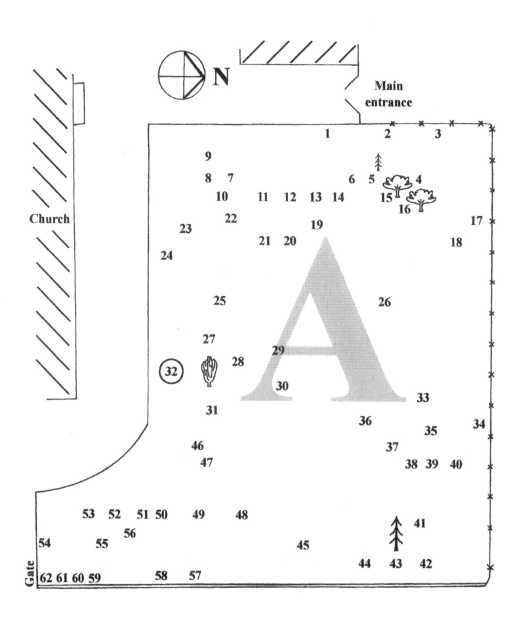

Churchyard Plan - Section A

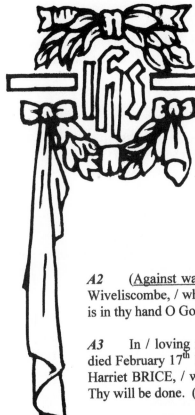

A1   Sacred / to the memory of / James SLOMAN / (of this parish) / who departed this life / July 27th 1869 / aged 82 years / Also of / Harriet SLOMAN / wife of the above / who died February 24th 1890 / aged 90 years / Thy will be done (E)

A2   (Against wall)   In memoriam / James PAYNE, / of Billey Farm, Wiveliscombe, / who died February 17th, 1911, / aged 64 years. / My time is in thy hand O God. (E)

A3   In / loving memory / of / James BRICE, / of Billey Farm, / who died February 17th 1915 / aged 75 years. / Peace Perfect Peace. / Also of / Harriet BRICE, / wife of the above / Died March 29th 1917, / aged 75. / Thy will be done. (E)

A4   In loving memory of / James DULBOROUGH / died Dec. 2nd 1916, / aged 49 years. / Also of his wife / Emma DULBOROUGH / died Jan 13th 1951. / Aged 79 years. (E)

A5   Sacred / to the memory of / Robert HOWE / of Billey Farm Wiveliscombe / who departed this life / July the 7th 1888 / aged 75 years / Blessed are the dead which die in the Lord   (W)

A6   In / loving memory / of / John GREEDY / died Feby 1st 1897, / aged 82 years. / Also of / Wilmot GREEDY, / wife of the above / died July 19th 1895, / aged 80 years. (E)

A7   In loving memory of / Edward HILL, / (Fleed) Wiveliscombe, / who died July 10th 1891, / aged 67 years. / Also of / Harriet, wife of the above / who died April 12th 1877, / aged 39 years. / He giveth his beloved sleep. (W)

A8   Sacred / to the memory of / Edward HILL / of Fleed in this Parish, / who died Septr. 28th 1853: / aged 67 years. / After the short illness of twelve hours. / Also Elizabeth his / wife who died March 13th 1868: / aged 69 years. / "I will sing unto the Lord because he hath / dealt bountifully with me." 13th Psalm 6 verse. (W)
<u>Reverse</u>:   E.H. / 1853.   E.H. / 1868.

A9 (Pillar) In memory of / John FIELD. / Died November 3rd 1837 / aged 92 years. / Myra FIELD, / died March 29th 1847 / aged 77 years. (N) Corelli Collard FIELD / Husband of / Susanna CHARTER / and Sarah FIELD / died January 7th 1875, / aged 72 years. (W) Susanna Charter FIE LD / died Sep$^{tr.}$ 10th 1847 / aged 49 years. / Sarah FIELD, / died Sep^{tr} 15th 1866 / aged 67 years. (S)

A10 In loving memory of / Harriet LOCK / who passed away / Feb, 6. 1933 aged 89 / Also Thomas / beloved husband of above / passed away Oct, 17. 1933 aged 93 (E)

A10a (Ground) In memory / of / John LOCK / 1871 – 1940

A11 (Surround) *[Blank]*

A12 In loving memory of / Samuel WESTCOTT / of Langley Marsh / Wiveliscombe / who departed this life / January the 18th 1880 / aged 51 years / Watch therefore for ye know not / what hour your Lord doth come (E)

A13 In loving memory of / Elizabeth / the beloved wife of / George R THORNE / of Jews Farm Wiveliscombe, / who died January 7th 1907, / aged 81 years. / "God loved her, and thought it best, / to take her home with Him to rest." / Also of / George Radley THORNE / who died March 21st 1914, / aged 76 years. (E)

A14 I.H.S. / In loving memory of / George THORNE / second son of / G R THORNE / of Jews Farm Wiveliscombe / ...... / In the midst of life we are in death (E)

A14a I.H.S. / Leonard Charles / MERCHANT / died June 10th 1889 (E)

A15 I.H.S. / In loving memory of / James CLAPP / of Whitefield Wiveliscombe / who departed this life / November the 11th 1880, / aged 52 years / I know in whom I have believed, and / am persuaded that he is able to / keep that which I have committed / unto Him against that day. / II Tim. 1 Chap. XII Verse / Also of Amelia / the beloved wife of the above / who died June 23rd 1909 / aged 75 years. / Also of James / grandson of the above / who died February 25th 1890 / aged 4 ½ months. R.I.P. *[Richards]* (W)

A16 Treasured memories / of our dear Brother / Edward John FURZE / who passed away 31st. Jan. 1950 / Aged 58 years. / In God's keeping. *[Carpenter, Bridgwater]* (E)

A17 In / ever loving memory / of / a beloved husband and Dad / Walter BURTON, / who fell asleep May 16th 1933, / aged 72 years. / Also of Mary BURTON, / beloved wife of the above / who fell asleep July 12th 1938, / aged 76 years. / At rest. (E) (F/H)

A18 In / ever loving memory of / my beloved husband / John Charles DUNN, / who fell asleep October 12th 1938, / Aged 47 years. / At rest. (E) (F/H)

A19   In loving memory of / Jessie / the beloved wife of / John GODDARD / who died September 25th 1885 aged .... / Also of the [above] named / John [GODDARD] who died .... Bristol / March .... / aged .... *[Manning, Taunton]* (E)

A20   (Surround) In loving memory of George STONE who died 19th Dec 1915 aged 63 (S) Resting (E) Also of Kate STONE who died 17th Jan 1923. Aged 67 (N)

A21   In / loving memory / of / Mary Alice ANDREWS / the beloved daughter of / M KIMBER / who passed away Novr 14th 1918 / aged 30 years / Gone but not forgotten (W)

A22   Sacred / to the memory of / Rachel BURFITT / died January 27th 1871 / aged 70 years / My days are like a shadow / that declineth and I am / withered like grass / Also / Thomas BURFITT / died August 1st 1875 / aged 77 years / He will regard the prayer / of the destitute and / not despise their prayer (W)

A23   My dear Mother / Elizabeth BROOK? / 7th....... 1909? *[Collard, Taunton]* (E)

A24   In / memory / of / .... 1866 ? (W)

A25   Sacred / to the memory of / Jane, / wife of James PAYNE, / who departed this life / Octr 22nd 1848 / aged 50 years (W)

A26   I.H.S. / Sacred / to the memory of / William JONES / who died January 15th 1889/ aged 73 years. / The Lord gave, and the Lord /hath taken away, Blessed / be the name of the Lord. *[S. Richards]*   (W)

A27   To / the beloved memory of / Ann / relict of the late / John BOUCHER / of Rodhuish / who died August 10th 1862 / aged 62 years / Also Benjamin / son of / John & Ann BOUCHER / born May 13th 1837 / died February 8th 1844. I will ransom them from the power of the grave / I will redeem them from death. (W)

A28   James KING / died Sept 15th 1828 / aged 30 years. (E)

A29   In ever loving memory / of / Henry John HARTNELL, / who passed away / April 7th 1911, / aged 57 years. / Also of Mary Ann / wife of the above / who passed away / April 29th 1939, / aged 86 years. / Peace, perfect peace. (E) (F/H)

A30   In memory of / William TREBLE / who died June 12 1876 / aged 23. (E)

A31   (Under tree)   Sacred / to the memory of / John COX / died February 3rd 1867 / aged 66 years / There is therefore now no con / demnation to them which are in / Christ Jesus, who walk not after / the flesh, but after the spirit. / Romans 8.C.1.V./ Also / Mary wife of the above / died August 20th 1867 / aged 75 years. / Blessed are the pure in heart / for they shall see God. / Matthew 5.C.8.V. (E)

A 32 – PREACHING CROSS

The red sandstone PREACHING CROSS is believed to date from the 14th century, and is probably the oldest stone structure still standing in Wiveliscombe. In a niche on the west side is a sculptured figure, whose identification is unknown, but is reputed to be either St. Mary, or John Drockensford, Bishop of Bath and Wells 1309-1329 'who built the adjoining manor house'. [See page 6] The shaft is octagonal, and tapers towards the top, which is missing. A more complete example of such a cross can be seen in the churchyard of the neighbouring parish of Fitzhead. [See page 6]

A33   Sacred / to the memory of / Joseph ROGERS / died Febr^y 2nd 1868, aged 90. / Ann ROGERS / wife of the above / died Augs^t 10th 1864. Aged 82. / Also children of the above / William ROGERS / died Augs^t 4th 1843. Aged 27. / Harriet LORD / widow died Decr 24th 1855. Aged 42. / Also Harriet LORD her / daughter died Novr 19th 1863. / Aged 18 years. (W)

A34   Sacred / to the memory of / John THOMAS / who departed this life / January the 25th 1875 / aged 66 years / Blessed are the dead, / which die in the Lord. (W)

A35   In the memory of / James THOMAS died 8th March 1822 / Aged 15 years. / Also of Ann THOMAS died 24th Decemb^r 1827 / Aged 16 years. / Also of Jane THOMAS died 4th January 1844 / Aged 21 years. / Sickness full Sore Long Time I Bore. / Physicians all in vain. / Till god *[sic]* did please by death to cease, / and ease me of my Pain. / Also John THOMAS died / March 10th 1855. Aged 71 years. / Also Jane THOMAS wife / of the above. Died Novr 9th 1856 / aged 71 years. / Also William THOMAS son / of the above died March 15th 1865 / aged 33 years. (W)

A36   (Cross) W.C. (E)

A37   In the midst of life we are in death / In / memory of / Thomas Ormlett MARTIN / who departed this life / February 23 1866 / aged 49 years /
Also / Mary MARTIN / wife of the above / who departed this life / February 24th 1876 / aged 56? Years
[Stone broken in two & poem illegible]   (W)

A38   (Broken stone)

A39   (Fallen stone) In / loving memory of / Frederick NORTH / of Wiveliscombe / died December 5th 1928 / aged 81 years.

A40   In loving memory of / John NORTH, / (of Clerks Pool, in this parish) / who died June 24th 1891, / aged 70 years. / In the Father's gracious keeping, / leave we now our Lov^d one sleeping. (W)

A41   Sacred / to the memory of / William HOLBOROW / late officer of Inland Revenue / of this town / who departed this life / on the 24th day of April 1869 / aged 85?(?38) years and 9 months. (W)

A42   (Ground)   Sacred / to the memory of / Mrs Elizabeth WALKER / relict of / William WALKER Esq / of E*[verley Lodge]* Herts / who died at Castle in this Parish / January 14th 1832 / in the 80th year of his age / Also to the memory of / her son-in-law / Capt I.N. FISCHER, RM / who died at Castle 8th November 185- / aged 76 years / Also to the memory of / Elizabeth Martha FISCHER / his widow and daughter of the said / William and Elizabeth WALKER / who died at Castle? *[?home]* June 29th 1870 / in the 78th year of her age. *[See T1]*

A43   Sacred / to the memory of / ..../ Major ....

A44   (Ground)   Underneath / are deposited the remains of / Lieut. Colonel BRUTON / of the North Devon Militia / who died April 20th 1846 / aged 76 years (N) / Also of / Gertrude his wife / who died July 22nd 1862 / aged 87 years. (S)

A45   Sacred / to the memory of / Thomas THRESHER / who fell asleep in Jesus / September the 8th 1877 / aged 73 years / He was a local preacher of the / Wesleyan Methodist Society / at Wiveliscombe for 50 years / Also of / Ann THRESHER / wife of the above / who departed this life / October the 12th 1863 / aged 56 years / Not lost but gone before (W)

A46   (Fallen Stone)   In / loving memory of / William DWELLY / who passed away / July 21 – 1924 / aged 82 years / Also of / Hannah KING / wife of the above / who fell asleep / Oct -27 -1926 / aged 80 years. / Peace perfect peace.
(Surround) John KING who died September 21 – 1873 aged 59 years (S) / Also Mary Ann his wife died December 13 – 1890   Aged 77 years. (E)

A47   Sacred / to the memory / of / Robert WEBBER / died June 25th 1843 / aged 39 years / Also / Mary WEBBER / died June 17th 1860 / aged 53 years. (W)

A48   I.H.S.   / I am the resurrection and the life / Sacred / to the / memory / of / Amelia / the beloved wife of / John MARTIN Esqr / of Argyle Square London / who departed this life / on the 28th day of September 1869 / aged 58 years .
[Richards] (W)

A49   In sacred memory of / Sarah BOUCHER / wife of William BOUCHER / of Ford Wiveliscombe / who died June 9th 1862 / aged 76 years / Also / Anna TYLER / sister of Sarah BOUCHER / who died November 26th 1862 / aged 80 years / Also / Anna BOUCHER / daughter of William and Sarah BOUCHER / who died at Weston-super-mare / November 28th 1888 / aged 74 years / Absent from the body, at home with the Lord. (W)

A50   Sacred / to / the memory of / Thomas TYLER / of Whitefield / died December 6th 1861 / aged 51 years / My flesh shall rest in hope / Psalm 16 Verse 19 / Also Elizabeth his daughter / died October 6th 1867 / aged 22 years (W)

A51   Sacred / to the memory of / Jane TIMEWELL / who departed this life / Jan 3rd 1857 / aged 67 years / Also / Catharine / her youngest daughter / who departed this life / July 29th 1859 / aged 28 years / Be ye also ready / Matt.24.v.44 / Also / John Comer TIMEWELL / died July 12th 1866 aged 78 years   (W)

A52   I.H.S. /   In / loving memory of / Thomas GAMLIN / who died November 22nd 1877 / aged 23 years / His end is peace / Also / William CHORLEY / who died February 9th 1870 /   aged 87 years / Also Lucy GAMLIN / who died March 6th 1879 / aged 13 years / asleep in Jesus / On the resurrection morning / all the graves of their dead restore / Father Mother Sister Brother / meet once more (W)

A53   In / loving memory / of / William BERRY / who fell asleep July 2nd 1892 / aged 68 / Also of Mary Ann his wife / who was called home / August 1st 1907, aged 74 / Also of their infant daughters / Clara & Alice / Until the day dawns (W)

A54   Not dead but gone before / In memory of / William MILTON / who departed this life July 16th 1842 / aged 85 years / Betty MILTON wife of the above / who departed this life August 30th 1846 / aged 87 years / Sylvia MILTON daughter of the above / who departed this life December 27th 1860 / aged 79 years / John MILTON son of the above / William & Betty MILTON / who departed this life December 1st 1877 / aged 82 years / Elizabeth Collard MILTON / daughter of the above John MILTON / who departed this life April 13th 1844 / aged 6 months. / The rich and poor meet together The / Lord is the maker of them all. Prov.22.2. (W)

A55   (Tiny remains of stone)

A56   In / loving remembrance / of / William GAMLIN / who died Feb. 8. 1882, / Aged 56 years. / Resting in hope. / Also of our dear mother / Elizabeth, / wife of the above / who died Sep 3 1907, / Aged 80 years. / Farewell dear children our lives are past / our love was true while life did last, / And now for us no sorrow make / But love your Saviour for his own sake / Erected by H & E B / Also William Henry / youngest son of the above / who fell in action Aug 9 1915 / Aged 44 years / Interred in Boulogne Cemetary *[sic]*, France   (W)   *[see page 180]*

A57   In / memory / of / William MILLETT / who died Novr 29th 1861 / aged 73 years / {line of illegible text} / Also of / Hannah / his beloved wife / who died April 3rd 1862 / aged 73 years / She is not dead but sleepeth / Also of / John / son of the above / who died June 17th 1849 / aged 26 years .... (W)

A58   (Cross) Sacred / to the memory of / Mary Louise Florence / infant daughter of / Cornelius and / Mary WAMBEY / who died Aug 8th 1863   (W)

A59   (Wall)   Henry DAVY / Died in Novr 1872 / aged 67. / Mary / his wife / died in Jany 1872, / aged 71. / William Charles / their son / died in Novr 1851, / aged 21.   (W)

A60   (Wall)   William COLLARD / died in Sep^{tr} 1843, / aged 75. / Phoebe / his wife / Died in Feby 1855, / aged 90.   (W)

A61   (Wall)   Joan COLLARD / died in July 1834 / aged 79. / Sylvia / her sister / died in August 1859 / aged 89.   (W)

A62   (Wall)   William COLLARD / died in Jany 1829, / aged 95. / Thomasin / his wife / died in June 1804, / aged 70. / Elizabeth / his second wife / died July 1839 / Aged 85. (W)

'IN RESPECTFUL AND LOVING RECOLLECTION'
Engraved in the wall above headstones A59, A60, A61 and A62

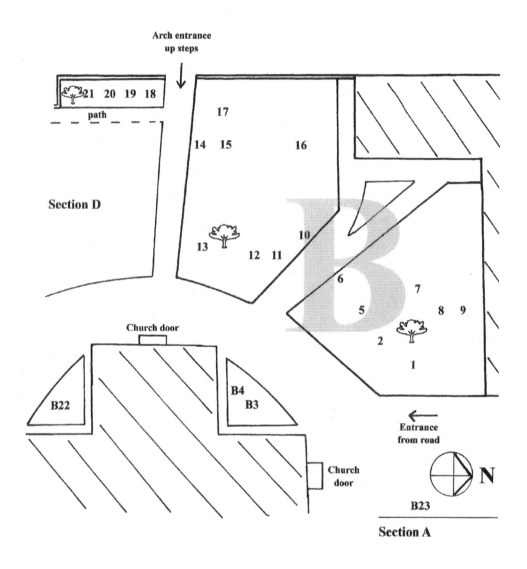

Arch entrance up steps

21 20 19 18

path

17

14 15   16

Section D

13 12 11

10

6
7
5
8 9
2
1

Church door

B4
B3

B22

Entrance from road

N

B23

Section A

Churchyard Plan – Section B

Churchyard
Section B

B1   I.H.S. In / affectionate remembrance / of / Eleanor Jane NORTH / who died April 14th 1878? / aged 26 years / ... In fleeting ... / ... in bodies ... / ... me thy vale of .. / ....sentence to ... / Also in memory of / Elizabeth Mary TUDBALL / sister of the above / who passed peacefully away / on the 22nd November 1914 / Aged 71 years (E)

B2   (Cross) In / memory of / Mary LYDDON / of Whitefield / Died March 26th 1906. Aged 59 / Erected by her niece / Annie L LYDDON / 1875 – 1933 / Interred at Stoke, Coventry. (E)

B3   (Memorial Cross)   THE GREAT WAR 1914-1919 / They whom this cross commemorates are numbered amongst those who at the / call of King and country left all that was dear to them, endured hardness, / faced danger, and finally passed out of the sight of men by / the path of duty and self sacrifice giving up their / own lives that others might live in freedom. Let those who come / after see to it that they be not forgotten.

B4   To the glory of God / and in memory of the / men of this parish /
(Wall)   who gave their lives in / the War 1939–1945.

Major W S CAPPER R.A.

Driver P C GREEDY R.A.S.C.

Corporal H J HANNON R.A.O.C.

Private M C C HAWKINS Som. L.I.

Marine D J HEMBURROW R.M.

Sub Lieut J A HEWLETT R.N.

Private W J D LEWIS Som.L.I.

Flying Officer V F D MEADE R.A.F.

Marine E F MILLETT R.M.

Ab. Seaman W A PROLL   R.N.

Gunner E J STONE R.A.

Flt. Sgt H P TEALE R.A.F.

O/Tel R WALSH R.N.

Flying Officer R WHELDON R.A.F.

Their name liveth for evermore. Ecclus 44.14.

[Herbert WAUTHIER del. - F Osborne & Co Ltd, London]

B5   Sacred / to / the memory of / Edward ROCKETT / who departed this life / December 15th. 1859. / Aged 71 years. / He died in the Lord. (E)

B6   I.H.S. / In loving memory of / Gertrude Elizabeth / the beloved wife of / W J POWLESLAND, / who died December 20th 1895. / Aged 44 years. / At rest. / (Small stone)   GEP / 1895   (E)

B7   (Cross) This monument is erected / in affectionate / remembrance of the / CHORLEY family / late of Sharpe House / of this parish / at the request of the late / Maria TRAINER / who departed this life Feby 2nd 1888 / Aged 85 years / Make them to be numbered with thy saints /   (E)

B8   (Marker stone) 149

B9   (Marker stone) 150

B10   ...John ...VERYARD ? / who died December 6th 18.. / aged 73 years / ....(E)

B11   In loving memory of / James HATSWELL / who died August 10th 1891 / Aged 69 years / And he took him aside from the multitude.   St Mark. VII.35 / Also of / Elizabeth Jane HATSWELL / who departed this life / October 15th 1903 / Aged 88 years. (E)

B12   In affectionate remembrance of / Herbert James HATSWELL / who died in London / February 9th 1878 / aged 22 years / Interred at Tower Hamlets Cemetery / also Edward HATSWELL / who died February 20th 1861   aged 1 year 10 months. We loved them – no tongue can tell / how much we loved them and how well / God loved them too and thought it best / To take them home with him to rest   (E)

B13   (Cross) I.H.S.   In loving / memory of / William STONE / who died May 12th 1915, / Aged 58 years. / "Peace Perfect Peace" (E)

B14   I.H.S. / In loving memory of / Edward John LUTLEY / youngest son of / William & Mary LUTLEY / of Fries Farm Wiveliscombe / who died February 2nd 1881 / Aged 43 years / Also of Mary Jane / sister of the above / who died Feby 23rd 1914 / Aged 80 years / Also of Anna Maria / sister of the above / who died March 14th 1917 / aged 81 years *[Richards]*   (E)

B15   I.H.S. / In memory of / William LUTLEY / of Fries Farm Wiveliscombe / He died Dec 25th 1837 / aged 58 years / and Mary his wife / who died April 11th 1869 / aged 75. (E)

B16   Them also who believe in Jesus / will God bring unto him   / Sacred to the memory of / Harriet NATION / who departed this life / September 14th 1885 in the / seventieth year of her age / May she rest in peace   (E)

B17   In / memory of / E CLATWORTHY / who died 5th May 1804 / aged 6 years / J CLATWORTHY / died 5th November 1831 / aged 60 years / A CLATWORTHY / died 9th August 1865 / aged 59 years / J CLATWORTHY / died 4 June 1873 / aged 55 years (E)

B18   In / loving memory of / a dear Husband & Father / Ivor Reginald / BURSTON Ex RN / died 29th Jan. 1988 / Aged 74. / And / Laura BURSTON / née GREEDY / a dear Wife & Mother / died 5 Jan. 1996 / aged 70 / Both lovingly missed / by all the family. (E)

B19   In / loving memory of / William J LYDDON / Died March 10th 1958. / Aged 83 years. / R.I.P. / Ada Rosa LYDDON, / died May 17th 1967, / Aged 95 years. (E)

B20   (War Grave)
Jellalabad / 1800 Private /
T BESLEY / Somerset Light
Infantry / 16th February 1917
Age 17. (E)

B21   Dorothy May /
HERBERT / 29. Dec. 1919
29. June 1999 (E)

B22   (Surround)
From strength to strength.
(W) / Howard McCRIRICK,
Priest, Born April 10: 1859,
Died May 26: 1922. (S) /
And of his wife Marion
Isabel. Died July 7: 1958.
Aged 95. (N)

B23   (Beneath asphalt)
Walter Kemp LUXTON.
Buried 27 November 1885.
Age 11 months.

B3
War Memorial
[see page 173]

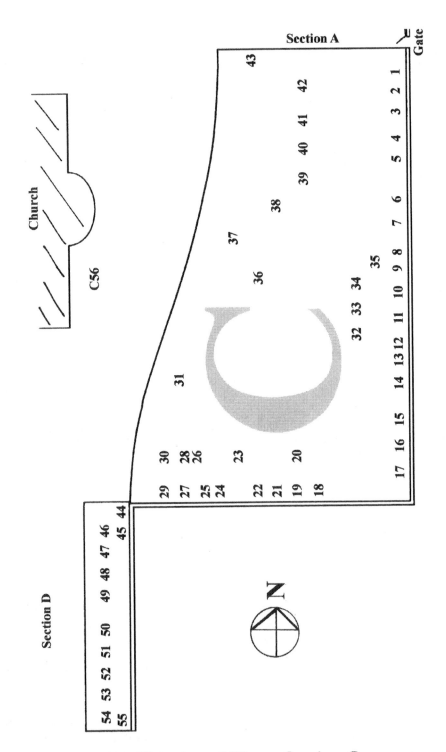

Churchyard Plan – Section C

C1 (Wall) In / memory of / Edward BOUCHER, / of Jews House, Wiveliscombe / who died March 9th 1885, / aged 47 years. / "Judge not, that ye be not judged" / Also of Anne, / the beloved wife of the above / who fell asleep in Jesus / April 2nd 1913, aged 73 years. / Interred in Winsham Cemetery. / We loved her Oh no tongue can tell / how much we loved her and how well / God loved her too and thought it best / to take her home with him to rest / Good bye until we meet / around the throne. (W)

C2 (Wall) In / loving remembrance of / Edward BOUCHER / of Prospect House / late of Jews Wiveliscombe / who died March 31 1881? / aged 80 years / Abide with us, for / toward evening a.... / the day is far spent / St Luke XXIV Chap XXXIX Verse / Also of / Mary Timewell / his wife / who died at Prospect House / December 27th 1888 / aged 77 years (W)

C3 (Wall) In / loving remembrance of / Ann BOUCHER / youngest daughter of / Edward and Mary Timewell BOUCHER / of Jews House Wiveliscombe who died January 14 1873 / aged 19 years / Father not my will / But thine be done / 1.SAM III Chap. XVIII Verse / Also of / Emma BOUCHER / third daughter of the above / of Prospect House, Wiveliscombe / who died February 20th 1877 / aged 29 years / it is the Lord, let him / what seemeth Him Good / 1 SAM. III Chap. XVIII Verse (W)

C4 Sacred / to the memory of / Thomas BOUCHER / of Jews and Lambrook / in this Parish / who died on the 23rd day / of September 1858. Aged 67 / also of / Mary Ann his wife / who died on the 24th day of / December 1858 Aged 65 (W)

C5 (Ground) Sacred / to the memory of / John CULVERWELL / Obit August 15th 1860? Aged 94? (N)

C6 I.H.S. Sacred / to the memory of / Robert CULVERWELL / who departed this life / January 16th 1848 / aged 89 years / also / Betty CULVERWELL / widow of the above / who departed this life / February 11th 1848 / aged 83 years / Behold we come unto thee for thou art / the Lord our God (W)

C7   I.H.S.   Sacred / to the memory of / Elizabeth CULVERWELL / who died on Easter Sunday / April 16th 1876 / aged 69 years (W)

C8   (Damaged stone)   ......Penelope ...../ Daughter / ...... / ... 182- /   (W)

C9   BISHOP CRANMER / Died / April 9th 1831. / Aged / 83.   (W)   *[Apothecary]*

WIVELISCOMBE INFIRMARY AND DISPENSARY

At the time of its inception in 1804, the nearest similar medical establishments were at Exeter or Bath. The Infirmary, therefore, pre-dates East Reach Hospital, in Taunton, by eight years. Supported by Mr William Hancock and private donations, the Infirmary was founded by Dr Henry Sully. It was in effect a forerunner of the modern National Health Service, as it was to allow for 'servants, labourers and apprentices to have free medical attention and care'. It was a considerable asset for the community and surrounding parishes: by the end of the first five years it is reported that there had been no less than 5,913 patients. The resident doctor was supported by visiting consultants, and pupils came to study medicine, some of whom were to stay on and work in the combined hospital/clinic. Dr Sully specialised in eye diseases and cancer and is described as being 'kind-hearted and benevolent'. He retired in 1832 and went to live near Taunton, where he 'died at a good old age, retaining to the last his sense of humour and eccentricity of character'. This unique and significant institution may have contributed to the reported longevity of the local inhabitants *[see page 192]*, but it was to close in 1948, being superseded by the newly instigated National Health Service (NHS).

1816   Institute moved to the High Street and by 1822 there were 12 beds.
1831   Dr Bishop Cranmer died (*C9* in the churchyard)
1832   Dr Sully retired. He was succeeded by one of his pupils, John Tudball, and
         Dr Andrew Francis Edwards (who was to die in an accident on 18 August 1876,
         after forty years as Doctor in Wiveliscombe – *T3* and *C33*)
1839   A further move took place as permanent premises were purchased for £600 on the
         High Street. '1804' can still be clearly seen over the door, with a house named
         after Dr Cranmer ['Cranmers'] just up the hill.
1841   On the death of Mr Tudball in 1841, Dr Edwards was joined by Mr Henry Weech
         Randolph, another of Dr Sully's pupils.
1856   On the retirement of Mr Randolph & Dr Edwards, Mr William Legge (Surgeon) took over
1857   Dr Randolph was appointed to Milverton where he remained until he resigned in 1885.
1866   Mr Legge resigned, to be succeeded by Dr George R Norris.
1888   570 patients recorded at the Dispensary – total annual patients number approx. 1,000.
1889   Accommodation for the nurse was made from rooms at the Dispensary.
1903   After 37 years, Dr Norris resigned. His successor was Dr G I J Turner.
1910   Dr W H Randolph began his long service to the town, continuing as a GP in the same
         premises after the introduction of the NHS in 1948.

"This was indeed an hospital within a cottage, but whether it was the first Cottage Hospital has to be a matter of semantics" - SOMERSET ARCHIVE & RECORD SERVICE

C10   In memory of / Lydia Charlotte BACK / who died August 21st 1835 / aged 23 years / Also of / George BACK / who died April 21st 1840 / aged 29 years. (W)

C11   (Broken cross on ground)   Sacred / to the / memory of / William Henry BACK / who was taken to his rest / on the 21st Sep[r] 1875 Aged 68 / Them also which sleep in Jesus / will God bring with him

C12   In memory / of / Margaret Minter BACK / who died 12th March 1854 / aged 70 / Also of / Laura Cecilia BACK / daughter of the above / Obit Feb[y] 28th 1906 / aged 86 / In death not divided .

C13   (Tomb)   In loving memory of (W) / Anne Catherine Edwards BACK (S) / died 23rd July 1879 / aged 77 years (E)   / Grant her O Lord eternal rest (N)

C14   (Tomb)   In / loving memory / of / my beloved husband / Edward Drake BACK, RN / who died / at Hartswell House / Wiveliscombe / June 18th 1888 / Aged 83 years / "I am with thee for I am thy / God" Ish XLI.10. / Father in thy gracious keeping leave we now thy servant sleeping (N) / His life was love – faith – charity and peace (S)

C15   In loving memory / of / Eland John GUNNINGHAM / 1903 – 1976 / Loved and remembered / always. / Also his wife / Elsie / 1906 – 1978 (W)

C16   Cyril Walter SELLICK / died April 19th 1976 / aged 61 years. / For 30 years / Beloved husband of Lilian / for 21 years churchwarden / of this parish. (W)

C17   In / loving memory of / Grace Elizabeth TWIGGER / (Betty) / Born 12th May 1923 / Died 29th December 1977 / Aged 54. / A devoted wife and mother. (W)

C18   In / loving memory of / Neil Alan / WILSON-SMITH / 1938 – 1996 (N)

C19   In / loving memory of / Gladys Winifred Mary / WILSON / 1899 – 1981 / Bernard Henry / WILSON / 1898- 1990 (N)

C20   (Ground)   Maud CLUTTERBUCK / Died 25th Jan 1985 / Aged 82 years (N)

C21   In loving memory of / Beryl Gertrude SMITH / Died 15th Oct. 1980 / aged 54 / and her husband / Herbert SMITH / Died 31st Jan. 1990 / Aged 71 / Together again   (N)

C22   In / loving memory of / my dear husband / Walter Charles CHIDGEY / Died May 19th 1970 / Aged 65. /Also his wife / Annie CHIDGEY / Died Dec 1st 1973 / Aged 63. (N)

C23   (Ground)   In memory of / John Thomas STEEL / died 24th September 1984 / Aged 78 (N)

C24   In loving memory / of / Bessie PECK / 1891 – 1970 / Rest in Peace. (N)

C25   To / a dear husband / and Father / Ernest MULLINS / Died Dec 15th 1969 / Aged 74. / Rest in Peace. / Also / Dorothy his wife / Died Jan 18th 1978 / Aged 71.   (N)

C26   William Henry LILLEY / Harry / Died 17th July 1983 / Aged 72. (N)

C27 (Wall) In loving memory of / my dear Husband / Ernest William STEVENS / Died Nov 19th 1969. Aged 67 / Also / Eileen Frances / Died Sept 20th 1996. Aged 68 (N)

C28 William John CONIBERE / 11th August 1923 / 19th August 1982 (N)

C29 Sydney PULSFORD / of Kingsmead / Born 23rd November 1901 / Died 19th July 1969 / Always remembered, greatly missed / Also Winifred Emeline / his wife / passed peacefully away / 21st Oct. 1974 / United with Sydney. (N)

C30 Herbert Charles DASCOMBE / of this parish / 1895 – 1974 / Also his wife / Dorothy Mary DASCOMBE / 1910-1999 (N)

C31 Sacred / to the memory of / Thomas COOKSLEY. / A respectable tradesman / of this parish / who departed this life / the 30th of January 1839 / aged 82 years. / Also Sara, his wife, / who departed this life / the 9th of April 1851 / aged 77 years. (E)

C32 Sacred / to the memory of / Mary THURTELL ...... / ...James THURTELL (E)

C33 (Ground) [mb] The memory of the just is blessed (E) / In sacred remembrance of Andrew Francis EDWARDS, MD (S) / of Bourne House, Wiveliscombe (W) *and* O rest in the Lord (E) / Also of his wife Anna Maria EDWARDS (N) / who fell asleep October 13th 1887 (W)

C34 (Cross) To the glory of God / In / loving memory of / Francis Henry EDWARDS, MM / son of Dr EDWARDS of this town / Died 1st Dec 1911 aged 71 / With Christ which is far better (E)

C35 In memory of / Thomas STEVENS / of Cotcombe in this parish / who died ……….. aged 80 years / Gone but not forgotten. *[S Richards]* (E)
Small stone C.S. / 1908

C36 Sacred / to the / memory / of / William KING / Died June 24th 1865 / aged 49 years / Also / Emma KING / Died July 28th 1865 / aged 9 years / Tho lost to sight, to memory dear / they are not dead but sleepeth here / Also Caroline KING / wife of the above / Died January 5th 1906 / aged 84 years / Also Mary Ellen FROST / 2nd daughter of the above / Died December 12th 1936 / aged 79 years (E)

C37 In loving memory of / Lilla Philipps / wife of Robert King CROSS, / second daughter of / Sir W[m] Philipps LAUGHARNE, Bar[t] / of Orlandin, Pembrokeshire, / who died May 29, 1868 / Aged 35 years / Also of Lilla Mary / infant daughter of R K and B E CROSS / who died July 13 1874 / aged 13 months / Not lost but gone before/ L.P.C. (E)

C38 In memory of / Thomas DUNN who / departed this life Dec[r] 2nd / 1829 aged 70 years / Also / Ann his wife who departed / this life Nov[r] 16th 1824 aged / 64 years. (W)

C39 Sacred / to the memory of / {Mary} CULVERWELL of this parish / who departed this life / the 23rd of April 1824 / In the 76th year of her age / Also Robert CULVERWELL son / of John and the above Mary CULVERWELL / who departed this life / the 21st of March 1827 / In the 36th year of his age. (W)

C40 (Tomb)[mb] The Revd John LLEWELLIN, MA late of the vicarage / in this parish / Obit December 28th 1869 Aetat 61 years. *[Wiveliscombe Curate 1860-1869]*

C41 (Cross) Sacred / to the memory of / Charlotte Ann Maria LANGLEY Born April 15th 1815 / Died October 27th 1837 / Aged 72 years / I know that my redeemer liveth (E)

C42 Sacred / to the memory of / Maria NURCOMBE / who departed this life / October 11th 1870 / Aged 85 years / Erected by her son Robert in Australia (E)

C43 In loving memory of / Charles LOVELL / Died 15th Feb 1917 / Maria LOVELL / Died 29th May 1955 / Ernest Peace LOVELL / Died 8th Feb 1993 / Rest in peace.   (W)
(F/H) In / loving / memory / Charles / LOVELL / Died / Feb. 15. 1917.

C44 (Wall) William Willoughby / WOOD / of Hartswell House / Born 4th Feb 1871 / Died 21st Aug 1966. (W)

C45 (Wall) Walter Willoughby / WOOD / of Hartswell House / Born 14th Oct 1906 / Died 2nd Oct 1974. (W)

C46 In loving memory of / Eveleen / dearly beloved wife of / Lt Colonel Henry JEFFERYS-TAYLOR / and daughter of / Major Carter O'NEAL, 5th Inniskilling Dragoons / of Ratcliffe, Leicestershire / Died 27th October 1949 / Buried at Great Holland, Essex (W)

[Oak cross at left - see page 51]
C46a To the memory of / Lt Colonel Henry JEFFERYS-TAYLOR, DSO / late / the Durham Light Infantry / of / Culverhead, Wiveliscombe / Born 24 May 1881 Died 24th January 1962 (W)

C47 In loving memory of / Frederick Mortimer HARVEY / Rector of Bolnhurst, Bedfordshire / from 1874 to 1888 / who died at Wiveliscombe / Oct 8 1912. Aged 67 /   Thou art my helper and redeemer. PS.XL.21 (W)

C48 (Surround) At rest (W) / Henry IRISH who died June 1st 1923 aged 83 years (N)

C49 In loving memory of / Emma IRISH who died July 19th 1919. Aged 82 years. (S)

C50 (Cross) Mary PENBERTHY / of Redruth, Cornwall, Died Oct 21st 1928 / Aged 73 years (W)

C51 In loving memory of / Edwin Southcombe DYER / of Manor Farm, / who died May 18th 1934 / Aged 69 years. (W)

C52 In loving memory of / Daisy Arscott CHANIN / At rest 17th July 1944, / aged 57 years. / Also Montie her husband / At rest 14th Nov 1956. / Aged 67 years. (W)

C53 In loving memory of / Amy Violet / beloved wife of Sidney John HILL / passed away 14 May 1950 Aged 53 / And of Sidney / passed away 18th July 1969. Aged 73 (W)

C54 In loving memory of / my dear husband / William David James / RAYSON / 22 Oct 1925 – 12 Feb 1985 (W)

C55 In / memory of / a beloved Husband & Father / Thomas Arthur DOBSON / 17.1.20 – 10.10.90 (W)

C56 Remember / Hannelore Emma Auguste LUXTON / 1924 – 2000 / Rest in Peace – Rise in Glory (E)

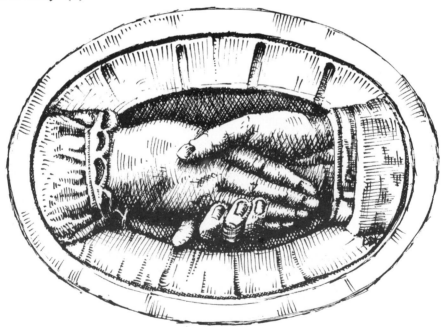

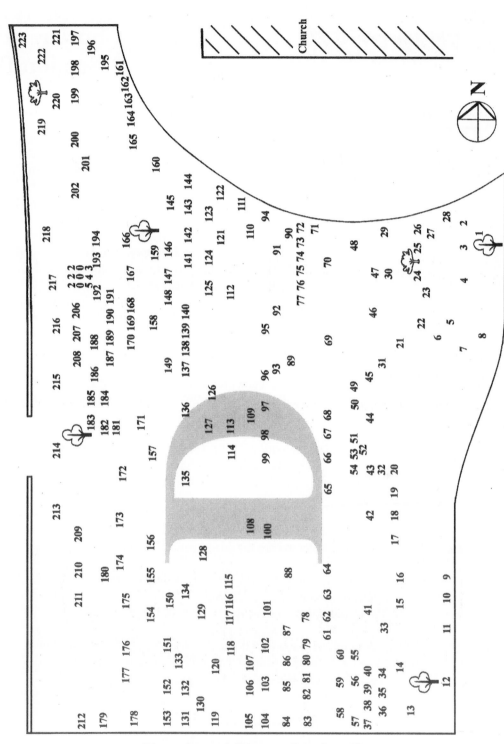

Churchyard Plan – Section D

73

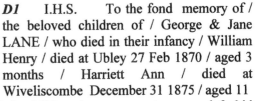

D1   I.H.S.   To the fond memory of / the beloved children of / George & Jane LANE / who died in their infancy / William Henry / died at Ubley 27 Feb 1870 / aged 3 months / Harriett Ann / died at Wiveliscombe December 31 1875 / aged 11 months / Jesus said Suffer little children / to come unto me and forbid them not / for of such is the kingdom of heaven (E)

D2   I.H.S. She is not lost but gone before / Sacred / to the / memory / of Ann / wife of Henry LARCOMBE / who departed this life / August 25th 1869 / in the 63rd year of her age (E)

D3   I.H.S. In / affectionate / remembrance of / Fred LARCOMBE / of Wiveliscombe / who died December 26th 1876 / aged 28 years / "Not my will, but thine be done" (E)

D4   In / loving memory of / William PEARSE / who departed this life / April the 26th 1874 / Aged 61 years. / also of / Mary Painter PEARSE / wife of the above / who died April the 2nd 1878 / aged 63 years. M.R.P. / 1878. W.P. / 1874   (E)

D5   In / memory of / Phillis ROGERS / who departed this life / on the 11th day of March 1875, / aged 80 years. / Blessed are the dead / which die in the Lord. (E)

D6   In memory of / Upham Routley TUCKFIELD. / Died December 27th 1902. Aged 59, / who was Sexton of St Andrew's Church, Walcot, Bath 1892 – 1902 / This stone is erected by members of the congregation / in appreciation of his services. (N)

D7   In loving memory of / William COOKSLEY / who departed this life / January the 9th 1877 / aged 68 years / Also of / Ann COOKSLEY / wife of the above / who died August 24th 1882 / aged 70 years / Blessed are the dead who die in the Lord (E)

D8   (Cross)

D9   Sacred / to the memory / of / Marian wife of / Major Thos. Geo. JOHNSON / who died on November 30th 1887 / Requiescat in pace (E)

D10 (Cross) In / loving memory of / Edward Paul POOLE, / of Prospect House / who died November 5th 1894, / aged 36 years. / Thy will be done / Also Edith Marianne POOLE, / wife of the above / who died October 29th 1899, / aged 37 years. (E)

D11 (Cross) In loving memory of / Samuel Henry WINTER, / who died Decr 5th 1895, / Aged 67 years. (E)

D12 (Broken Cross) *[Blank]*

D13 (Ground) In loving memory of / Nora Ethel (Lally) COX / 20 Nov 1915 – 22 July 1989 / and her husband / Reginald Noel COX / 8 Dec 1911 – 18 Oct 1991. (W)

D14 In / loving memory of / our dear sons / Thomas KELLOW, / who died March 9th 1895, / aged 30 years. / His end was peace / Also / Walter KELLOW / who died August 18th 1898, / aged 31 years. / In life beloved in death lamented. (E)

D15 In loving memory of / Robert King CROSS / who died February 19th 1895 / Aged 62 years / also of / Florence Mary CROSS / daughter of the above / who died May 2nd 1895, / aged 32 years. / In caelo quis. / Also Bessie Eliza / widow of the above / Robert King CROSS, / who died March 3rd 1925, / aged 79 years. / Nearer my God to thee / (E) (Foot Stone) In / loving memory of / Percy Godwin CROSS / beloved husband of / Cissie CROSS / who passed away / Novr 16th 1928. / R.I.P. (E)

D16 (Cross) In loving / memory of / George Arscott / the beloved son of / George & Annie BOXALL / Born Christmas Day 1887 / Died Easter Monday 1910 / A light is from our household gone / a voice we loved is stilled / a place is vacant in our home / which never can be filled.
(Foot Stone) In loving memory / of / Sidney John Manley HILL / beloved son of / Sidney & Violet HILL. / who died November 14th 1938 / aged 16 years / Safe in the arms of Jesus. (E)

D17 (Cross) I.H.S. In loving / memory of / George BOXALL / who passed away suddenly / May 26th 1927 / aged 67 years / Until the day break and the shadows flee away / Also of Annie / beloved wife of the above / who passed away Christmas Day 1930 / aged 69 years (E)

D18 In / loving memory of / William ARSCOTT / of Langley, Wiveliscombe, / son of Robert ARSCOTT, of Ford, / who passed away Novr 12th 1916, / aged 58 years. / God be with you till we meet again (E)

D19 There remaineth therefore a rest to the people of God / I.H.S. / In affectionate remembrance of / Eliza / the beloved wife of William ARSCOTT / of Langley / who died Octr 11th 1878 / aged 67 years / Also of William ARSCOTT / husband of the above / who died July 1st 1887 / aged 77 years (E)

D20   Until the day break and the shadows flee away / In affectionate remembrance of / Charles ARSCOTT of Wiveliscombe / youngest son of / William ARSCOTT of Langley / who was born January 2nd 1848 / Died December 31st 1877 / Aged 29 years / Seek ye the Lord while he may be found / Call ye upon him while he is near. VV Isaiah 6 v. (E)

D21   In memory of / James TUCKFIELD / For 44 years Sexton of this parish / Died April the 21st 1885 / Aged 69 years / Just as I am without one plea / but that thy blood was shed for me /   Also of / Maria TUCKFIELD / wife of the above / who died January 19th 1894 / aged 77 years. / Thy will be done (E)

D22   *[Blank but possibly base for D23]*

D23   In loving memory of / Henry John TUCKFIELD, / who died November 19th 1872 / Aged 3 years. /
Also of Elizabeth TUCKFIELD / mother of the above and the / beloved wife of / Upham Routley TUCKFIELD, / Sexton of this Church / who died February 8th 1891 / aged 48 years. / Grant them, Lord, eternal rest. /
Also / Upham Routley TUCKFIELD / who died at Bath / December 27th 1902 aged 59. / Thy will be done. (S)

D24   [mb]   Sacred / to the memory of / Ester Wills NORTH / wife of David NORTH / of Whitefield / who died April 15 1820? / Aged 79 years. (E)
also
Sacred / to the memory of / David NORTH / of Whitefield / who died April 5th 1807?/ aged 65? Years   (W)

D25   …..remembrance of / …… of this parish who died Novr 1844 / ….. Sarah his widow who died July 5th 1872 / ….. memory of their eight unmarried children / William Luff died AD 1830, Mary Carpenter 1854, Thomas 1836,   /   Luff 1841, William 1841, Purnell 1865, Luff 1844, Sarah Ann 1865 (N)

D26   In loving memory of   / I.H.S. / Eliza / The beloved wife of / William LARCOMBE / who departed this life / November the 17th 1879 / Aged 36 years / Thy will be done / Also the above / William LARCOMBE / Born June 5th 1848 / Died on Xmas Day 1921 (E)

D27   (Ground) Until the day dawn. *[Richards]*

D28   Sacred / to the memory / of / Richard WOOLAWAY, / who died Sep^t. 11th 1909, / aged 57 years / In the midst of life we are in death / Also of Aubrey Richard / the beloved son of the above / who died Decr 20th 1912 / aged 26 years / Peace perfect peace (E)

D29   (Cross) Happy / memories of / Robert Walter LUTLEY, / of Sharpe House / Died 13th December 1959. (E)

D30 In loving memory of / Eliza HAYDON / Born Feby 16th 1828, / Died April 21st 1910, / wife of the late / Frederick HAYDON, / The Castle Tiverton / and daughter of the late / W J HANCOCK, of Wiveliscombe. / R.I.P. / Mary Ann LUTLEY, / daughter of Eliza and Frederick HAYDON / Died May 19th 1939, aged 82. (E) / William John / HANCOCK, / Died March 7th 1878, / aged 78. / Son of / William (1753-1813) & Jenny (1776-1860) HANCOCK (S) / Mary Ann / HANCOCK / Died July 28th 1828 / Aged 25 / wife of / William John HANCOCK / of / Wiveliscombe (N) / All those who lie in this grave were (S) / of Sharpe House (E)

D31 (Cross) Sacred to the / memory of (W) / Jane Eliza BACK / widow of Fleet Paymaster / E D BACK, RN.

D31a (Fallen/ground) In loving memory of / John COX / who died April 28th 1889 / aged 54 years / asleep in Jesus / Also of / Martha H COX / daughter of the above / who died October 22nd 1899 / We cannot Lord thy purpose see / but all is well that's done by thee / Also of Martha / wife of the above / who entered into rest Feby 12th 1933 / aged 95 years / He giveth his beloved sleep.

D32 I.H.S. / In loving memory of / George HODGE / who died April 16th. 1917 / aged 79 years. / Also of / Mary Ann HODGE / his wife / who died April 10th. 1915 / Aged 80 years. / Also of / Victor Albert WARREN / Grandson of the above / and beloved son of / James & Emily WARREN / fell in action in France / June 7th 1917 / aged 20 years / Peace perfect peace (E) *[see page 184]*

D33 In loving memory of / Mary Jane ARSCOTT, / of Langley, Wiveliscombe, / who fell asleep June 21st 1917, / aged 72 years. / Also of her sister / Emma ALLEN, / who fell asleep Octr 9th 1916, / aged 64 years. / Resting. / Also of their brother / Frederick ARSCOTT, / who passed away Novr 7th 1930, / aged 87 years. (E)

D34 (Cross) I.H.S. / In / loving memory / of / James ARSCOTT, / of Langley, Wiveliscombe, / who departed this life January 4th 1896 / aged 53 years. / I heard the voice of Jesus say / come unto me and rest, / lay down thou weary one lay down / thy head upon my breast. / Also of / Thomas ARSCOTT / who departed this life March 4th 1916, / Aged 69 years. / Thy will be done. (E)

D35 I H S / In / loving memory of / Robert Manley ARSCOTT, / of Ford, in this parish / Died January 17th 1898, / aged 60 years. / "The memory of the just is blessed" / Also of / Mary Anna STONE / beloved wife of the above / who fell asleep October 21st 1939, / aged 88 years. / At rest. (E)
(Small stone) R.M.A. / 1898 / M.A.S. / 1939 (E)

D36 (Cross) In / loving memory / of / John ROSS / Born Aug 24th 1831 / Died Aug 3rd 1897 (E)
Anne Winifred ROSS / Died Sept 4th 1955 (N) Mary R E ROSS / Died Jan 21 1951 (S)

D37 (Cross) William BOUCHER / formerly of Lambrook House / of this parish / Died Sept 25th 1881 / at Minehead / "Eternal rest give unto him / O Lord and may perpetual / light shine upon him" / His widow dedicates this / cross to his memory /
Also Elizabeth Madeline / PEAKE – 1863 – 1945 / daughter of William and / Eliza BOUCHER (E)

D38 (Cross) In / loving memory of / Eliza BOUCHER neé LUTLEY / who passed away on the 20th March 1898 / Also Beatrice Helen Lutley / (Nell) BOUCHER 1872 – 1947 / Daughter of William and / Eliza BOUCHER (E)

D39 (Cross) In loving memory of / James SIMONS / Born June 13th 1818 / Died May 28th 1894 / With Christ which is far better /
Also in loving memory of / Emily his wife / born November 11th 1822 / died April 10th 1898 (E)

D40 In loving memory of / Richard John STONE, / late of Croford Mills, / who died March 18th 1914, / aged 63 years. / Also of Mary his wife / who died March 8th 1926. / Aged 79 years. / R.I.P. (E)

D41 In loving memory of / I.H.S. / Mary ROBBINS, / of Crowcombe, / who died November 5th 1891, / aged 63 years. / Gone from all sorrow, sickness and pain, / gone where the ransomed eternally reign, / Gone where all heartrending partings are past, / gone where we all hope to gather at last. (E)

D42   In loving memory of / I.H.S. / Mary Anne / the beloved wife of / Richard Bowerman WYATT / who died at Croford in this parish / June the 15th 1886 / aged 44 years / Not lost but gone before
(Small stone) M.A.W. / 1886   *[Richards]* (E)

D43   (Cross)   In loving / memory of / Joseph & Harriet PARKMAN / Died April 21 1882,   Aged 59. / May 23 1912,   Aged 80. / Also their three sons / John, James and Robert   (E)   In loving / memory of / William PARKMAN / their son / who died Feby 4th 1935 Aged 71 / At Rest   (N)

D44   In loving memory / of / James SUMMERS / who passed away / February 25th 1919, / aged 64 years / Also of / Mary SUMMERS / wife of the above / who passed away / March 25th 1935 / Aged 83 years / "Until the day break / and the shadows flee away"(E)

D45   Sacred / to the memory of / Edward HILL of this parish / who departed this life / the 20th of May 1809 aged 61 years / also Betty HILL his wife / who departed this life / the 8th of May 1831 Aged 81 years (E)

D46   Sacred / to / the memory of / Betsy COLLARD / who departed this life / November 1st 1855 / aged   ? years (E)

D47   In / loving memory / of / Jane Ann MOORE / of London, / who died at Wiveliscombe / on October 21st 1924, / Aged 65 years. (E)

D48   In loving memory of / William COLLARD, / of this parish / who died April 22nd 1879 / Aged 64 years. / Also / Mary COLLARD / wife of the above / who fell asleep Nov 7th 1897, / Aged 82 years / "Till he comes"   (E)
(Small Stone) M.C. / 1897.

D49   Sacred / to the memory of / Henry SKINNER / who died 3rd May 1867 / Aged 44 years. / I know that my redeemer liveth / Also of Charlotte / widow of the above / who died 2nd January 1910 / Aged 81 years / O rest in the Lord (E)

D50   I.H.S. In loving memory of / John ROGERS / who died November 28th 1882 / aged 58 years / For me to live is Christ / and to die is gain / Philippians, 1 Chap. XXI.V / Also of / Harriet ROGERS / wife of the above / who departed this life / August 11th 1888 / Aged 57 years / Christ is all sufficient (E)

D51   (Cross)   *[Blank]*
D52   (F/H)
D53   (F/H)

D54   (Cross) I.H.S. / Sacred / to the memory of / John WILDMAN / who departed this life / December the 4th 1876 / Aged 41 years   *[Richards]*   (E)

D55 (Broken Cross) I.H.S. / In loving memory of / Agnes SNAPE / wife of Chas SNAPE, MD / of Lambrooke House, Wiveliscombe / daughter of the late / Revd Thos. EDWARDS / Rector of Alford, Cheshire / Passed away on March 27th 1895 / Not lost but gone before (E)

D56 (Cross) In / affectionate / remembrance / of / Janet dearly loved wife of / John FOSTER / who died 12th June 1887, / Aged 37 years / "God is love" (E)

D57 (Cross) In loving memory of / Frederic PEARSE / born 27th February 1855 / died 27th June 1859 / And of Edward Boucher PEARSE / born 6th Dec 1851 died 18th Nov 1880 / Sons of Nicholas and Catherine PEARSE / "O God make them to be numbered with / thy saints in glory everlasting" (E)

D58 (Cross) Cecil / the loving & dearly loved / son of John & Madeline BIRD / Born 8 March 1875 / Died 29th June 1879 (E)

D59 (Cross) I.H.S. / In affectionate / remembrance of / Maria EDWARDS / daughter of the late / Revd J W EDWARDS / of Aldford, Cheshire / died May 10th 1891 / We which have believed do enter into rest. HEB.IV.3 *[Thatcher]* (E)

D60 (Cross) Jesu Mercy / In / loving memory of / Harriet HITCHCOCK / who fell asleep in Jesus / January 12th 1893 / Aged 38 years / Thy way not mine O Lord (E)

D61 In memory / of / Frank KING / who died / from / the effects of an accident / Novr ......1893 / ......faithful servant / ....a few things / ....over many things / enter thou into the joy of thy Lord / Matt........ (E)

D62 I.H.S. / In tender and cherished memory / of / Horace Tom, / the very precious child of / T & E WARREN. / Born Octr 8th 1890 – Died May 6th 1892 / He shall gather the lambs with his arm and / carry them in his bosom / Also his father / Tom WARREN / Died Sept 28th 1928. Aged 68 (E)

D63 (Small Stone) J.R. / 1891. (E)

D64 In affectionate remembrance / of / George LOCK / who died October 13th 1877 / aged 52 years / Well done good & faithful servant. Thou / hast been faithful over a few things. I will / make thee ruler over many things. Enter / thou into the joy of thy Lord. (E) (Small Stone) G.L. 1877 (E)

D65 In loving memory of / Elizabeth / the beloved and devoted wife of / Joseph COLLER of London / who died July 10th 1889 / aged 60 years / Also Maria GREEDY / mother of the above / who died June 29th 1880 / aged 86 years / Also John GREEDY / father of the above / of ..../ who died ..... 1888 ....
(Small Stone) E.C. 1889 / M.G. 1880 / J.G. 1888. (E)

D66   In loving memory of / Mary WARREN / died June the 5th 1882 / aged 58 years / Also of / Thomas WARREN / died June the 30th 1882 / Aged 4 years / Their home is in heaven / Also of William WARREN / husband of the above / died February the 4th 1890 / aged 59 years *[Richards]*   (E)

D67   (<u>Small Stone</u>)   W.W. / 1890

D68   In loving memory of / Alice WARREN / Died October the   31st 1885 / aged 15 years / In the midst of life we are in death /   She is not gone from memory she is not / gone from love but gone to the Father's / throne above. The cup is a bitter one / the sting most severe to part with one / we loved so dear. The trial is hard but / we'll not complain but trust in Christ / to meet again   (E)

D69   *[Blank]*

D70   I.H.S. / In / loving memory / of / Daniel STONEFROST / who fell asleep in Jesus / October 6th 1890, / aged 20 years. / Jesus I do trust thee / trust thee with my soul; / guilty, lost, and helpless / Thou hast made me whole, / there is none in heaven, / or on earth like thee: / Thou hast died for sinners, / therefore Lord, for me. / Verse written and handed by him / to his mother / Also of / Alfred STONEFROST, / who died May 7th 1903, / aged 53 years. (E)

[D73]

D71   In / memory of / Mary Louisa RUSSELL / widow of the late / Captain RUSSELL / of the 93rd Highlanders / who died on the 6th February / 1867 / in the 56th year of her age (E)

D72   (Small Stone) A.R. / 1866.

D73   Sacred / to / the memory of / Thomas RICHARDS / who departed this life / Septr 7th 1857. / Aged 63 years / Also of / Ann RICHARDS his wife / who died June 30th 1866, / aged 82 years. / Also / John Francis RICHARDS / grandson of the above / who died March 4th 1849, / in the 9th year of his age. / Also of / Sylvia wife of John RICHARDS / Died June 1st 1862, / aged 54 years. / Also / John RICHARDS / who died August 27th 1882 / aged 67 years / Also / Sarah RICHARDS / who died March 6th 1908 / aged 81 years (E)   *[see page 81]*
(Small Stone) J.F.R. 1849   (Small Stone) T.R. 1857.

D74   *[Blank]*

D75   S.R. 1862

D76   (Cross) D.S. 1890.

D77   (Against Railing) I.H.S. / Sacred / to the memory / of Anna wife of / Thomas RICHARDS / who died January 14th 1862 / aged 38 years / also / Sarah Lansdown RICHARDS / their daughter / who died February 24th 1853 / aged 2 years & 8 months. *[Richards]* (S)

D78   (Cross)   I.H.S. / In loving memory of / William HANCOCK / born August 20th 1810, / died December 2nd 1896. / In as much as ye have done it unto one of the / least of these my brethren ye have done it unto me / And of Mary his wife / born August 29th 1834, / died August 22nd 1909 / Whosoever liveth and believeth in me shall never die (E)

D79   (Cross)

D80   (Cross)   Here beneath / rests the body of / John HANCOCK / Vicar of Haslebury Plucknett / in this County   / who departed this life / on the 5th of September 1881 / aged 69 years / And now Lord what wait I for / my hope is in thee (E)

D81   In memory of / Harry Egerton NORTON / Lt Col 15th Hussars / 14th August 1950. / and of his wife / Mary Froude Llewellyn / Bellew NORTON / formerly of Oakhampton Manor / in this Parish / 4th December 1962 (E)

D82   (Cross)   I.H.S. / In / loving memory / of / Harry Bawden BELLEW / of Oakhampton Manor / Born 31 Jan 1854 / Died 17 Sep 1904 (E)

D83   (Cross)   In loving / memory of / Ethel / the sweet child of / Benjn and / Ada BOUCHER / Born March 17th 1873 / Died Octr 26th 1878 (E)

D84 BENNETT / (Ground) In loving memory / George Edward BENNETT / 1902 – 1988 / Edith Henrietta BENNETT / 1907 – 1988 / And their son John / 1932 – 1986 / Ashes scattered at sea (E)

D85 In loving memory of / Thomas DINHAM / who died April 16th 1891 / Aged 59 years. / Also of Sarah Frances / wife of the above / died April 14th 1920 / aged 85 years. / Gone but not forgotten / Also Charlotte Selina COOMBS / of Lambrook Villa, Wiveliscombe / late of Damerham, Wiltshire / who died Sept …2nd? 1906 / aged 85 years / Until the day break (E)

D86 In / loving memory of / Frederick LUTLEY / Manor Farm, Wiveliscombe / who fell asleep / August 13th 1886 aged 63 / In the midst of life we are in death / Also Mary Anne / widow of the above / died June 3rd 1901 / aged 66 years *[Richards]* (E)

D87 (Cross) In / loving remembrance of / Frances widow of / Captain J S KEATS RN / Died February 4th 1898 / Out of weakness we're made strong (E)

D88 (Cross) In memory of / Louisa Philippa BELLEW. / eldest daughter of / John Prestwood BELLEW / of Stockleigh Court, in the County of Devon / Died Nov. 16th 1909 / A friend loveth at all times. PROV. XVII.17 (E)

D89 I.H.S / In loving memory of / George SULLY / who departed this life / May the 11th 1857 / aged 65 years /
Also of Ann SULLY / wife of the above / who departed this life / March the 24th 1885 / aged 78 years /
Also / Sidney Alfred COLLARD / their grandson / Died October 28th 1885 / aged 5 months / Not lost but gone before *[Richards]* (E)

D90 [mb] In / memory / of / Catherine Eliza / infant daughter of / Charles and / Ann BOUCHER / of this parish / who died Jany 29th 1863 / aged 9 months / The Lord gave and the Lord / hath taken away. Blessed / be the name of the Lord
[Pollard, Taunton] (E)

D91 (Cross) [mb] In / loving memory of / Charles BOUCHER / of Greenway in this parish / who died August 16th 1886 / aged 78 years / Also of / Ann BOUCHER / his wife / who died Jany 5th 1925 / aged 90 years (E)

D92 In / loving memory of / Gordon Dennis / BRIDGES / Died 16 Sept. 1996 / aged 62 years (E)

D93 (Cross) In / treasured remembrance of / John CHORLEY / Lieutenant and Paymaster / the First Somerset Militia / who died at Taunton / February 22nd 1839 aged 65 years / and of Ann his beloved wife / who died at Wiveliscombe / February 25th 1845? aged 40 years (E)

D94 In / affectionate / remembrance of / Caroline / the beloved wife of / John VICKERY. Painter / Wiveliscombe / who departed this life / the 9th day of December 1876 / aged 39 years / Also her infant George / the tenth child / aged 2 days   (E)

D95 Thomas TYLER / who died June 30th 1793 / aged 46 / Also Ann his wife / who died October 3rd 1831 / aged 82 / Also Benjamin their son / who died July 27th 1794 / aged 15 / Also Edith their daughter / who departed this life / the 18th of December 1849 / aged 69 (E)

D96 Sacred / to the / memory of / John TYLER / of Ford in this Parish / who departed this life / August 15th 1865 / aged 32 years (E)

D97 (Small Stone) W.H. / 1881

D98 In memory / of / Mary NURCOMBE / Died January 28th 1863 / aged 76 years / Also of / John NURCOMBE / husband of the above / Died June 17th 1871 / aged 86 years (E)

D99 Sacred / to / the memory of / Charles NURCOMBE / son of John and Mary NURCOMBE / of this parish / who departed this life / the 20th of December 1827 / Aged 3 years / Also Philip NURCOMBE / another son who departed this life / 2nd June 1839 / aged 19 years / .... remembrance ....

D100 In / affectionate / remembrance / of / Admonition NURCOMBE / Died 28th Feby 1872 / aged 50 years / Until the day break and the / shadows flee away / Also of Eva NURCOMBE / daughter of the above / Died 27th October 1882 / Aged 28 years (E)

D101 *[Blank]*

D102 In / loving memory of / George Henry BOND / who died May 30th 1883 / aged 50 years / Also of / Sarah / widow of the above / who fell asleep / Jan 17th 1898 / aged 60 years / Peace perfect peace / I am the resurrection / and the life whosoever / liveth and believeth in me / shall never die / William Dean BOND / Born March 1872 / Died April 1912 (E)

D103 *[Blank]*

D104 In / loving memory of / Francis Audley son of / Th^{os} C L & Annie LEMPRIERE / who died December the 25th 1880 / aged 10 years. / Also of / Walter Herbert LEMPRIERE / son of the above / who died February the 2nd 1882 / aged 7 weeks / Not lost but gone before / also / Thos.(?) L. LEMPRIERE / Father of the above / who died October 14th 1908 (E)

D105 Sacred / to the memory of / Mary MILTON / who departed this life / July 15th 1876 / Aged 70 years (E)

D106   *[Blank]*   (Small stone)   T.C. / 1889   (E)

D107   In loving remembrance of / William NORTH / of Langley, Wiveliscombe, / who died February 19th 1891. / Aged 81 years. / Also of / Jane, wife of the above / who died April 22nd 1887. / Aged 80 years. / The blood of Jesus Christ his son cleanseth us / from all sin   (E)

D108   In loving memory of / Isabella Minnie THRESHER / who died February 12th 1892, / aged 22 years. / "He bringeth them unto their desired haven"   (E)

D109   In / affectionate / remembrance of / Jane HAWKINS / the beloved wife of / William HAWKINS. / of the Lion Hotel in this / parish, who departed / this life April 17th 1870. / Aged 70 years. / "It is the Lord. Let Him do what / seemeth Him best." / 1st Saml. 3.18./
Also the aforesaid / William HAWKINS, / who died December 31st / 1881 aged 78 years / "Remember not the sins of my youth / nor my transgressions, acco - / rding to thy Mercy remember / thou me for thy goodness' sake / O Lord" / Psalm XXV. 7 verse (E)

D110   (Cross) In loving memory of / John Ellis PAYNE / the dearly loved son of / John Ellis & Sybella Bevan PAYNE / who went to be with Jesus Novr 10th 1906 / Aged 11 years. Safely folded on his breast / For ever and forever blest.   (E)

D111   In ever loving / memory of / Mabel Annie DOWN / died Oct. 2nd 1928 / aged 37 / Also of / Arthur Henry DOWN / died July 23rd 1947 / aged 80   (E)

D112   I.H.S. / In affectionate memory of / Elizabeth WERE / who died Dec 16th 1869 / aged 37. A few more years shall roll / A few more seasons come / And we shall be with those that rest / Asleep within the tomb.   (E)

D113   I.H.S. / In loving memory of / John NEWTON / of this Parish / who died March 28th 1858 / aged 61 years / Also / Betsy NEWTON / wife of the above / who died August 5th 1882 / Aged 84 years / The memory of the just is blessed. Proverbs Xth chapter. 7 v.   *[Richards]*   (E)

D114   In / loving memory of / William SULLY / who departed this life / October the 2nd 1885, / aged 61 years. / Thy will be done. / Also of / Ann SULLY / who died April 21st 1898 / aged 76 years / Her end was peace.   (E)

D115   (Ground) Kathleen Mary CARR / S.R.N. Sister H.V. / 25th April 1913 / 23rd May 1989. / Rest in peace

D116   (Ground) Cherished memories of / a dearly loved wife & mother / Winifred Alice BURTON / 1898 – 1990 / Also / a beloved husband & father / George Alick BURTON / 1894 – 1983.

D117 (Ground) Louisa A BIRD / "Bobbie" / Dearly loved / 26th November 1904 / 1st July 1991 / Rest in peace

D118 In / loving memory of / William Lawrence Weston / the beloved son of / H & E CAUSLEY / who fell asleep in Jesus Feb[y] 16th 1909 / aged 3 years 10 months / Suffer little children to come unto me / And of his Grandma / Elizabeth Daniel CAUSLEY / died April 1st 1909 (E)

D119 Cherished / memories of / A dear / husband & father / James CLARKE / died 29th Feb. 1988 / aged 82. (E)

D120 In loving memory of / Jane BULL / who departed this life / December 31st 1890 / aged 65 years / Also of Selina / youngest daughter of the above / who died December 6th 1886 / aged 26 years (E)

D121 Sacred to the memory / of / William HILL son of / George and Sarah HILL / who died Oct 8th 1858 / aged 21 years / "Boast not thyself of tomorrow / For thou knowest not what a day may bring" / Also Ann HILL daughter of the above / George and Sarah HILL / who died Dec 8th 1841 / aged 35 years / "What is your Life? It is even a vapour / which endureth for a little time / and then vanisheth away". (E)

D122 In / loving memory of / Raymond CHUBB / who died 31st August 1995 / aged 69 / Also of his brother / Ronald CHUBB / who died 8th September 1933 / aged 13 / May they rest in peace / together (E)

D123 (F/H) In loving / memory of / Job STENNER / 8th Jan 1922 (E) / Also / his wife / Elizabeth / 18th Aug. 1954. (N)

D124 In loving memory of / Elizabeth, / the beloved wife of Henry BALE, / who departed this life August 13th 1888, / aged 50 years. / "In the midst of life we are in death" / Also of / Henry BALE, / husband of the above / who died Oct[r] 12th 1910, / aged 87 years. (Small stone) E.B. 1888 / H.B. 1910 (E)

D125 In / memory of / Sarah BALE / who departed this life / January 15th 1864. / Aged 79 years. / She was a true and dutiful wife / A dear and tender mother / She said good by all / I am going to my Blessed Saviour. / Blessed are the Dead which die in the Lord / William BALE / Died April 26 1872. / Aged 72 years. (E)
(Small stone) S.B. / 1864

D126 W.W. / 1884 (E)

D127 (War Grave) Honi Soit Qui Mal y Pense / Royal Army Service Corps / R4/139894 Private / G RAWLE / Royal Army Service Corps / 22nd September 1915 Age 47 / Ever loving memory / from brothers and sisters (E)

D128 I.H.S. / In / affectionate remembrance / of / Mary HURFORD / who died August 27th 1878 / aged 19 years / In the midst of life we are in death   (E)

D129 In loving memory of / Mary / wife of Joseph BAILEY / of Clatworthy Cottage / Wiveliscombe / who fell asleep in Jesus / December the 8th 1879 / aged 67 years / Mary had chosen that / better part which shall / not be taken from her   *[Richards]* (E)

D130 I.H.S. / In affectionate remembrance of / Mary Ann DRURY, / who died February 22nd 1881 / at Wiveliscombe, Somerset / Blessed are the dead which / die in the Lord / Rev. 14.13 (E)

D131 In loving memory of / William James / GADD / Died 19th Oct. 1987 / Aged 83. / Also his wife / Florence / Died 27th June 1997 / Aged 95 / At rest together (E)

D132 In memoriam / Jessie RICHARDS / Died November 10th 1888 / Aged 13 years. / At rest. / Also of / Simon RICHARDS / Died November 11th 1915 / Aged 89 years / Also of his wife / Harriett RICHARDS / Died December 20th 1915 / Aged 78 years (E)

D133 In / loving memory / of / my dear husband / Thomas Charles CROSS, / who died suddenly / March 3rd 1898. / Aged 62 years. / "In the midst of life / we are in death" / Also of / Hannah / wife of the above / who died Aug. 23rd 1924, / aged 99 years. / "With long life will I satisfy thee" (E)

D134 In / loving / memory of / John R COCK, / who died at Clatworthy House / April 17th 1895. / Aged 44 years / "Thy will be done." (E)

D135 In / loving memory / of / Mary Ann DUNN, / who died Sept 3rd 1928, / aged 69 years. / At rest.   (E)

D136 (Cross)   In / loving memory of / Sarah WERE, / wife of James WERE, / who departed this life / July 20th 1893, aged 64 years. / Her end was peace / Also / James WERE / Died April 12th 1894, / aged 64 years. / Gone to be with Jesus (E)

D137 *[Blank]*
D138 E.W. / 1863
D139 J.W. / 1863
D140 M.J.W. / 1859

D141 Be pleased O Lord to Deliver / In / memory of / Jane wife of / William BALMAN / who departed this life / March 8 1867 in the / 38? year of her age / Also of / William BALMAN / who departed this life / October 27th 1869 / Aged 38? years / Thy rod and thy staff / they comfort me / Also of / Catharine / infant daughter of A. R. and M. A. BALMAN / who died January 5th 1868 / Aged 16 months (E)
(Small stone)   W.B. / 1869   J.B. / 1867

D142 In / memory of / William BUR- / STON who depart / ed this life the 30 / April 1823 Aged 15(?) / years *[Illegible poem]* In / memory of / Nancy BURST - / ON who departed / this life the 5th of / Feby 1825 Aged –5(?) / years / A gentle mother / …in life / ….in / …. (E)

D143 In memory of / William BURSTON / Saddler of this Parish / who died 27th June 1860 / aged 50 years / Deeply lamented and respected / by all who knew him *[Hays]* (E)

D144 (Cross) In memory of / Cath^n Elizth ALBERTUS / Died Novr 16th 1870 Aged 62 (E)

D145 In / memory / of / Phillip Blundell HILL / Died / July 2nd 1862 / aged 47 years. / To the Lord our God belong mercies / and forgiveness (E)

D146 Sacred / to / the memory of / the beloved children of / Edwin & Elizabeth MIDDLETON / Annie Beatrice / Died October 24th 1863 / aged 9 months. / Elizabeth Ellen / Died October 27th 1863 / aged 7 years and 10 months. / Kate Jessy / Died November 29th 1863 / Aged 3 years and 2 months. (E)

D147 In / memory of / Frances Laura / infant daughter of / William & Laura LEGGE / who died / Decr 10th 1860 / Aged 18? months (E)

D148 Sacred / to the memory of / William WERE / who departed this life / October the 9th 1820 / aged 57 years / And of / Mary WERE / wife of the above / who departed this life / November the 5th 1878 / Aged 86 years / The toil some way thou'st travelled oe'r / and borne the heavy load / ……… But Christ hath taught thy languid feet / To reach his blest above. (Small Stone) M.W. / 1878 (Small Stone) W.W. 1820. (E)

D149   In / memory of / George SLOCOMBE / died July 2nd 1872, / aged 67 years. / Thou hast delivered / my soul from death, / mine eyes from tears, / and my feet from falling. / Psalms 116.Verse 8 / Also of / Maria SLOCOMBE / wife of the above / died January 15th 1890. / Aged 84 years (E)

D150   In loving memory of / our dear Mother / Salome Ellen HILL / who died Sept 15th 1932, / aged 77 years. / R.I.P. (E)

D151   Peace for ever / Catherine MARRYAT / Died / February 13th 1883 (E)

D152   (Cross)   In / loving memory of / Eleanor Mary / daughter of / Thomas & Eleanor RICHARDS / who died November 15th 1891, / aged 24 years. / Her end was peace. (E)

D153   (Cross)   In / loving memory of / Thomas RICHARDS, / who died 13th October 1892 / aged 70 years. / Also / Eleanor, his wife / who died 14th December 1892 / aged 67 years. / Thy will be done. (E)

D154   In / loving memory of / William FROST / who died June 23rd 1887 / aged 67 years / He waited patiently / for the Lord / Also of / Elizabeth FROST / wife of the above / who died February 3rd 1900 / aged 77 years / Her end was peace   (E)

D154a   (Reverse) In memory of / Thomas DINHAM / Born Aug 16th 1898 / Died Sept 6th 1898 (W)

D155   (Cross)   In / loving memory of / John Henry STACEY / died 5th December 1947 / aged 94 years. / Also of Lisa Bella STACEY / his wife / died 18th August 1906 / aged 53 years. (E) Also of three of their children / Cecil Edward aged 13 years. / Evelyn Kate aged 11 years. / Ewart Henry aged 6 years. / All died 4th November 1893. (S)

D156   In affectionate remembrance of / Sarah Anna / the beloved wife of / James HILL / who died at Withycombe Octr 30th 1892, / aged 56 years. / The Lord was her guide through Life. / Also of / James HILL / husband of the above / who died Jany 15th 1923 / aged 89 years (E)
(Small stone) S.A.H. 1892   J.H. 1923

D157   In / memoriam / Elizabeth (Lizzie) A WEBBER / Died 13th January 1922. / Aged 70 (E) (Small stone) E.A.W.

D158   I.H.S. / In memory of / James HAYES / died October 12th 1864 / aged 74 years / Also / Jane HAYES / wife of the above / died January 17th 1883 / aged 89 years (E)

D159   In loving memory of / John BENNETT, / (Pyncombe Wiveliscombe) / died Jan. 14th 1893, / aged 71 years. / also of / Louisa wife of the above / who died Jan. 11th 1869, / aged 39 years. / Thy will be done. (E)

D160 In affectionate remembrance of / Joseph BURTON / who died August 9th 1886. / aged 66 years. / He giveth his beloved sleep. /
Also / Elizabeth. Youngest daughter of the above / who was drowned near Auckland, / October 29th 1894: aged 31 years. / Peace perfect peace. /
Also / Caroline BURTON, / wife of the above / died April 14th 1908, / aged 86 years. (E)

D161 (Cross)   In / memory of / Henry John DUNN / Died December 23rd 1874 / aged 31 years / Safe in the Arms of Jesus / Erected by his loving wife / Emma (E)

D162 I.H.S. / In loving memory of / John KELLAND / who died November 27th 1883 / aged 48 years / Dying Daily / Also of / Mary Ann KELLAND / his wife died May 17th 1871 / aged 59 years / Also / Mary Ann KELLAND / their daughter / Died March 20th 1875 / Aged 9 years *[Richards]* (E)

D163 In / memory / of / John KELLOW / Died November 9th 1862. / Aged 37 years / Precious in the sight of the Lord / Is the death of his Saints. Psalm 116. Verse 15.   (E)

D164 In / loving memory / of / Thomas COWLING / who died Oct 25th 1885 / aged 61 years / Also of / Mary Ann his wife / who died Nov 14th 1909 / aged 79 years. / Also of / their two daughters / Elizabeth / who died Oct 27th 1900 / aged 45 years / And of Eliza / who died Jan 26th 1901 / aged 44 years / And their daughter Edith / who died May 1st 1931 / aged 62 years (E)

D165 Sacred / to the memory / of Jane the / wife of James GAMLIN who / departed this life 14th Dec[r] 1861 / aged 65 years / Also of / John GAMLIN / son of the above who departed / this life 21st June 1864 / aged 46 years / Also of / James GAMLIN / who departed this life / November 5th 1874, aged 78 years / Blessed are the dead / which die in the Lord (E)

D166 I.H.S. In affectionate remembrance of / Elizabeth / the beloved wife of / John LUTLEY / of Hartswell in this parish / who died Dec[r] 24th 1876 aged 56 years (E)

D167 Sacred / to the memory of / Mary / the beloved wife for one short year / of / James Dyer BLAKE of Langport / and daughter of Thomas EDBROOKE / of Croford in this parish / who died Oct[r] 19th 1850 / aged 30 years / Blessed are the dead which / die in the Lord. Rev.14. (E)

D168 In / memory of / George EDBROOKE / of this parish / who died March 13th 1815 / Aged 57 years / .....on tombs are titles vainly spent / man's good name is his best monument /
Also Betsy, the wife of / George EDBROOKE / who died December 26th 1828 / aged 66 years / Blessed are the dead which die in the Lord (E)

D169 *[Blank]*

D170 I.H.S. / Precious in the sight of the Lord is the death of his Saints / In memory of / Thomas EDBROOKE / of Old Cleeve / who died at Wellington / the 9th Sep 1873 aged 60 / Also Anna / wife of the above / who died at Exeter / October 9th 1905 (E)

D171 (Ground) In ever loving memory of / my darling Dad / William PAYNE / who entered into rest / August 9th 1928 / aged 67 years. / Blessed are the peacemakers: for / they shall be called the children of God (E)

D172 (Ground) My darling Mum / Emma PAYNE / who entered into rest / April 9th 1934 / aged 70 years / Nothing in my hand I bring / simply to thy cross I cling.

D173 (Ground) In / affectionate / remembrance of / Robert ALLEN / who departed this life / November 29th 1874 / aged 94 years / Also Betty wife of the above / who departed this life / May 18th 1875. / aged 96 years. / Cheerful husband, wife most dear / tender parents lieth here / free from malice, void of pride / in love they lived in peace they died *[Stagg, Taunton]* (W)

D174 [mb] In loving memory of / our dear Father / John BALE, / (who fought in the battle of Waterloo) / died December 8th 1861, aged 72 years. / Dearest loved one we must leave thee / in the peaceful grave's embrace / But thy memory shall be cherished / Till we see thy Heavenly face. / This stone is erected by his loving / daughter Anna MIDDLETON, of Australia (E)

D175 …….. 1888 / …….. 1885 / …….. / who d…. 1887 / also William KING / died August 22nd 1902 / Aged 70 years (E)

D176 In / loving memory of / John JENKINS, / died 11th Octr 1896, / aged 63 years. / "In the midst of life we are in death" / Also of / Lilian JENKINS. / died 7th Feby 1894, / aged 5 years. /
Also of / Ernest C JENKINS, / died 10th April 1896, / aged 33 years. /
Also of Annie / wife of John JENKINS, / who passed home July 16th 1926, / aged 73 years. (E)

D177 In loving memory of / John SALTER / died June 19th 1895, / aged 79 years. / Also Ann SALTER / his beloved wife / died October 30th 1904, / aged 81 years. (E)

D178 Ernest GREEN, / 1987. / Forever in our thoughts. (E)

D179 (Ground) In / loving memory of / Gordon Charles / FUDGE / Died 8.12.1996 / Aged 73

D180 In loving memory of / Maria HILL / who departed this life / October 20th 1894 / aged 68 years / Not my will but thine be done / Also of / William HILL / husband of the above / who departed this life / December 21st 1898 / Aged 86 years (E)

D181 In / affectionate remembrance of / James CRUWYS / who died the 25th day of Feby 1878 / aged 58 years (E)   Also Sarah wife of the above / who died the 13th day of Feby 1867 / Aged 56 years / Also Emily their daughter / who died the 26th day of May 1874 / aged 15 years / Also Sarah their daughter / who died the 23rd day of June 1874 / aged 21 years *[Manning, Taunton]* (E)

D182 (Surround)   In loving memory of our dear Father (E) / George QUICK died Decr 4th 1915 aged 77 (S) / Also our dear Mother (W) / Elizabeth QUICK. At peace May 25th 1921 aged 78 (N)

D183 E.L. / 1893

D184 (Cross)   In / ever loving memory / of / Clifford Charles / the beloved child of / George & Clara / QUICK / who died June 6th 1918 / aged 3 years. / Jesus called a little child / unto him (E)   Also of / Leonard / John QUICK / who died / January 4th / 1925 / aged 4 years (S)

D185 In loving memory of (E) / Herbert TRELIVING late of Upingtons, Wiveliscombe, who fell asleep Feb 7th 1919 (N) Aged 64 years / I know that my redeemer liveth (W) Also of Alice Ann his wife / who died on October 19th 1958 Aged 89 (S)

D186 [mb]   John LEAN / son of / John and Georgina LEAN / of this Parish / Died January 3rd 1887 / Aged 73 (E)

D187 In / memory of / Elizabeth PUGSLEY / who died December 12th 1868 / aged 78 years / Also of / John Follet PUGSLEY / who died August 3rd 1880 / aged 95 years (E) (Small stone) J.F.P. / 1880 and E.P. / 1868.

D188 [mb]   Lucy LEAN / daughter of James LEAN Esqr of Clifton, Bristol, / who died in this parish August 29th 1866. / Aged 61. / Looking unto Jesus the author and finisher of our faith / Hebrews Ch. XII.V.2. (S)   Elizabeth Sarah LEAN / daughter of James LEAN Esqr of Clifton, Bristol, / who died in this parish July 8th 1878 / aged 63. / As thy days so shall thy strength be / Deut. Ch. XXXIII.V25th (N)

D189 (Cross)   Susanna Risdon PUGSLEY. Died 23rd March 1909 Aged 75 years   (N)

D190 (Cross)   I.H.S. In / memory of / Maria Follett PUGSLEY / who died Oct 10th 1868 / Aged 1 year & 7 months / She is not lost but gone before   (E)

D191 In loving memory of / Lutley PUGSLEY /of Whitefield / Died 5th May 1882 aged 65 / I heard a voice from heaven saying / Blessed are the dead which die / in the Lord. Rev.14 v.13. (N)

D192 In / loving memory / of / Maria PRICE / who died June 14th 1917 / aged 91 years / Also of / Betsy GOVIER /sister of the above / who died April 24 1908 / aged 86 years (E)

D193   Sacred / to the memory of / Thomas CULLIFORD / of this parish who departed this life / March 19th 1846 / Aged 61 years. / Also / of / Betty his wife / who departed this life / November 9th 1851 / Aged 65 years (E)

D194   In affectionate remembrance of / Thomas CULLIFORD / who died May the 17th 1855 / aged 7 months. / Also of / Thomas CULLIFORD / who died October the 18th 1861. / Aged 5 years. / also of Charles CULLIFORD / who died September the 16th 1878. / Aged 13 years. / Children of Thomas and / Mary CULLIFORD (E)
(Small stone) T.C. 1855 / T.C. 1861 / C.C. 1878

D195   (Cross) In / memory of / Anna Maria LIGHT / who departed this life / August 13th 1878 / Aged 36 / Blessed are they who die in the Lord / Also of Jane LIGHT / who departed this life / May 22nd 1871 aged 47 years (E)

D196   *[Blank]*

D197   To the memory / of / Charles Hartree BROWN / who died on / the 5th day of March 185? / aged 50 years./ Also / Charles Herbert BROWN / son of the above who died / on the 3rd day of May 1856 / aged 3 years. (E)

D198   Sacred / to the memory of / Elizabeth BROWN / who died the 4th of Novr 1848. / Aged 72 years. / Also of / Joseph BROWN / husband of the above / who died the 18th of Octr 1864 / Aged 98 years / Blessed are the dead which / die in the Lord (E)

D199   To the memory / of / James CLATWORTHY / who died 4th Decr 1865. / Aged 60 years. (E)

D200   In / affectionate remembrance / of Hannah / the beloved wife of / William TICE / who departed this life / February the 11th 1861 / aged 52 years / This stone is erected by her / children in loving memory / of a devoted parent / She is not dead but sleepeth (E)

D201   In / loving memory of / Jane POCOCK / died January 7th 1862 / aged 76 years. / Also / Thomas POCOCK / husband of the above / died March 12th 1867 / aged 86 years. / Looking unto Jesus, the author / and finisher of our faith / Heb. Chap. XII . Verse 2 / And of / Caroline POCOCK / daughter of the above / who entered into life / May 7th 1887, aged 72 years. (E)

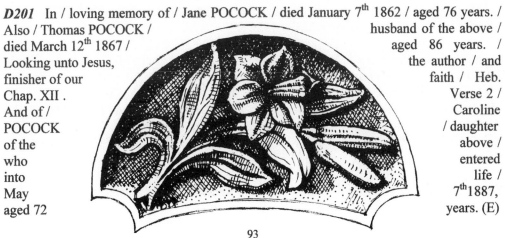

93

D202 Sacred / to the memory of / John NATION / who departed this life / February 8th 1874 / aged 74 years / Also Ann NATION / wife of the above / who departed this life / November 14th 1869 / aged 56 years / Their end was peace *[Richards]* (E)

D203 *[Grave with no headstone]*
D204 *[Grave with no headstone]*
D205 *[Grave with no headstone]*

D206 (Cross) I.H.S. / In loving memory of / Betsy / the beloved wife of / Thomas BELLEW / who fell asleep / March 27th 1906 / aged 61 years / "Arise shine for thy light is come and the / Glory of the Lord is risen upon thee" (E)
Side Also of / their son / Henry John BELLEW / who was drowned whilst bathing / in the Coly. June 20th 1891 / aged 25 years *[Manning & Son, Taunton]*

D207 In loving memory of / Elizabeth KELLAND / of this parish / who died Decr 19th 1871 / aged 45 years / This memorial is erected by her unknown / faithful son-in-law William WEBER, May 1887 / With deep sympathy of her surviving children (E)

D208 In / loving memory / of / Anthony MILLETT / who died Octr 20th 1916 / aged 70 years. (E)

D209 I.H.S. / In memory of / Anna Maria MILLETT / Died September 13th 1884 / aged 35 years / My hope hath been in thee O Lord / Also of James MILLETT / father of the above / who died April 22nd 1869 / aged 70 years / Christ is all sufficient / Also of Eliza MILLETT / wife of the above / who died August 10th 1885 / aged 87 years / Her end was peace (E)

D210 (Cross) In affectionate / remembrance of / Edwin LUCAS. / Died November 10th 1901 / aged 66 years / Also of Eliza his beloved wife / Died May 4th 1893
(Small Stone) E. L. 1901 *[Hann]* (E)

D211 (Cross) In / remembrance of / Caroline J LUCAS / Died April 29th 1926, / aged 63 years. (Small Stone) C.J.L. / 1926 (E)

D212 In / memory of / a dear husband and father / Alec Ralph SMITH / Died 14th July 1986 / aged 62. / Loved and remembered always (E)

D213 Sacred / to the memory of / Sarah the beloved wife of / Samuel KELLAND / who died June 8th 1888 / aged 84 years. / I sleep but my heart waketh / Also of Samuel KELLAND / husband of the above who departed / this life August 26th 1899 aged 92 / Rest in peace (E)

D214 In / loving memory of / our brothers / James TURNER / who died March 30th 1883, / aged 16 years. / /cont............

94

D214 cont.   Robert TURNER / who died March 25th 1895, / aged 34 years, and was interred / in the New Cemetery Cardiff. / And our sister / Elizabeth Maria TURNER / who died April 2nd 1908, / aged 37 years. / Also our Mother and Father / Sarah Featherstone TURNER / who died December 28th 1915, / aged 82 years. / William TURNER, / who died September 25th 1920, / aged 87 years. (E)
(Surround)   And our sister Emily who departed this life November 10th 1929 at Huish Champflower Schoolhouse (S)

D215   In loving remembrance of / Elizabeth / wife of George DAVIS, / who died Feb[y] 1st 1889, / aged 40 years. / "In the midst of life we are in death." / Also of / George DAVIS / who died Dec[r] 26th 1923, / Aged 78 years. / Faithful unto death / And of / Frances SUTTON / who died April 12th 1915, / aged 80 years. / At rest.

D216   [Blank]

D217   In / memory of / the beloved children of / William and Martha LANSDOWN / Sarah / died Dec[r] 4th 1864. Aged 7 years. / William / died Dec[r] 5th 1864, aged 3 years. / Harry / died Dec[r] 8th 1864. Aged 5 years. / Mary / died Sep[tr] 6th 1870, aged 2 years. / Tom / died Nov[r] 4th 1876, aged 5 years 6 months. / Louisa / died Nov[r] 9th 1876, aged 11 months. (E)

D218   In loving memory of / Joseph YANDLE / who departed this life / October 21, 1887 / in his 80th year. / Also of Charlotte / his beloved wife / who died February 12, 1893 / aged 79 years. / "How sad we mark the closing eye / of those we loved in days gone by / yet sweet in death the parting song / we'll meet again t'will not be long" (E)

D219   In / affectionate   remembrance / of / Harriet BRANFIELD who died ..... November 1871 / Also / William BRANFIELD / ..../ husband of the above / who died ......1878 / aged ?? years.   (Small Stones) W.B. / 1878. H.B. / 1871. (E)

D220   Richard SULLY / Died 10 of November / 1841 aged 96. / A humble Christian / Trusting in his redeemer (E)

D221   Sacred / to / the memory of / Maria STONE / who departed this life / on the 6th day of Sept[r] 1858 / Aged 78 years /   Also / Robert STONE / her husband / died April 3rd 1864 / aged 74 years (E)

D222   In / loving memory of / Edward R D(?) COX / who departed this life / October the 12th 1878 / aged ...years / There is but a step between / me and death. [1 Sam 2 v.3] (Small Stone) E.C. 1878 (E)

D223   In the midst of life we are in death / In / affectionate / remembrance of / Elizabeth / the beloved daughter of / William and Eliza HODGES / of this town / who departed this life / June 14th 1867 aged 21 years / Her end was peace. *[Richards]* (E)

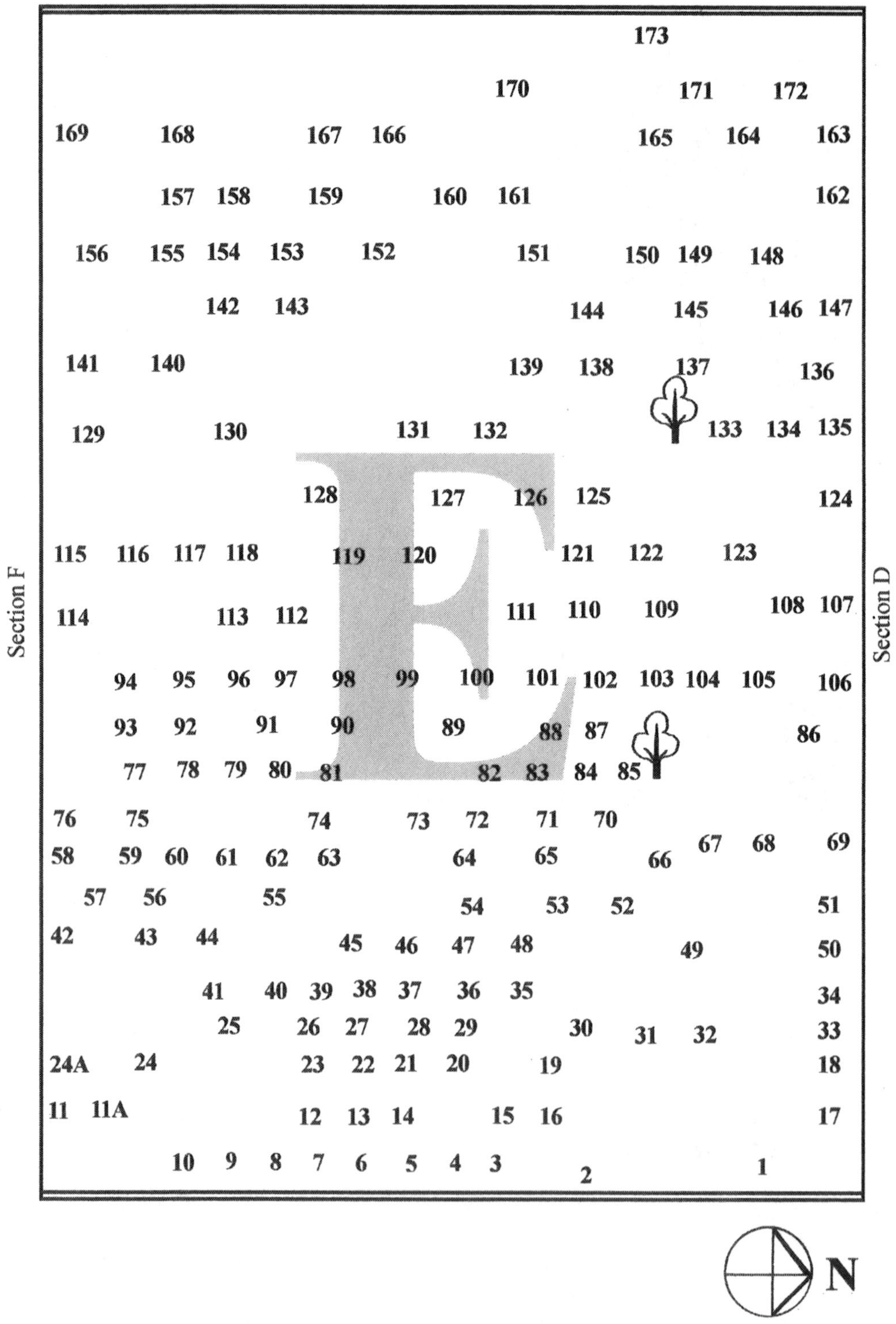
173
170 171 172
169 168 167 166 165 164 163
157 158 159 160 161 162
156 155 154 153 152 151 150 149 148
142 143 144 145 146 147
141 140 139 138 137 136
129 130 131 132 133 134 135
128 127 126 125 124
115 116 117 118 119 120 121 122 123
114 113 112 111 110 109 108 107
94 95 96 97 98 99 100 101 102 103 104 105 106
93 92 91 90 89 88 87 86
77 78 79 80 81 82 83 84 85
76 75 74 73 72 71 70
58 59 60 61 62 63 64 65 66 67 68 69
57 56 55 54 53 52 51
42 43 44 45 46 47 48 49 50
41 40 39 38 37 36 35 34
25 26 27 28 29 30 31 32 33
24A 24 23 22 21 20 19 18
11 11A 12 13 14 15 16 17
10 9 8 7 6 5 4 3 2 1
E
Section F
Section D
N

Churchyard Plan - Section E

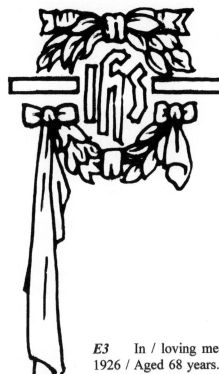

E1 In memory of / Mary Elizabeth KELLOW / who died Feb[y] 21st 1935. / Aged 77 years. / Erected by her sister Florrie. (E)

E2 (Surround) In loving memory of (W) Roy the beloved only child of (N) C & M BARRINGTON (E) who died 30th March 1932, aged 8 years (S)

E3 In / loving memory of / Edward BARRINGTON / Died Dec 1st 1926 / Aged 68 years. / Also Mary Ann his wife / Died Feb. 11th 1940 / Aged 77 years. / Also Kathleen. Their daughter / Died Dec. 4th 1904 Aged 6 months (E)

E4 (F/H) In / loving / memory / ....

E5 In / ever loving memory / of / Catherina Alice, / the dearly beloved wife of / John HURLEY / who passed peacefully away / October 28th 1928, / Aged 53 years. / Also of / John HURLEY / the dearly loved husband of / Maud HURLEY, / who passed peacefully away / February 9th 1950, / Aged 75 years. (E)

E6 In memoriam / Reginald STONE / Died 3rd May 1930 / Aged 50 years. / Also of Ethel May STONE / Beloved wife of the above / who fell asleep 20th September 1953 / Aged 70 years. / At rest. (E)

E7 In / loving memory of / Aden STONE / of Langley. / who passed away May 21st 1931, / Aged 49 years. / In God's keeping. (E)

E8 (Cross) In ever loving memory of / my dear husband / Leonard Edwin BOXALL / who passed away suddenly / October 23rd 1933, / Aged 43 years. / In the midst of life we are in death. / In loving memory of our dear Mother / Beatrice Helena BOXALL / peacefully on Feb 26th 1985 Aged 95 years / In death they are united (E)
In / ever loving memory of / George Gordon / BOXALL / Died 18th March 1991 / Aged 66 years (E)

E9   In loving memory of / Ella STONE / who fell asleep Sept 1ˢᵗ 1935 / Aged 60 years. / She was beloved by all who knew her / Also B J STONE / Called to rest March 16ᵗʰ 1953 / Aged 80. Reunited. (E)

E10   In / loving memory of / Mary Annie ARSCOTT / who fell asleep / June 18, 1936 / Aged 70. / At rest. / also / William Edward ARSCOTT / her husband / who fell asleep / Jan 16, 1951 / Aged 83. / and their daughter / Minnie ARSCOTT,   1902 – 10.9.1983 (E)

E11   (Flat stone) *Florence Hilda LUXTON. Buried 5 September 1938. Aged 58 years.*

E11a In loving memory of / Reuben JEWELL / the dearly loved husband of / Bertha Helena JEWELL / who passed away Novʳ 12th 1937, / Aged 82 years. / And of his wife / Bertha Helena JEWELL / who fell asleep Octʳ 19ᵗʰ 1951, / Aged 95 years. (E)

E12   (Surround)   In ever loving memory / of our dear parents   (E) / Jane HOYLE who died October 25ᵗʰ 1930 aged 70 years (N) / John   HOYLE who died August 6th 1935 aged 79 years (S) / Till memories fade and life departs they will live forever in our hearts (W)

E13   In / loving memory / of / Fred KELLOW, / who died December 15ᵗʰ 1928, / Aged 56 years. / Also his beloved wife / Ann KELLOW, / who died August 15ᵗʰ 1959, / Aged 86 years. (E)

E14   (Cross)   Sacred / to the memory of / James Christopher FRANCE / who died September 30ᵗʰ 1928 / aged 16? Years / And Eleanor his mother / who died January 3ʳᵈ 1930 Aged 45 / the wife of William Ashburner FRANCE / The Lord bless thee and keep thee (E)

E15   (Cross) In loving / memory of / Thomas BISHOP / who passed away Dec 18ᵗʰ 1924 / Aged 52 years. / At rest / And of his wife / Elizabeth Hannah / who died May 20ᵗʰ 1965   (E)

E16   In loving memory of / Elizabeth VICARY, / who died August 6ᵗʰ 1925, / Aged 73 years. (E)

E17   In / memory of / Francis GREENSLADE / who fell asleep Decʳ 20ᵗʰ 1912, / in his 90ᵗʰ year. / "Thy redeemer is strong" / "Nothing in my hand I bring / Simply to thy Cross I cling" (E)

E18   (Fallen/ground) In loving memory of / my dear husband / Thomas KELLOW, / of Langley Marsh, / who died September 5ᵗʰ 1898, / aged 65 years. / Also of / Mary Ann KELLOW, / wife of the above / who died February 24ᵗʰ 1909, / aged 73 years. / "Blessed are the dead which die in the Lord" / Also of Edward KELLOW, / youngest son of the above / who died July 9ᵗʰ 1905, / Aged 27 years. / Interred in Fulham cemetery.

E19 (Ground)   In loving memory of / Emma VICARY, / Born May 13th 1846, Died Decr 15th 1922, / Thy will be done. (N)
Also of John VICARY, / her beloved husband / who died 22nd Sep^t 1937, Aged 89 years. / At rest (S)

E20 (Cross)   Rest in peace. (Surround)   In loving memory of (E) / Frederick & Charlotte [L] EWIS, (S) / who passed away May 1926, aged 80 & 77 (N)

E21 (Surround)   In loving memory of / Francis James VICARY / who died Oct 2nd 1927, Aged 42 years / Thy will be done (E)

E22 (Cross)   In / loving memory / of / Eliza Jane GREEDY / Died Oct 10th 1927 / Aged 72 years (E)

E23 (F/H)   In / loving memory of / my dear husband / Thomas WALKER, / who passed away June 6th 1932 / Aged 62 years. / Thy will be done. /
Also of his wife / Florence / who fell asleep May 7th 1955 / Aged 85 years. (E)

E24 (Surround)   In loving memory of our dear sisters (E) /
Eliza REEVES, died April 28th 1938 aged 76 years (S) / Peace perfect peace (W) /
Also of Mary Ann RAWLE, died Feby 27th 1941, aged 86 years. (N)

E24a (Unmarked) *Clifford Forrest DOBLE. Buried 7 September 1938. Aged 63 years.*

E25 (Surround)   In loving memory of my dear husband Walter BARWICK, who died Decr 28th 1937, aged 77 years (S) Thy will be done (W)
Also of his wife Charlotte BARWICK, who died November 2nd 1945, aged 78 years (N)
(F/H) In loving / memory of / Frederick ADAMS / Died Dec 29, 1936 / Aged 62 years /
Also / Elizabeth ADAMS / Died Oct 3, 1949 / Aged 76 years (E)

E26   In memory of / our dearly loved parents / Elizabeth Ann CUMMINS, / who died Sept 19th 1935 / Aged 67 years. /
Harry CUMMINS / who died Decr 21st 1951 / Aged 93 years. / Together in God's care (E)

E27 (Cross)   In / loving memory of / Kate / wife of A E GERRARD, / who passed away on / the 28th September 1925, / Aged 49 years. / At rest. (E)

E28 (Cross)   (Surround)   In loving memory (E) Emily wife of John RISDON died at Storey's Close August 13th 1924 (S)

E29 (Cross)   To the dear memory of / Frances Mary / FEATHERSTONE, / December 6th 1916. / "Love never faileth" / Elizabeth Anne her sister / Died May 8th 1934 / The true light now shineth   (E)

E30   (Broken Cross)   In memoriam / Harriet Ann TYLER, / Died Nov. 20-1939. / Ida Caroline TYLER, / Died Feb. 1-1915. / Florence Geraldine TYLER, / Died Jan. 13-1935. / Mabel Sarah Maud TYLER, / Died Nov. 25 -1916 / all of Ford, Wiveliscombe (E)

E31   In loving memory / of / my dear husband / Henry LEE / who fell asleep in Jesus / August 22nd 1904, / Aged 31 years. / "His memory is as dear today / as in the hour he passed away" /
Also of Minnie / wife of the above / who died March 21st 1937, / Aged 58 years. (E)

E32   In loving memory of / Sarah, / the beloved wife of / John ADDICOTT, / of Pitt Farm / who died September 7th 1907 / Aged 81 years. / I am the way the truth and the life / no man cometh unto the Father but by me /
Also of / John ADDICOTT, / husband of the above / who died September 21st 1914 / Aged 81 years / His end was peace (E)

E33   In loving memory of / Annie / the beloved wife of / Charles TAKLE, / of Grants Farm in this parish, / who died August 2nd 1905, / Aged 25 years. / Sleep dearest wife thy task is o'er, / thy loving hands shall toil no more, / no more those weary eyes shall weep. / Sleep, dearest wife, gently sleep / Also / Charles TAKLE / who died March 19th 1956. / Aged 82. / Also / Annie TAKLE / who died April 19th 1952 / aged 75 (E)

E34   (Ground)   Ethel Louise / GIBBS / died / 18th Aug 1988 / Aged 77 / R.I.P.

E35   In memory of / Horatio MAINWARING / late Indian Woods & Forests / son of Admiral MAINWARING / of Whitmore Hall, Staffordshire / Died 20th July 1913, Aged 64. / Rest in peace. (E)

E36   (Cross) R.I.P. (Surround) To the dear memory of George PROUT, June 8th 1917. (S) and of his dear son Gilbert, May 6th 1933. (N)

E37   (Cross)   I.H.S. / In / loving memory of / William BAKER. / who died Feb 26th 1925, / Aged 65 years.   (E)   (Surround)   In loving memory of Olive Mary HILL née BAKER / died 16th June 1983, Aged 87.

E38   (Cross)   R.I.P (Surround) To the dear memory of Enid Madge CUMMINS, November 20th 1926. (S) / and of her Mother Mary PROUT, October 22nd 1935 (N)

E39   (Cross)   R.I.P.   (Surround) To the dear memory of Annie Elizabeth THORNE March 15th 1935 (S)

E40   In / loving memory of / my dear husband / Joseph PARKMAN / who died July 29th 1935, / Aged 64 years. / Gone but not forgotten. (E)

E41   (F/H)

E42 In / loving memory of / Mary Hannah, / wife of / Tom JONES, of Ford. / who died July 27th 1938 / Aged 66 years. / At rest. / Also Tom, her husband / who died Aug 20th 1958. / Aged 92 years. (E)

E43 In memory of / my beloved husband / Frederick Joseph HAWKINS / who passed away / January 28th 1936, / Aged 59 years. / Thy will be done / Also of Emma Jane / beloved wife of the above / who passed away / March 3rd 1957, / Aged 81 years. / Also of / Doris Mary HAWKINS / passed peacefully away Sept 22nd 1972, / Aged 68 years. / Also her husband / Richard Frederick / passed peacefully away Mar 29th 1982, / Aged 77 years. (E)

E44 R.I.P. / Sacred to the memory of / my dear husband / Thomas James WHEBBY / 28-6-1933, / Aged 43. (E)

E45 In / loving memory / of / Ethel Annie / wife of / William Henry HAWKINS, / who died May 7th 1927, / Aged 38 years. / Rest in peace. (E)

E46 PEACE / In loving memory of / Mary Elizabeth BENNETT / who departed this life / July 15th 1926, / Aged 66 years. / At rest. / Also of / William Leversha BENNETT / who passed away / July 27th 1932, / Aged 73 years. / Peace perfect peace (E)

E47 (Cross) In loving memory / of / Herbert Crane STREETEN / who died November 16th 1921, / Aged 64 years. / Peace perfect peace / Also of Selina STREETEN, / beloved wife of the above / who died April 30th 1947 aged 86 (E)

E48 In loving memory of / James DUNN, / of Jews Farm, / who died November 11th 1912, / Aged 66 years. / Peace perfect peace, with sorrows surging round / on Jesus' bosom nought but calm is found. / Also of / Sarah DUNN, / beloved wife of the above / who died October 23rd 1924. / Aged 78 years. (E)

E49 In loving memory of / Richard WATERMAN / who died July 23rd 1903. / Aged 59 years. / Also of Annie / daughter of the above / who died September 18th 1903. / Aged 25 years / "Until the day break" / Also of Benjamin, / son of the above / who died August 16th 1919. / Aged 49 years. / Also of Mary wife of / Richard WATERMAN, / who died August 25th 1921, / Aged 87 years. / Peace perfect peace (E)

E50 (Cross) I.H.S. / God is love / In / loving memory of / Samuel John LUTLEY / who fell asleep April 29th 1901 / in his eighteenth year / The Lord is my Shepherd I shall not want Psalm 23.1. (W) /
Rev Abraham / Daniel REECE / Vicar of West Hatch 24 years / At rest Novr 20th 1904 / aged 58. / Also of his widow / Anna Elizabeth REECE / who died February 21st 1940 / aged 95 years (E) / Father I will that / they also whom thou / hast given me be with me / where I am. St John 17.24. (N) / Jessie Eliza / LUTLEY / At rest March 18th 1928 / Aged 46 years. / Forever with the Lord (S)

E51   In memory of / George DYKE, / Died April 10th 1900. / Aged 60 years. / He lived for 35 years in the service of / Mr & Mrs Henry BELLEW / of Oakhampton House in this Parish, / and was highly esteemed and / deeply regretted (E)

E52   (Cross)   In loving memory / of / James Whitfield, / the beloved husband of / Ida Beatrice   WILKES / who departed this life / December 20th 1905 / Aged 48 years (E) / Also / Ida Beatrice / his wife / died April 28th 1907 / aged 47 years (N)

E53   (Cross)   In memory of / Geoffry Woodhouse HANCOCK / born 6th July 1875 died 17th Sep 1937 (E)

E54   (Cross)   In loving memory of / Alice Sophia / wife of the Rev L R HANCOCK / and second daughter of / the fifth Baron DYNEVOR / 1862-1939 / A shining light that shineth more and / more unto the perfect day. Proverbs IV.18 / Also of her husband / Leonard Rhys HANCOCK, MA / sometime Archdeacon in Brazil and / Chaplain of Christ Church, Rio de Janeiro / Born 17th May 1867 – Died 26th May 1943. / "The trumpet shall sound". I.Cor.XV.V2 (E) / Also of their son / George Leonard / Rhys HANCOCK MA / tutor biologist at / Makerere, Uganda / born 26th February 1900 / died 22nd June 1940 / buried in the European / Cemetery Kampala / "The Lord gave and the Lord / has taken away" Job.1.21. (N)

E55   In ever loving memory of / a dear husband and father / Robert SELLICK, / who died August 27th 1930 / Aged 71 years, / Peace perfect peace. / Also / Sarah Ann SELLICK, / Dearly beloved wife of the above / who died June 8th 1934, / Aged 67 years. / Thy will be done. (E)

102

E56   In / loving memory of / Albert TRICKEY / who fell asleep Decr 11th 1936, / Aged 76 years. / Also his beloved wife / Mary Jane TRICKEY / who fell asleep Jany 18th 1937, / Aged 74 years. / In God's keeping. (E)

E57   (Cross)   In loving memory of / Sarah Frances POWELL / Beloved wife of / Norman POWELL / Died 9th March 1938 / Aged 30 years. / Also Florence Bessie DINHAM / Died 23rd Nov 1943, / Aged 38 years. (E)

E58   In loving memory of / my dear wife / Maria CROWCOMBE / Died 27, July 1938. Aged 68 years / Also / Tom CROWCOMBE / Died 5, May 1954. Aged 84 years. / Re-united. (E)

E59   PEACE / In / loving memory / of / John TUDBALL, / who fell asleep 6th Aug. 1937, / Aged 61 years. / "At Rest".   / Also his wife / Mary Ann TUDBALL / Died 6th March 1969 / Aged 89 years. (E)

E60   I.H.S. / In loving memory / of / Ellen M COX / who entered into rest / 31st July 1936, / Aged 72 years. / Abide with me. / Also of / John C COX / husband of the above / who fell asleep / 10th February 1942 / aged 78 years. (E)

E61   R.I.P. / In loving memory / of / Lennox Gore TUDBALL / 19.12.1933. / Aged 60 (E)

E62   In / loving / memory of / John Babbage SAUNDERS / of Fry's Farm / who entered the homeland / on Sep 9th 1929 / Aged 58. / I know that my redeemer liveth / whom I shall see for myself. / Also his beloved wife / Bessie / who passed away / on Nov. 21st 1962 / Aged 85. / I shall be satisfied when / I awake in his likeness. (E)

E63   In / loving memory / of / Bessie / the affectionate, devoted wife of / Ernest Frank CATFORD, / Died June 21st 1929, / Aged 67 years. / And the light of his life gone out. / Also of / Ernest Frank CATFORD / husband of above / Died May 24th 1935 / Aged 75 years. / In death not divided (E)

E64   (Cross)   In loving memory of / Francis Escott HANCOCK / Born 7 December 1859 / Died 29 October 1943 / and of his wife / Mary Elizabeth HANCOCK / Born 21 September 1864 / Died 24 June 1958 (E)

E65   (Cross)   Steadfast in the faith / I.H.S. / In ever loving memory of / Edward Dawbney HANCOCK / MRCS LRCP / Dearly loved husband of / Flora Caroline / and eighth son of / William and Mary HANCOCK / of Court House, Wiveliscombe / at rest 29th December 1925 / Aged 56 years / They also which sleep in Jesus will / God bring with him / 1. Thess.IV-10   (E)
(Ground) And of his wife / Flora Caroline HANCOCK / At rest 11th December 1959 / Aged 80 years.

E66 (Cross)   In tender / and / loving memory / of / Flo the dearly loved wife of / Herbert LUCAS, / who passed away Sep^t 15th 1902 Aged 29 / "Oh for the touch of a vanished hand / And the sound of a voice that is still"   (E) /
Also of / Herbert Harry LUCAS / died March 18th 1936 / Aged 68 years / Peace perfect peace (N)

E67   In / loving memory / of / Mary Anne / Devoted wife of /Amos WILLIAMS / of Manor House / Born May 10th 1854, / Died May 21st 1916. / The Lord is good unto them that wait for / Him, To the soul that seeketh him. Lam: 3.25 /
Also of / Amos WILLIAMS / husband of the above / Born September 20th 1854, / Died August 27th 1916. / Thy will be done in earth, as it is / in Heaven. Matt.C.10 (E)

E68   In / loving memory / of / Charles WILLIAMS, / who died at Manor, / Wiveliscombe Decr 8th   1900 / Aged 81. / I waited patiently for the Lord, and / he inclined unto me and heard my cry. (E)

E69   (Ground) Always remembered / J. J.   KIRK / 1926 – 1988 / A. H. KIRK / 1898 – 1977 / For ever loved   /
(F/H)   In loving memory

E70   In / loving memory / of / Alfred Albert ROBINSON / who died November 24th 1908, / Aged 63 years. / Until the day break and the shadows flee away (E)

E71   (Cross) In loving memory of / William Ilbert HANCOCK / F.R.C.S.E. / Born April 10th 1873, / Died January 26th 1910. / Ninth son of the late / William and Mary HANCOCK, / of this parish / "Until the day break" (E)

E72   (Cross)   In / ever loving memory of / Philip Froude HANCOCK / At rest / 16th Oct 1933 / Aged 68 years / "Which I have / loved long since / and lost awhile" /
And of his wife / Jessie Violet HANCOCK / At rest 12th Dec 1959 / Aged 89 years (E)

E73   (F/H)   Jack HANNON / Died tragically / 13th July 1927 / Aged 31 / R.I.P. (E)

E74   In / loving memory / of / James COLE / who passed away (suddenly) May 12th 1930 / Aged 70 years. / Until the day break and the shadows flee away /
Also of Christianna his wife / who fell asleep January 25th 1935 / Aged 63 years / Peace perfect peace. (E)

E75   In loving memory of / our dear Mother / Emily Ann CHEDZEY / who died April 9th 1938, / Aged 83 years. / At rest. (E)

E76   In / memory of / my dear parents / of Culverhay / Wiveliscombe / John TIDBOALD / Died 14th Nov 1941 / and Caroline Beatrice / TIDBOALD / Died 20th Nov 1961 / Reunited (E)

E77   In loving memory of / Thomas / the beloved husband of / Margaret MERCHANT / who fell asleep Dec 25. 1937, Aged 85, / Thy will be done. / Also of Margaret MERCHANT / wife of the above / who died March 19. 1940, Aged 89. / In God's keeping. (E)

E78   In loving memory / of / John Southcombe MERCHANT / who died Dec. 3rd 1936, Aged 85. / Also of his wife / Mary Ann / who died Sep[t] 17th 1946, Aged 83. (E)

E79   In ever / loving memory / of / Thomas Richard HILL / who died May 25th 1935 / Aged 63 years. / Peace perfect peace. / Also / Elizabeth HILL / Devoted wife of the above / who died July 10th 1954 / Aged 82 years (E) / No. 129 (W)

E80   (Surround)   In loving memory of (E) / William PULSFORD / who died October 2nd 1959. Aged 68 (S) / At rest (W) /   Lilian Margaret PULSFORD who died August 8 1933. Aged 42 years. (N)

E81   (Cross) In loving memory / of / Tom SELLICK / who passed away / December 21st 1929, / Aged 66 years. / Also Edith his wife / who passed peacefully away / Sept 21st. 1952. Aged 81. / Peace perfect peace. (E)

E82   (Cross)   In / loving memory of / William COLLARD / who died March 18th 1912, / Aged 68 years. / Also of Fanny / wife of the above / who died December 12th 1922, / Aged 77 years. (E)

E83   In / loving memory of / Elizabeth Jane RICHARDS. / who departed this life / October 8th 1910, / aged 73 years. / She hath done what she could. / Also of Edwin Henry RICHARDS / husband of the above / who died Dec. 15th 1912 / Aged 80 years / Peace perfect peace (E)

E84   In ever loving memory / of / Thomas Joyce MERCHANT, / of Clerkspool, Wiveliscombe, / who was born January 19th 1826, / At rest December, 19th 1906. / He died trusting alone in the merits / of his redeemer. / And of Mary his wife / who was born April 17th 1825, / At rest June 5th 1913 / There remaineth therefore / a rest to the people of God / Heb.IV.9. (E)

E85   In ever   loving memory / of / George WHITE, / of Shirley, Southampton, / who was born July 10th 1829, / At rest July 7th 1906. / Gone to receive the crown of life which the / Lord hath promised to them that love him / Also of / Mary SOUTHCOMBE, / wife of the above / Died June 10th 1935, / Aged 79. / Peace perfect peace. (E)

E86   In / loving memory / of / Daisy Eleanor / second daughter of / William & Annie PARSONS / of Wiveliscombe, / Died May 3rd 1907, / aged 18 years. / Also Francis George / youngest son of the above / Drowned at sea Nov[r] 19th 1910, / Aged 17 years. / Thy will be done. /   /cont ....

E86 cont. Also / Frederick William PARSONS R.M.L.I. / Eldest son of the above / Died of wounds as prisoner of war in / Germany April 9th 1918, age 28 / Duty nobly done / Also Violet Annie BARRY, / beloved wife of William BARRY / and daughter of the above / Died Feby 9th 1920, Aged 33 years. / R.I.P. (E) *[see page 183]* (F/H) Our darling / Joyce / always / remembered by / Mum and Dad.

E87 In loving memory of / Charles OXENHAM / who died Feby 12th 1927, / Aged 62 years. / Also of Hannah / Beloved wife of the above / who died April 22nd 1950 / Aged 91 years. / Also of Mary Hannah / beloved daughter of the above / who died Jany 7th 1910. / aged 22 years. / "Until the day break" / Also of / Charles Henry OXENHAM / Grandson of the above / Died June 4th 1940, Aged 19 years. (E)

E88 In / loving memory / of / Jane ROGERS, / who died June 23rd 1911, / Aged 75 years. (E)

E89 In / memory / of / Mary Evans Jeffries BOND, / who passed away April 26th 1920 / Also of / Hugh Clarke BOND, / husband of the above / who died Aug. 16th 1928. (E)

E90 (Cross) In / loving memory of / Eliza HODGE / beloved wife of / Francis HODGE / who passed away / August 2nd 1929 / Aged 65 years / Also of William George / only son of the above / who fell in action in France / May 5th 1915 / aged 26 years (E)

E91 I.H.S. / In / loving memory of / Bessie DAVEY / eldest daughter of / Thomas and Emma DAVEY / who died January 20th 1933, / Aged 55 years. / Also of Emma / Beloved wife of Thomas DAVEY, / who passed away February 26th 1939, / Aged 82 years. / At rest. / Also of the above / Thomas DAVEY / who died July 14th 1946, / Aged 90 years. / Resting. (E)

E92 (Surround) In memory of Georgiana Kate KETTLEWELL died May 24th 1936 (S)

E93 In / loving memory / James LAND / 1868 – 1937 / Helena Ethel LAND / 1879 – 1958 / James LAND Jnr / 1910 – 1973 / Geoffrey Herbert / QUICK / 1910 – 1982 / Gertrude Mary / QUICK / 1916 – 1996 (E)

E94 (Surround) In loving memory of (E) / Frederick BUNT, died Feby 17th 1937. Aged 68. At rest (S)

E95 (Cross) In loving memory of / Ann PULSFORD / who died Octr 24th 1936, / aged 75 years. / Also of / William George PULSFORD / husband of the above / who died May 27th 1947 / Aged 85 years / (At Foot) No. 15. (E)

E96 (Surround) In loving memory of / Thomas CRIDDLE, who passed away May 14th 1935, aged 57 years (S) / At rest (W) / Also of his wife Margaret CRIDDLE, who passed away Decr 23rd 1950, aged 72 years (N)

E97   In / loving memory / of / Tom WINDSOR, / of Challick Farm, Wiveliscombe, / who passed away Jan[y] 22nd 1931, / Aged 70 years. / At rest. / Also of his wife / Lucy WINDSOR, / who died Sept 29th 1948, / Aged 76 years. (E)

E98   (Surround)   In loving memory of Ellen CHIDGEY, beloved wife of Charles Gilbert CHIDGEY. Died May 24th 1930 aged 49 years (S) /   Also of Charles Gilbert CHIDGEY died Oct 22nd 1952 Aged 73 years (N) / Peace perfect peace (E)

E99   In / memoriam / Linda FOLLETT / Died 27th May 1927, / Aged 53. (E)   L.F.

E100 In / memoriam / Henry LARCOMBE / Died 25th April 1916, / Aged 72. / Also / Mary Jane LARCOMBE / wife of the above / Died 24th December 1919, / Aged 78. (E) (Stone at Foot) H.L. / M.J.L. (E)

E101 I.H.S. / In loving / memory of / Florence Lydia / the dearly loved wife of / Walter John BALMAN / of Minehead and only daughter of / Benjamin and Bessie COLLARD / who passed away Feb[y] 8th 1909 / Aged 29 years. / "He giveth his beloved sleep" / Also of / Benjamin COLLARD / who passed away June 18th 1917 / Aged 65 years. / Also of / Elizabeth Jane COLLARD / Beloved wife of the above / who passed away Sep[t] 23rd 1932 / Aged 71 years. (E)

E102 [mb](F/H) In / loving memory / of / Charles Hayes / WEBBER / who died / January 20th 1907 / aged 45 years (W)   (F/H) Also of / Mary Ann/ his widow / who died / April 17th 1930 / aged 68 years (E)

E103 In / loving memory / of /Jane CLEEVE / Died Oct 9th 1904 / Aged 67 years / Also Richard / beloved husband of the above / died Jan 12th 1915 / Aged 72 years At rest (E)

E104 In loving memory of / Elizabeth / the beloved wife of / Isaac WINDSOR, / who died March 3rd 1906, / Aged 78 years. / It is enough, earth's struggles all have / ceased. Jesus has called her to his / perfect peace / Also of / Isaac WINDSOR, / who died February 3rd 1910, / Aged 80 years. / Not gone from memory, / not gone from love, / but gone to his Father's home above. (E)

E105 In loving memory of / Emily Ida / the beloved wife of / Robert HAWKINS, / who died June 4th 1901, / Aged 34 years. / "Not gone from memory, / not gone from love, / but to our Father's home above" / Also of / Robert HAWKINS / who died Oct 7th 1956. / Aged 86 years (E)

E106 [mb] *[Blank]*

E107 In loving memory of / William COLLARD / who entered into rest / November 9th 1898, / Aged 77 years. / Also of Sarah, / wife of the above / who entered into rest / May 2nd 1909. / Aged 80 years. / "Until the day break / and the shadows flee away" (E)

E108 In loving memory of / Lavinia, / beloved wife of / John WALDRON / who died February 24th 1905. / Aged 68 years. / Also of the above / John WALDRON, / who died April 4th 1908, / aged 76 years. (E)

E109 In / loving memory / of / Emma, / beloved wife of / William CHEEK, / who died July 6th 1902, / aged 53 years. / "Her end was peace" / Also of / William CHEEK, / husband of the above / who died February 13th 1913 / aged 75 years (E)

E110 (Cross) In / loving memory of / Walter WALDRON, / who died Jany 7th 1909. / Aged 29 years. / Also Lavinia WALDRON / sister of the above / who died Novr 21st 1911 / aged 63 years *[Manning, Taunton]* (E)

E111 In loving memory of / Amos MARKS, / who fell asleep March 31st 1914, / Aged 77 years. / With Christ which is far better. / Also of Selina / wife of the above / who died Oct 31st 1926, / Aged 89 years. (E)

E112 In loving memory of (E) Mary SNOWDEN died February 22nd 1931 aged 84 years (S)

E113 In / loving memory of / Mary EASTMENT / died 12 Dec 1933, / Aged 78 years. / and / John Frederick EASTMENT / Died 5. Feb. 1938, / Aged 74 years. (E)

E114 In loving memory of / Sidney James FURZE / who died April 30th 1938, / Aged 47 years. / At rest. / Also of / Eva beloved wife of the above / who died April 10th 1964. / Reunited. (E)

E115 (Ground) Joyce CHORLEY / née TWENEY / 18 Dec 1988

E116 (Ground)   Alfred Stephen / and / Lilian Maud / TWENEY / 4th April 1985

E117 (Ground)   Frederick John / CASLEY / Born 8th Aug 1914 / Died 19th June 1985

E118 (Cross) In / memory of (W) / Mabel BRELEY / Died August 15th 1933 / Aged 52 (E)

E119 (Cross)   In / loving memory of / James Thomas HARRISON / Died July 13th 1926, / Aged 81 years. / Also Ellen Jane / Beloved wife of the above / Died Dec 16th 1938, Aged 78. / Also Archibald their son / Somerset L.I. who fell in Flanders / July 6th 1915, Aged 23. (E) *[see page 182]*

E120 (Surround)   In loving memory of (E) / Thomas RICHARDS who died September 18th 1920, aged 70 years/ (S) / At rest (W) / also of Jane RICHARDS who died August 15th 1925, aged 74 years. (N)

E121 (Cross, broken)   In / loving memory of / William Albert BALMAN / Born Feb 10th 1870 / Died Decr 7th 1908 / The Lord is my Shepherd. / Also of Jane BALMAN / wife of the above / died May 12th 1931. (No. 56) (E)

E122 In / loving memory of / Frederick Radford COOK / 1850-1907 / and of his wife / Mary Ann COOK / 1857-1927 / Also of / Frederick Hammond COOK / 1880 – 1962 / and of his wife / Edith Maud COOK / 1889 – 1970 (E)

E123 (Cross) In loving / memory of / Gerald BRANSTON / Died Feb 12th 1919 (W)

E124 In / loving memory of / our darling babies / Ivy Maud KING, / Died March 16th 1907 / Aged 3 months. / Also / Violet Doreen KING, / died March 20th 1914 / Aged 2 years. / Safe in the Arms of Jesus. (E)

E125 In / loving memory / of / Alfred NEWTON, / who passed away November 16th 1909. / Aged 67 years. / The dead in Christ shall rise first. / And of his wife / Mary NEWTON, / who died February 18th 1911, / Aged 76 years. / Her end was peace / And their youngest son / Fredrick John NEWTON, / Aged 82 years. / His ashes laid here 24th July 1953. / Mark the perfect man and behold / the upright, for the end of that / man is peace. PSALM.37 (E)

E126 In loving memory of / William Langdon COX / who died July 5th 1915 / aged 44 years. / Entered into rest. / And of his wife / Florence Mary COX / who died January 1st 1946, / aged 76 years. / Reunited. / Also of / Ernest COX / son of the above / who died December 8th 1917 / Buried at Quievy, Aged 21 years / Thy will be done (E) *[page 180]*

E127 (Cross) In loving memory of / Minnie / the beloved wife of / Frank GREEDY / who died May 18th 1919, / Aged 32 years. / "Peace perfect peace". (E)

E128 (Cross) In loving memory of /our dear Father / Willie BERRY, / who passed away 16th March 1927 / Aged 64 years /
Also of our dear Mother / Emily Ida BERRY / who fell asleep 25th January 1933 / Aged 69 years / Ever remembered by their children (E)

E129 (Surround) In loving memory of (W) / Charles SYMONS died June 24th 1937. Aged 76 years (S) / also Rosa Ann his wife died May 29th 1941. Aged 75 years (N)

E130 In remembrance of / James HOWELL / Died 10th Oct. 1931 / Aged 68. / Also his wife / Sarah Ann / Died 26th Feb. 1953 / Aged 93. (E)

E131 In loving memory / of / Robert STONE, / who passed away July 4th 1921, / Aged 73 years. / Peace perfect peace. / And of Jane STONE, wife of the above / who died at Newport March 20th 1928, / Aged 74 years. / Her end was peace. (E)

E132 (Surround)   Mildred Annie NATION   September 13th 1964   Aged 54 (S) Frederick John NATION. Son. Died Jany 4th 1958   aged 52 (N)
(Open Book)   In loving memory of / Frederick Henry NATION / Died Jan 5th 1919 / Aged 38 / Elizabeth Ann NATION / Died Feb 26th 1947 / Aged 68 (+ text) (E)

E133 In loving memory of / Hugh MILES, / who departed this life / May 6th 1900. / Aged 71 years. / I heard the voice of Jesus say / come unto me and rest. / Also of / Mary Ann MILES, / wife of the above / who died April 15th 1911, / Aged 83 years. / "Peace perfect peace" (E)

E134 [....] memory / of / the beloved [...] of / George Branfield KNIGHT / who departed this life / February 20th 1905 / aged 69 years /
Also of George Branfield KNIGHT / who died May 24th 1913 / Aged 76 years / "Peace perfect peace" (E)

E135 In memory of / Peggy SOMERS / loving wife and mother / Sept. 4th 1987 / Aged 56 / Rest in peace (E)

E136 (Cross) [mb] I.H.S. / In loving memory of / Bessie Harris, / the beloved wife of / Frederick William GREED / who died Feby 20th 1900 aged 32 years / "Peace perfect peace" / Also Jessica GREED / daughter of the above / Died Dec 25th 1943 / Aged 48 years (E)

E137 In loving memory / of / John TREBLE, / who entered into rest July 26th 1871 / Aged 60 years. / Also Elizabeth TREBLE, / the beloved wife of the above / who fell asleep in Jesus / April 27th 1901. Aged 82 years. / Not lost but gone before. / Erected by their loving children. / Also Elizabeth, / daughter of the above / who departed this life (at Edinburgh) / September 3rd 1904, Aged 43 years. / Also Sarah ADAMS, / who died September 7th 1925. / Aged 75 years. (E)

E138 In / loving memory / of / Mary / the beloved wife of / George Henry ELLIOTT, / who died January 8th 1913. / Aged 51 years. / Her end was peace. / Also of / George Henry ELLIOTT / who died March 19th 1942, / aged 87 years / Rest in peace (E)

E139 (Cross) At rest / In / loving memory of / Jane / the beloved wife of / George M. WILLIAMS / who passed away May 17th 1919 / aged 59 years (E)

E140 PEACE / Kate / The beloved wife of / Allan HATSWELL / who slept peacefully away / June 15 1935. / Also / Allan HATSWELL / who passed over / October 7 1937 (E)

E141 (F/H) In loving / memory of / Walter / and / Jane BABB / 1st June 1937 11 July 1945 (E)

E142 In / loving memory / of Elizabeth BOND / who died Dec 27th 1931 / Aged 75. / Also / Walter her husband / who died Dec. 27th 1940. / Aged 84 / "Reunited" *[Phippard]* (E)

E143 (Broken metal cross) Reverse ETNA / 229-30-10

E144 (F/H) William / George / PARSONS (S) / Died after / 5 years / RAF / Service / from Mum (E)
(Surround) William RICHARDS. Died March 27th 1919. Aged 79 years. (E) / William George PARSONS died Feb 13th 1946. Aged 33 years. (S) / Sarah RICHARDS. Died March 17th 1928. Aged 84 years. (W) / George Henry PARSONS. Died Dec 2nd 1921. Aged 46 years. (N)

E145 [mb] *[text flaked off]* In loving memory / of / Elizabeth MORGAN / [passed aw]ay March 21st 1913 / [aged] 66 years / …. And the shadows flee away (E)

E146 In loving memory of / Fanny, / wife of Robert BICKNELL, / who died January 8th 1900, / Aged 64 years. (E)

E147 Phyllis Audrey / MOGFORD / 1925 – 1987 / You fell asleep without goodbye / but memories of you / will never die. (E)

E148 In / loving memory / of / John FOX, / late 40th Reg^t Foot / who died March 17th 1904, / aged 81 years (E)

E149 In memory of / Levi LUXTON, / at rest 11th January 1905 Aged 56. / and / Lucy LUXTON, / at rest 17th February 1918 Aged 74. / Also of / Clement Henry LUXTON, / at rest 5th June 1957 Aged 74. / and / Mabel Elizabeth LUXTON, / at rest 28th April 1973 Aged 90. *Lucy LUXTON. Died 12 October 1960. Aged 1 ½ days. Alexandra LUXTON. Died 11 October 1960. Aged 1 day. Clement Mark LUXTON. Died 17 April 1962. Aged 2 days.* (E)

E150 In / loving / memory of / Lucy May CUMMINS / Died 6, Dec 1905 / Aged 21. / In God's keeping. (E)

E151 In loving memory of / Augusta / Beloved wife of / Edwin SLOCOMBE, / who passed away / August 7th 1919. / Aged 36 years / A loving mother true and kind, / a beautiful memory left behind /
Also of the above / Edwin SLOCOMBE / who died July 19th 1940 / Aged 60 years (E)

E152 In / loving memory / of / Edith Mary / the beloved wife of / James STONE, / who died Feby 23rd 1921. / Aged 48 years. / Peace perfect peace. /
Also of / James STONE / husband of the above / who died June 28th 1960 / Aged 87 years. (E)

E153 (Cross)   In loving memory of / Annie / the beloved wife of / G D VARNEY / (Master Mariner) / who died Dec 28th 1923 / Aged 39 years / With Christ which is far better (E)

E154 In / loving / memory of / John CUMMINS / Died 4 Jan. 1938. Aged 82. / Also Sarah, his wife / Died 21, June 1931. Aged 71. / Again united. / Arthur John CUMMINS / Died 30 Nov 1985. Aged 92 ....is wife / Died 20 Nov 1984 Aged 88 (E)

E155 In memory of / William ARTHUR / of Quaking House in this Parish / who died Oct 14th 1940 / Aged 76 years / Also of Lavinia Mary his wife / who died May 4th 1936 / Aged 78 years / RIP / This stone was erected by their / grandchildren in 1942 (E)

E156 (Surround) In loving memory of William PARROTT / Fell asleep 2nd Jan 193(7?) aged –9 years / At rest (E) Also of his wife Florence Jane / Fell asleep January (1?)9th 1944. Aged 67 / "Goodnight. Not goodbye" (W)

E157 In / loving memory of / Sarah BAKER / Died 6th May 1934 Aged 63 years / Also / Charles BAKER / died 30th September 1934 Aged 70 years / Rest in peace (E)

E158 In / loving memory of / Bessie CHIPLIN / 1869 – 1932 / Also / William CHIPLIN / 1872 – 1944   (E)

E159 In / loving / memory / of / Sidney William UPHAM / died April 11th 1929 / Aged 37 years./ Peace perfect peace./ Also of his wife / Edith Mary / Died March 21st 1949 / Aged 59 years./ At rest (E)

E160 In loving memory / of / Catherine / beloved wife of Alfred BARRINGTON / at rest July 7th 1922 / Aged 56 years./ Wisdom and love have ordered all the past / all shall be blessedness and joy at last./
Also of Alfred BARRINGTON / husband of the above / who died January 3rd 1949 / Aged 84 years.(E)

E161   In memory of / Jane / the beloved wife of / Henry RAWLE, / Died December 17th 1920. / Aged 50 years. / At rest /
Also of / Henry RAWLE / died January 31st 1952 / Aged 81 years. (E)

E162   (Ground)   Janie LANG / 1893 – 1986 / Perfect in every / good work

E163   (Cross)   I.H.S.   /   In / loving memory / of / my dear husband / Edward John MEARS / who departed this life July 25th 1905 / Aged 30 years / Also of Jane his widow / who died July 3rd 1953 / Aged 81 years / Also of / Edward William / son of the above / who died December 18th 1902 / Aged 5 months (E)

E164   (Cross)   In / memory of / Maria Elizabeth / Widow of / Lt Col John Smith KEATS / who died Decr 5th 1901 aged 87 (E)

E165   Sacred to the memory of / Emily Mary BAILEY / who departed this life December 30th 1903 / Aged 17 years. / Let your light so shine. /
Also of / Emma BAILEY / Died January 5th 1929 / Aged 73 years. /
Also of / James BAILEY / Died May 18th 1929 / Aged 72 years. (E)
Reverse: Bernard BAILEY MM / 1895-1966 / Pauline 1939 / Aged 3 weeks (W)

E166   *Ernest Charles WOODBURY. Buried 26 February 1927. Aged 14 years.*

E167   (F/H)

E168   (F/H)

E169   (Surround)   In loving memory of (E)   / James FURZE, / who died August 17th 1934, Aged 76. (S) / At rest. (W) /
Also of his wife Mary Jane, who died January 22nd 1939, Aged 80 years. (N)
(F/H) In loving memory

E170   In / loving / memory of / James Horswell TREBILCOCK / Died 28th January 1935 / Aged 58 years. / Also Ellen his wife / Died 8th February 1967 / Aged 89 years. (E)

E171   (Ground)   Nicholas A. / PEAPLE / 21-7-85 / aged 32 years

E172   (Ground)   In / loving memory / of / Arthur Robert / GENREY / 1910 – 1985 / Ellen GENREY / 1905-1994

E173   (Ground)   Cherished memories / of / A wonderful wife / Mother & daughter / Pamela Rose DEER / 1960 – 1990 / Her life a beautiful memory / Her absence a silent grief

E174   (Ground)   *[Blank]*

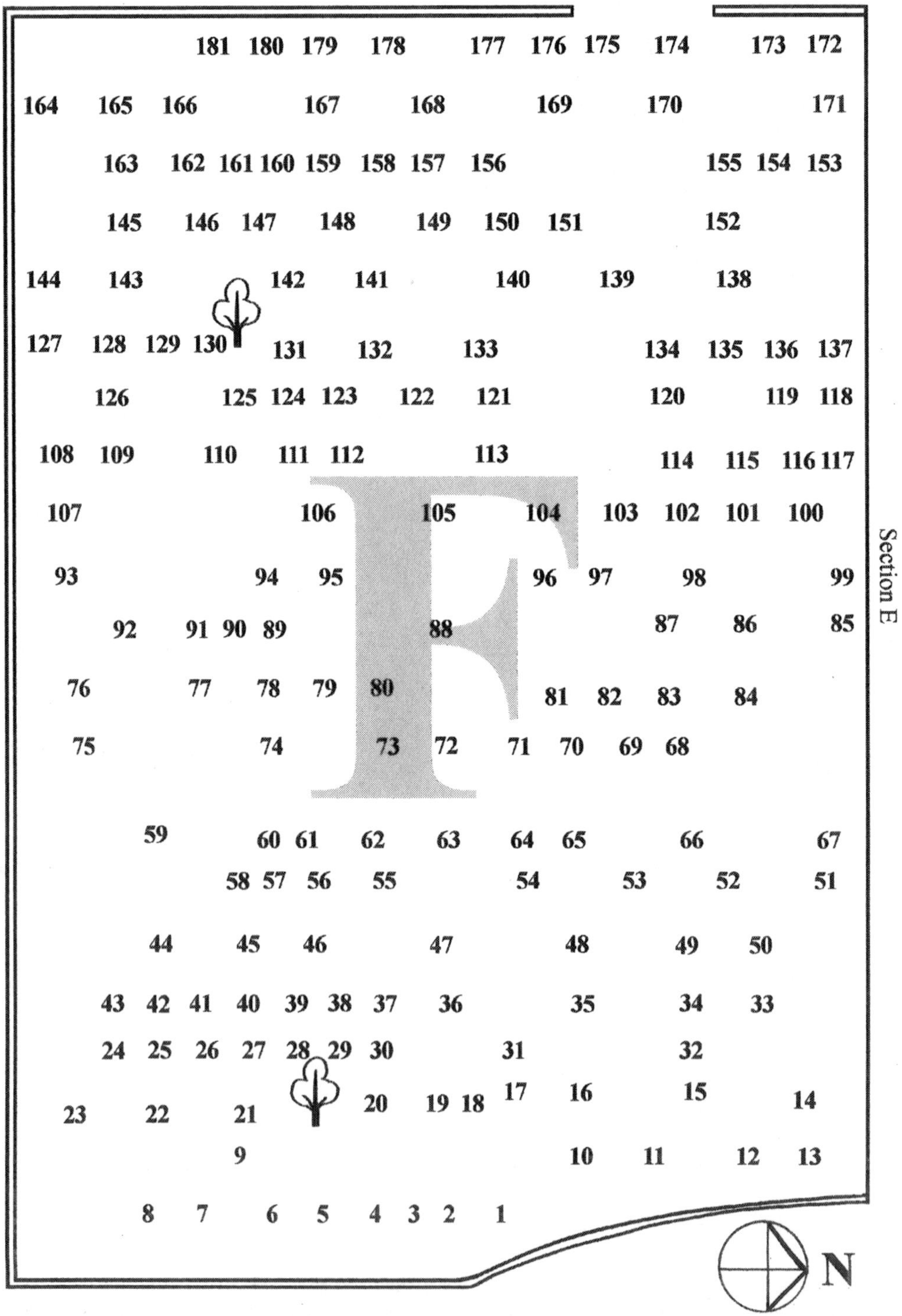

181 180 179 178　　177 176 175 174　　173 172

164 165 166　　167　　168　　169　　170　　171

163 162 161 160 159 158 157 156　　155 154 153

145 146 147 148　149 150 151　　152

144 143　　142 141　　140 139 138

127 128 129 130　131 132 133　　134 135 136 137

126　125 124 123 122 121　　120　119 118

108 109 110 111 112　113　　114 115 116 117

107　106　105　104 103 102 101 100

93　94 95　96 97 98　99

92 91 90 89　88　87 86 85

76 77 78 79 80　81 82 83 84

75 74 73 72 71 70 69 68

59 60 61 62 63 64 65 66 67

58 57 56 55 54 53 52 51

44 45 46 47 48 49 50

43 42 41 40 39 38 37 36 35 34 33

24 25 26 27 28 29 30 31 32

23 22 21 20 19 18 17 16 15 14

9 10 11 12 13

8 7 6 5 4 3 2 1

Section E

N

Churchyard Plan - Section F

114

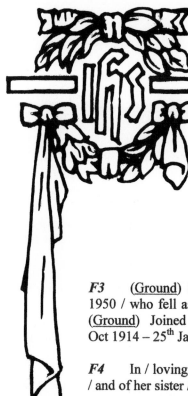

F1   (F/H)

F2   In / loving memory of / Lily SEARLE / died 15th Oct 1979, / aged 84 years, / Also Regina PRIDDLE / died 18th Feb 1958 / aged 5 years / Safe in the arms of Jesus (E)

F3   (Ground) Sharyn Patricia / THOMPSON / Born 5th November 1950 / who fell asleep / 18th October 1968. / Lovingly remembered. (E) (Ground) Joined by / her dear mother / Olive Marguerite / POPE / 31st Oct 1914 – 25th Jan 1993 / Precious memories / and cherished love (E)

F4   In / loving memory of / Valerie Anne / SEDGBEER / 1943 – 1950 / and of her sister / Lynne Anne / 1952 – 1967 (E)

F5   In / loving memory / Vera Ellen SELLICK / died 12th Dec. 1959 / aged 49 years (E)

F6   In treasured memory of our darling daughter / Judith Ann HOLE / suddenly taken 30th Jan. 1960. Aged 16 years / Lovingly remembered /Also her mother / Alice Constance HOLE / died 15th Feb. 1985. Aged 69 years (E)

F7   In / loving memory of / Hubert LOVELL / died 14th Jan. 1979. / Aged 82. / And / Florence Mary LOVELL / died 27th Oct. 1988 / aged 89 (E)

F8   In / loving memory of / James Bartlett DAWE / died 5th Sept. 1960 / aged 54. / Mabel DAWE / died 27th June 1986 / aged 82. (E) (F/H) In loving memory of / James Bartlett / DAWE / died / 5th Sep 1960. / Aged 54 years

F8a   *Arthur James SHEPHERD. Died 3rd April 1960. Aged 64 years.*
Ada SHEPHERD. Died 11th February 1960. Aged 61 years.
[Parents of Ursula J SHEPHERD and Phyllis J SPENCER]

F9   (Ground) In loving memory of / Clifford H BELLAMY. / died 14th January 1956 / aged 50 years / Always in our thoughts / Also his wife / Emily / who died 2.3.89 / aged 80 (E)

F10 (Surround) Albert SEDGBEER. Died 2nd Feb. 1947. Aged 84. (S) / Celia SEDGBEER. Died 7th Sept. 1950. Aged 85. (N)
(F/H) Ever thoughtful / loving, kind / Never forgotten / by those left behind.

F11 (Surround) In loving memory of (W) Joseph BANFIELD died 26th Jan. 1947 Aged 73. (S) Also his wife Ellen BANFIELD died 21st Sept. 1953. Aged 78. (N)

F12 (Ground) In loving memory of / Emma, / the beloved wife of / William HEYWOOD / of Whitefield. / who fell asleep 14th May 1941. / Aged 73 years / Also of William HEYWOOD, / who passed away 26th June 1966 / Aged 88 years. / At rest. (E)

F13 (Surround) In loving memory of (E) / Rachel HEYWOOD who passed away February 5th1940, aged 90 years. (S) / At Rest (N) / And of her beloved husband James H HEYWOOD. Interred at Clayhanger, Devon (N)

F14 (Surround) In loving memory of (W) / Mabel Florence NATION 1893 – 1951 (S) Frank NATION 1889 – 1940 (N)

F15 (Surround) In loving memory of (W) / our dear daughter Patricia Margaret SMITH (S) / who died Novr 30th 1944 aged 5 years and 11 months (N)

F16 In loving memory of / Frank Thomas Walter COLDREY / died Dec 14th 1946 / aged 80 years. (E)

F17 In loving memory of / Ann Amelia NEWTON / who fell asleep 30th Oct. 1947. / Aged 64 years. (E)

F18 In loving memory / of / Alma Louisa STONE / beloved wife of Samuel STONE / who died March 1949 aged 66 years / Also / her beloved husband / Samuel / died September 5th1966 Aged 84 years / Also / Dorothy Ada STONE / beloved wife of / Leonard George STONE / who died May 8th 1992 aged 84 years / Also her beloved husband / George / who died April 10th 1997 aged 90 years (E)

F19 In / loving memory of / Leila May BARRINGTON / who died 18th January 1950. Aged 59 years. / And / Edward BARRINGTON / husband of the above / who died 15th September 1981. Aged 79 years. / At rest (E)

F20 In / loving memory of / Bessie GIBBS / died Feb 2nd 1960 / aged 71 years / and / Walter GIBBS / husband of the above / died Aug 7th 1962 / aged 83 years. (E)

F21 (F/H) In / loving / memory ....

F22 In / memory of / Anna VICKERY / May 11th 1957 / aged 73. / William James VICKERY / March 13th 1972 / aged 86. (E)

F23   In loving memory of / Wilfred John HOLLEY / son of / William and Alice Mary HOLLEY / who died Feby 2nd 1961. / Aged 65 years. (E)

F24   In loving memory of / William Thomas BRICE, / who died 24th Nov 1958. / And his wife / Minnie Amelia, / who died 7th Oct. 1959. (E)

F25   In loving memory of / my dear husband / Rudolf KUHN, / who died 14th June 1957. / Aged 68 years. (E)

F26   (F/H) In / loving memory of / Beatrice May / HARTNELL / 29 June 1969 aged 77 / Also of her sister / Olive / died 10 Dec 1971 aged 82

F27   (F/H)   Louisa / STONE / died July 14 / 1955. / Aged 77 years / Rest in peace

F28   In / loving memory of / my dear mother / Lucy PROUT / At rest 17th April 1953. / Aged 65. (E)

F29   In loving / memory of / Elizabeth / REED / died 19th Dec 1952 / aged 73. / Also / Thomas / REED, / her husband / died 27th July 1953 / aged 71. (E)

F30   In / loving memory of / Ruth, / beloved wife of Harry NATION / died 10th June 1951. Aged 64 / Also Harry / beloved husband of Ruth / died 28th April 1967 Aged 85 (E)

F31 In / loving memory of / James HARGREAVES / who died February 13 1948 / aged 71 years / and his wife Gertrude Mary / who died February 2nd 1960 / aged 77 years (E)

F32   In loving memory of / Mary Bessie BOOKER / who died October 8th 1944 / aged 89 years. (E)

F33   In / affectionate remembrance / of / William DINHAM / who died June 4th 1941, / aged 67 years. / His end was peace. (E)

F34   In loving memory of / Robert ARSCOTT / who died November 12th 1944, / aged 79 years. (E)

F35   (Surround) In ever loving memory of (E) / Ellen SEAMAN who died August 16th 1946 aged 60 years (S) / At rest (W)

F36   (F/H)

F37   Ltn. Vilis SAKNE / *25.11.1913 Zvarde, Latvia / + 24.1.1952 Wiveliscombe, England (E)

F38   Treasured memories / of my dear parents / George and Elizabeth / ROACH. / Until we meet again (E)

F39   Janis CALIS / *9.9.1923, Valka, Latvia / + 5.11.1953, Wiveliscombe, England

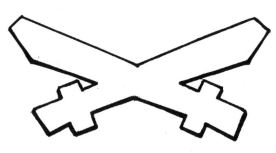

[F37 and F39] Built by the US Army, and later occupied by German POWs, after the War the camp at Culverhead became home to displaced servicemen, firstly from Poland and then Latvia. 87 Latvians were resident between 1947 and 1952, when the camp closed. The crossed swords on the headstone signify the burial of a serviceman.

F40   Treasured memories / of my dear husband / Albert John CONIBERE / who fell asleep 1st July 1955. Aged 59. / Till we meet again. / Also Frances Hope CONIBERE / wife of the above / who passed away 10th June 1966. Aged 64. / Peace. (E)

F41   In / loving memory of / our dear parents / William Henry CONIBERE / died April 27th 1956 / aged 70. / Emily CONIBERE / died May 20th 1973 / aged 78. (E)

F42   In proud and loving memory of / Lt Colonel E J E STRONG, R.A. / June 18th 1957 / Until the day break and the shadows / flee away. SOL. C2.V17. / and also of his wife / Joan Beatrice STRONG / September 23rd 1967 (E)

F43   In loving memory of / my dear husband / James Gore TUDBALL, / who died 30th Nov 1958. / At rest. / Also / Jessie Emma TUDBALL / wife of the above / who died 5th May 1961. / Aged 83. (E)   (F/H) In / loving / memory ……

F44 In / loving memory of / Thomas Edwin / CHAPMAN / called to rest / 12th July 1957 / aged 59 years / Also his wife / Elsie / called to rest / 22nd January 1985 / aged 80 years (E)

F45 (F/H) John / DRISCOLL / died / June 1. 1955 / aged 63 (E) Janet / DRISCOLL / 1893 – 1984 (N)   (F/H) Albert & Mary / REED / 1890 – 1954 / 1911 – 2000

F46 To / the dear memory of / Francis Ernest PROUT / beloved husband and father, / who died 22nd Nov. 1952. Aged 74. /   Also of his dear wife / Mary Ann / who died 17th July 1975. Aged 96. (E)

F47 (Surround) In loving memory of (E) / Sarah Jane FERRIS / Died 9th Nov 1950. Aged 66. / Also Fred her husband / died 14th Oct. 1952. Aged 72.   (N)

F48 In loving memory of / William Henry MARTIN / of Grants Farm / who passed away / August 4th 1946 / aged 70 years. / Also Annie his dear wife / who passed away / May 23rd 1969 / aged 85 years. / At rest. (E)

F49 (Fallen) In loving memory of / Minnie Anna DWELLY, / passed away 27th May 1944 / aged 77 years. (E)

F50 In ever / loving remembrance of / James WARREN, / who fell asleep April 25th 1940, / aged 71 years. /   Also Emily Sarah / beloved wife of the above / who fell asleep Sep[t]. 30th 1953, / aged 83 years. / Also Lilian Kathleen, / beloved wife of Sidney G J WARREN / who fell asleep March 3rd 1954, / aged 58 years. / Also Sidney G J WARREN / who fell asleep June 30th 1958, / aged 63 years. / At rest. (E)

F51 (Cross) In loving / memory of / George Jesse / VINING / died Feb 3rd 1939 / Aged 61 years / Also of Minnie his wife / died May 14th 1959 / aged 81 years / Peace perfect peace (E)

F52 (Cross) In loving memory of / Amelia, / beloved wife of / William COLLARD / who fell asleep / 19th August 1942, / aged 67 years. / And William COLLARD / who fell asleep / 16th May 1951 / aged 75 years. (E)

F53 (Ground) In loving memory of / Annie, beloved wife of / Richard BENNETT of Croford, / died 23rd January 1945 (E)

F54 Treasured memories / of a dear husband and dad / Ernest SALTER, / who entered into rest 10th November 1949 / aged 58. / Also Alice / wife of the above / who passed away 24th June 1972 / Aged 80 / Reunited (E)

F55 To / the dear memory of / Sophia COLES / died 14th March 1952 / aged 60. / And her husband / Leonard Claude COLES / died 22nd Aug. 1965 / aged 84. (E)   /cont……..

F55 cont. (F/H) In loving / memory of / Sophia COLES / died 14th March 1952

F56 In / loving memory / of / Mary Enstice / KELLOCK / died 18th Nov 1952. (E)

F57 (Surround) In loving memory of Millie VICARY died 12th December 1953. Aged 72 years. (S) and Bessie STEVENS her sister, died 14th May 1955. Aged 72 years. (N)

F58 (Ground) Charles LOVELL / 14th April 1955. / May his memory be blessed. / Elizabeth S LOVELL / passed away 31st May 1984. Aged 86. / Together may they rest in peace. (E)

F59 (Surround) Martha Eliza BIRD died 20th November 1957 aged 96 years (S)

F60 In / loving memory of / my dear wife / Louisa Annie BAKER, / who died October 6th 1953 / aged 65 years. / "God be with you" / Also of Ernest James, her husband / who died May 27th 1961 / aged 72 years. / Reunited (E)

F61 (F/H) In loving / memory of / Clifford Walter / HARTNELL / died Nov 4 1952 / aged 43 years

F62 (Surround) In memory of (W) / Sydney Becket HURST, died March 5th 1952. (N) / At rest (W)

F63 (Small flat stone)
F64 (Buried surround / bird bath / F/H)

F65 In / loving memory of / Alfred SMITH / died 1945 / Ellen SMITH / died 1964 / Alfred LAWRENCE / died 1993 / Margaret LAWRENCE / died 1998 (E)
(F/H) In / loving memory / of / Alfred & Ellen / SMITH *[Manning & Knight]*

F66 (F/H) In / loving memory / of / Ada Caroline / STONE / July 16th 1948 / aged 47 / R.I.P.

F67 (F/H) In loving / memory of / Annie / CORNISH / died / 6 April 1939 (W) / Phyllis / Ruby / FUDGE / died / 30 April 1979 (E) Arthur / Leslie / CORNISH / died / 28 June 1981 (N) William / John / CORNISH / died / 23 June 1946 (S)

F68 Sacred / to the memory of / Jeffery Clifford RICHARDS / who entered into rest / September 14th 1944, / aged 39 years. / And also his wife / Enid Doris / who joined him / on January 17th 1983, / aged 77 years (E)

F69 In / loving memory of / Marjory Alice RICHARDS / who died April 28th 1949, / aged 70 years. / Also of / Clifford Cyril RICHARDS / husband of the above / who died September 6th 1965 / aged 85 years. / Reunited. (E)

F70   In / loving memory of / a beloved husband and father / John GADD, / fell asleep 8th June 1948, / aged 77 years. At rest. / Also Edith Emma, his wife / died 27th April 1961, / aged 87 years. (E)
Mary Jane "Polly" POOLE. Died 4 May 2001. Aged 92 years.

F71   (F/H)

F72   (F/H)   In loving / memory of / Arthur H. / WRING / At rest / 26 June 1950 / Aged 57. (E)

F73   In / loving memory of / Ernest William / WRIGHT / 1898 – 1952 / and his wife / Florence May / WRIGHT / 1899 – 1977 (E)
(F/H)   At rest / Ernest W WRIGHT / 24th Jan. 1952 / Aged 53. (E)

F74   In / ever loving memory of / my dear husband and dad / Caleb PRIOR / who died 12th August 1953. / Aged 51 years.   Also his dear wife and mum / Eva Kathleen / who died 14th January 2000 / Aged 92 years. (E)
(F/H)   In loving / memory of / Caleb PRIOR / died August 12 1953 / aged 51 years.

F75   Erected by her children in proud / and loving memory of their mother / Bessie Annie LANGDON / died 5th March 1959. / Aged 77 years. (E)

F76   In loving memory of / Reginald WINSLADE / 24th March 1959. Aged 56. / In God's keeping. (E)

F77   In memory of / Florence Mary, / beloved wife of Thomas H PRESCOTT / who died   May 2nd 1955. Aged 57. / Till we meet again. / Also of / Thomas Henry PRESCOTT / who died June 15th 1973. Aged 78.

F78   (F/H)   In memory of / S J SHOPLAND / Died April 19. 1953. (W)   Also of / Ada SHOPLAND / died 12th Jan. 1981 / Aged 92 (E)

F79   In memory of / Ernest George WHITE / "Johnson" / 1905 – 1952 / and of his wife / Dorothy Lilian May / 1903 – 1990   (E)

F80   In / memory of / Francis David THOMAS / Higher Ford / Wiveliscombe / died August 22 1951 (E)

F81   In / loving / memory of / Albert John NEWCOMBE / Died 7th Sept. 1976 / aged 78. / Also of his wife / Eliza Ann / died 16th Jan. 1987 / aged 85. / Reunited (E)

F82   (Surround) In loving memory of / our dear parents (E) / Charles George HAINES died 17th April 1946 Aged 67 (S) / Re-united (W) / Jane HAINES   died 8th April 1960 aged 82 (N)

F83 (Ground) In / loving memory of / Frederick William / FLOOD / 26th April 1944 / Also his wife / Ellen Louisa / 27th April 1958 / Also their daughter / Dorothy Ann / 24th April 1999 / Reunited (E)

F84 (Surround) In loving memory (E) / Fred^k W HILL who died June 3rd 1942, aged 62. (S)

F85 (Surround) In loving memory of (E) Kenneth McLEANNAN passed on June 18th 1939. (N) / And his wife Helen passed on March 18th 1949 (S)

F86 (Cross) In remembrance of / William WHITE , / who died May 25th 1940, / aged 78 years. / Also of / Verina WHITE, / wife of the above / who died October 1st 1940, / aged 75 years. / At rest. (E)

F87 (F/H)

F88 (Surround) In loving memory of Henry GREEDY who died 19th May 1950 Aged 72 years (S) also Mary Ellen, his wife who died 4th Feb 1959, aged 90 years. (N) / At rest (E)

F89 Treasured memories / Sarah Jane / ORCHARD, / died 14th April 1953 / aged 86 years. / And / Martha ORCHARD / died 8th June 1960 / aged 91 years (E) / (F/H) In loving / memory of / William GREEDY / died / 11th Feb. 1955 / aged 76 years.

F90 (F/H)

F91 Edwin / SIMONS / died / Feb 21 1956 / Aged 74 (E) / (F/H) Louisa / SIMONS / died / July 29th 1958.

F92 In / loving memory of / John, / beloved husband of / Edith May CLAPP, / died 8th Oct 1957. Aged 71 / Also his wife / Edith May / died 20th June 1969 Aged 74. RIP (E) / (F/H) (Broken) A.... / 13th A..... 9 / A .....

F93 (Mound with no stone)

F94 (Ground) In loving memory of / Edwin John ARSCOTT, / died 31st March 1953 aged 83 / also Annie his wife died 26th Oct 1956 aged 83

F95 In / loving / memory of / our dear parents / Geoffrey WEBBER / died 12th June 1952 Aged 60 / Gertrude T WEBBER / died 5th Dec. 1970 Aged 74 (E)

F96 In / treasured memory of / a devoted wife / Mary Ann WHITE, / passed away Feb. 21st 1948, / aged 62 years. / Love's greatest gift remembrance / Also / Francis John WHITE, / husband of the above / who passed away April 24th 1956 / aged 70 years (E)

F97   (Cross) In loving memory of / Robert James WYATT / who entered into rest / March 12th 1946. / aged 74 years. / And Sarah his wife / who passed away / June 24th 1956.
(Ground) In loving memory of / George Robert / ELLIOTT / 18-1-1927 - 29-7-1992 / A loved husband and father   (E)

F98   To / the ever / loving memory of our / beloved parents. / Together / in God's loving care. / William & Eliza PAIN   (E)

F99   (F/H)

F100   (Surround) Alice Maude PROUT, who passed away October 8th 1940, aged 64 years (S) / Edward Leonard PROUT, who passed away April 8th 1951, aged 71 years (N)

F101   In loving memory / of / Emma Louise COX / who died February 27th 1942, / aged 69 years / Also of / Elizabeth Mary L COX / who died April 25th 1945, / aged 84 years (E)

F102   In memory / of / Charles MAY / died 6th April 1943, / Aged 78 years / Also his wife / Edith / died 27th Sep 1959 / aged 73 years / R.I.P. (E)

F103   (Surround)   In loving memory of (E) / Cordelia Louisa Philipps CROSS (S) / who died April 16th 1944, aged 80 years. (N)

F104   In / loving memory of / Frederick Charles ALFORD / who passed away 23rd Sept. 1947 / aged 54. / Also his wife / Susan Jane ALFORD / who passed away 1st Sept 1962 / aged 75. / Peace perfect peace. (E)

F105   In loving memory / of / Henry James HODGE / At rest 19th April 1950. / Aged 79 / Also Mary Ann, his wife / At rest 20th Oct. 1952. / Aged 79. / In God's keeping (E)

F106   (Parallel marble kerbs)   In loving memory of Isaac Stanley WEBBER, beloved husband and father, who passed over / on October 5th 1951.   Aged 67 years. (Churchwarden of this parish for 23 years) / Also Laura his wife / who passed away on January 19th 1968. Aged 86 years. / William GREEDY / died 19th June 1981. Aged 74 / Also / Gwen his wife 1909-1989. (W)

F107 (Ground) In loving memory of / Herbert GUY / who died 7th August 1959 / aged 76. / I will be with thee whithersoever thou goest. / Lucy Pool GUY / his wife / who died 28th April 1971 / aged 94. (E)

F108 (Ground) In ever loving memory of / Ivan, / the devoted and loving son of W. and W. WILSON / and brother of Lorna, Alan, Colin / died 22nd August 1959, / aged 25 years. / Treasured memories. (E)

F109 (F/H) In loving / memory of / George A SLOCOMBE / died 4 Dec 1957 / Aged 65 years
(Ground) In loving / memory of / Frederick / George / SLOCOMBE / 1914 – 1989

F110 (F/H) Albert W HOBBS / died / Dec 31st 1953   (Surround) In loving memory of (E)   E Charles BROWN died Nov[r] 12th 1954 aged 59 years (S) /   also his widow Emily BROWN died 27th Oct[r] 1968 aged 78 years (N) / At Rest (W)

F111 (F/H) In loving / memory of / Charlie / HODGE / from wife / and family

F112 In / memory of / Arthur Edward / PARSONS / died 9th June 1951 / aged 62 years / also his wife / Sarah / died 13th Dec 1989 / aged 99 years (E) *[G.F.S.]*
(F/H) In / loving memory of / Arthur / E PARSONS / died 9th June 1951

F113 (Cross) In loving memory of / Charles Langdon COCKS / died 2nd April 1949 / aged 69 years / and of his wife / Eva Mabel COCKS / died 16th August 1964 / aged 76 years / "And the spirit shall return / unto God who gave it." (E)

F114 In / loving memory / of / Beatrice Mary LUCAS / beloved wife of / Ernest Charles LUCAS / who died 8th February 1943 (E)

F115 To / the beloved memory of / Mary WARREN / dear wife of Herbert John WARREN / Dec. 25th 1872 – Jan. 26th 1942. / and / Herbert John WARREN / Aug. 1st 1874 – May 8th 1965. /
Also / Elsie Elizabeth WARREN / their daughter / Feb. 16th 1909 – Nov. 30th 1986 / Rest in peace (E)

F116 (Cross) To / the dear memory / of / John Wyatt PRATT / died May 23rd 1943 / aged 97. / and Jane Eliza his wife / died November 27th 1940 / aged 90. / "He that believeth on me hath / everlasting life" (E)

F117 (F/H) *George WHITE. Buried 2 July 1955. Aged 55 years. And his wife Adelaide Lillian WHITE. [Parents of Stanley WHITE]*

F118 In loving memory of / Mary Helena, / wife of Cyril SELLICK / who passed away / November 20th 1939, / aged 33 years. (E)

F119 In loving memory of / William Henry Thorne THOMAS / died Jany 14th 1941, / aged 71 / Also of his wife / Elizabeth THOMAS / died Jany 14th 1944 / aged 70/ R.I.P. (E)

F120 In / loving memory / of / my dear sister / Annie Beatrice Gore / TUDBALL / who died Jany 31st 1943 / aged 70 years / R.I.P. (E)

F121 (F/H)

F122 In loving memory of / John GIBBS / died 19th Feb. 1950. Aged 62. /   Also his wife / Lettice Bancroft GIBBS / died 28th March 1969. Aged 79. (E)

F123 (F/H) In loving memory of / William H BROOM / died 29 March 1951 / aged 69 (E)

F124 In / fondest memory of / William Robert WARREN / died 30th January 1970 / aged 80. / Also / Hilda Annie WARREN / wife of the above / died 23rd October 1970 / aged 80. / Together at peace   (E)

F125 In / loving memory of / Francis James / MORLE / who died 19th Feb 1953 / aged 57 / and his beloved wife / Amy Margaret / MORLE / who died 22nd Feb 1992 / aged 97 (E)

F126 (F/H)   In / loving memory / Annie WOODBURY(E) *Died 18 December 1957. Aged 64 years.   Charles WOODBURY. 5 February 1888 – 20 August 1975.*

F127 (Ground)   In ever loving memory of / Winifred, / the loving wife of W WILSON / and devoted mother of / Lorna, Alan and Colin. / Died 15th October 1960. / Aged 62 years. / Treasured memories. / Also William Edward, / devoted husband and father of the above / died 13th March 1964. Aged 65 years. (E)

F128 Treasured memories of / a devoted husband / Edwin KING / who fell asleep / January 30th 1960 / aged 63 years. / Till we meet again. / Also / Eva Ellen KING / died June 30th 1975 / aged 80 years. (E)

F129 In loving memory of / Arthur John THOMAS / who fell asleep / September 3rd 1956 / aged 59 years. / Till we meet again. / And / Victor THOMAS / who died on the / 26th November 1993 (E)

F130 In / loving memory of / Charles Henry HILL / who died September 24th 1954 / aged 71 years. / Also of Kate his beloved wife / who died December 16th1963 / aged 77 years. / Reunited. (E)

F131 (F/H)

F132 (F/H)   In loving / memory of / Ernest J / HUMPHRIES / died Feb 3 1950 / aged 41 (W)

F133 In loving memory of / a devoted husband and dad / Frederick Charles GREEDY / called to rest Jan. 19. 1949 Aged 51. / There's a face that is ever before us / a voice we would love to hear, a smile / we will always remember of the ones / we loved so dear. / Also a devoted mum / Daisy GREEDY / called to rest Feb. 13. 1957. Aged 59. (E)

F134 In / loving memory of / Florence Edith MULLINS / died 9th May 1980 / Aged 74. / At rest (E)

F135 In / loving memory of / Emily FRY / who departed this life / Nov 19th 1941 / aged 77 years / Peace after pain / Also John FRY / Husband of the above / who died July 24th 1950 / aged 94 years / His end was peace (E)

F136 In / loving memory of / Frederick Charles / WEBBER / died 14 Feb 1941 / aged 52 years. / Also his wife / Lily / died 27 Jan 1990 / aged 93 years. (E)

F137 George Christopher SANDFORD / passed away 6th January 1940 / Happy memories / Mildred Agnes SANDFORD / died 27th August 1975. Aged 86 / In loving memory (E)

F138 In proud and ever loving / memory of our dear son / Joseph Anthony HEWLETT / Paymaster Sub/Lieut, R.N.V.R. / who was killed whilst on / duty in H.M.S. VERNON / March 11th 1941, aged 24 years. / All he had hoped for, / all he had he gave, / to save mankind. / Himself he scorned to save. / And / Francis Gilbert HEWLETT / his beloved father, / who joined him Dec 4th 1944. / And Annie Beatrice HEWLETT / beloved mother and wife, / who joined them Feb. 14th 1967. (E) *[see page 185]*

F139 In ever loving and treasured memory / of a most dearly loved and devoted / father and mother / William HOLLEY / who passed away 16th December 1949 / aged 82 years / and Alice Mary wife of the above / who passed away 31st March 1905 / aged 34 years / Also Eliza second wife of the above / who passed away 4th January 1944 / aged 69 years. (E)

F140 Treasured / memories of / our dear parents / Frederick Charles EASTMENT / died 6th May 1947 / aged 57 / and / Anna EASTMENT / died 31st Oct 1972 / aged 82 / Rest in peace (E)

F141 Treasured / memories of / our dear brothers / Richard John EASTMENT / died 16th May 1949 / aged 34 / and / Alec Ronald EASTMENT / died 13th March 1973 /aged 49 / Rest in peace / Frederick Charles EASTMENT / died 30th November 1975 / aged 60 (E)

F142 In loving memory / of / James Henry SHOPLAND / died 23rd June 1952 / aged 54 years. / Edith SHOPLAND / died 29th July 1982 / aged 83 years. / R.I.P. (E)

126

F143   In loving memory of / Eliza GREEDY / who fell asleep 18th Jan. 1958 / aged 68 years. / At rest. / Also William / husband of the above / died 30th Dec. 1968 / Aged 80 years. (E)
(F/H) In / memory of / Wilfrid STRICKLAND / died / 30th Jan 1985 / aged 71 years (E)

F144   In loving memory of / William George RAPPS / beloved father of Cecilia VAULTER / died 25th April 1960. Aged 83 / Until we meet again. / Cecilia VAULTER died 13 Feb. 1975 / beloved wife of Sydney VAULTER (E)

F145   In / loving memory of / Ethel Mary WARREN / died 9th April 1958 / aged 71. / Also her brother / Alfred John WARREN / died 31st Dec 1969 / aged 70. (E)

F146 (F/H) In / loving memory / of / Sidney William / SLOCOMBE / died / January 7th 1957 (E)   (F/H)   Also wife / Mary / 1899 – 1993 (E)

F147 (F/H) In / loving / memory of / John / DULBOROUGH / died May 3 1992 / aged 59 years

F148 (F/H) In loving / memory of / Walter HOWE / Died Feb 14. 1951 (E)

F149   (Surround) In loving memory of Evelyn BELLAMY (S) / died 30th Aug 1948, aged 59 years (S) / R.I.P. (W) / Also Henry BELLAMY (N) / died 12th Dec 1949 aged 64 years (N)

F150   (Surround) In loving memory of (E) /   Alice Mary BAKER who died April 12th 1947, aged 37 years. (S) / At rest (W)
(F/H)   In memory of / Lucy CHUBB / died July 26 1950 / aged 62 (S)

F151   (Cross) To / the dear memory of / Victor F D MEADE / Flying Officer, R.A.F., V.R. / killed in aircraft accident / May 17th 1945, / aged 23. (E)   *[See page 185]*

F152   In loving memory of / Maurice C C HAWKINS, / Som. L.I. / who passed away October 30th 1941, / aged 24 years. / At rest. (E)

F153   (Surround) In loving memory of (E) / Robert FURZE, born 25th August 1865, died 31st January 1941. (S) / At rest (W) / Also of his wife Clara FURZE, who died May 31st 1944, aged 77 years. (N)

F154   (Surround) In loving memory of (E) / Hannah RAWLE who died March 16th 1941, aged 76. (S) / also of Jane RAWLE who died November 19th 1947, aged 84. (N)

F155   (Surround) In loving memory of (E) / Elizabeth WOOLAWAY who died Octr 3rd 1941 aged 85 years (S) / also of Edith WOOLAWAY who died Sep^t 14th 1948, aged 67 years (N) / At rest (W)

F156 In / loving memory of / Harry VICKERY / died March 4th 1947 / aged 61 years / also his wife / Annie Alma / died June 18th 1971 / aged 80 years (E)

F157 In / memory of / Jemima Helen BRISTOW / who died on 2nd Oct 1948. / Aged 84. / Mother of / Winifred May BAKER / who died on 4th Nov 1966. / Aged 59. (E)

F158 (F/H) In loving / memory of / Maurice / WOODLAND / died Jan 13 1950 / aged 24 (E)

F159 (Cross) In / loving memory of / my dear husband / Raymond Wilfred LOCK. / who passed away / 1st February 1951 aged 48 years. / "Thy will be done" (E)

F160 In / loving memory of / Elizabeth Lucy LOCK / who died 13th December 1963 / aged 85 / And her husband / William LOCK / who died 20th September 1973 / aged 99 (E)

F161 Sacred to the memory of / a devoted husband & father / Wilfrid Amos MILLER / died 12th February 1952. / Aged 38. (E)   (F/H) His pupils / remember / with / affection and / gratitude.   (Ground) Marjory / Anne MILLER / 1914 – 1996

F162 (Ground)   In ever loving memory of / my devoted mother / Constance CHALKLEY / who fell asleep 5th May 1957. / Aged 59 years.

F163 In / loving memory of / Mary / the beloved wife of Ian THORNE / who passed away 21st May 1958. Aged 72. / Rest in peace. / Also of Ian THORNE husband of the above / who departed this life 18th Jan 1960. Aged 73. / Until the day dawns (E)

F164 In / loving memory of / Florence Mary BAKER / died 31st August 1960. Aged 49 years. / Also / Arthur John BAKER / died 14th December 1960. Aged 59 years. / Rest in peace. (E)

F165 In memory of / Frederick John ELLIOTT / 1890 – 1958 / and his wife / Sarah Margaret / 1899 – 1976 (E)

F166 In loving memory of / Arthur Luscombe / TESTER / 1881 – 1959 / and / Muriel TESTER / 1881 – 1989 (E)

F167 (Surround) In loving memory of Nellie Margaret Witton FLEMING who passed within the veil Nov 19th 1950 aged 67 years (S)

F168 In / ever loving memory of / Evelyn Effie ELLIOTT / 1891 – 1967 / and of her husband / Harold George ELLIOTT / 1891 – 1973 / Their grandson / Peter WEALE / 1957 – 1996 / R.I.P. (E)

F169 (F/H)

F170 (Surround) In loving memory of (E) / Richard Bryant BURGE, who fell sleep Nov[r] 21st 1942, aged 16 years. (S) / Peace. (W) / Also his father R T BURGE. Died Jan 7th 1968. Aged 65. (N)

F171 (Surround) In loving memory of (E) / Frank GREEDY who passed over March 3rd 1940, aged 57 years. (S) / In thy presence is fullness of joy / Psalm 16.11 (W)

F172 In / loving memory of / Eliza CLAPP, / the beloved wife of / William B CLAPP / of Perry's Farm, Wiveliscombe / died March 11th 1940, aged 64. / R.I.P. / Also of the above / William B CLAPP / died October 13th 1953, aged 70. / At rest.(E)
(Ground) William Roy Branfield / CLAPP / died 29th April 1991 / aged 77 years.
(F/H) Loving memory / from / Colin. Heather. / Keith (E)

F173 In loving memory of our dear parents / William LEWIS / who passed away on April 13th 1941. / Aged 70 years. / And / Ada LEWIS / who passed away on March 6th 1962. / Aged 88 years. / Also our dear brother / Wilfred John Dennis LEWIS / 1st Bn Somerset Light Infantry / killed in action at Buithidaung, Burma / on Jan 26/27th 1944 (E)

F174 In loving memory of / James Henry / Anstey ROCKETT / who passed away November 21st 1942, / aged 72 years. / Thy will be done. / Also of Florence / wife of the above / who passed away / March 27th 1945, / aged 67 years. / At rest. (E)

F175 In / loving memory of / Laura Eva WARREN / died 21st Oct. 1943. Aged 56. / Also of Eva STOWELL her mother / died 16th Feb 1950. Aged 89. (E)

F176 In loving memory of / Emma GREEDY / died 30th Oct 1944 aged 67 / also of her husband / William / Died 19th March 1961 aged 85 (E)

F177 Annie Storey STACEY. / Wife of John Henry STACEY. / Died 17th December 1946, aged 79. / She is gone and all her anxious thoughts are over / her weary head shall bow with pain no more (E)

F178 Treasured memories of / Cynthia June, / the beloved only child of / John and Elsie HAYES / who fell asleep 12th Oct. 1950. / Aged 7 years. / Safe in the arms of Jesus. (E)

F179 (Ground) Jack LUMBER / died 1963 / aged 43 years / Happy memories of a dear husband & father (E)

F180 (F/H) *Margaret Mary "Peggy" LANG. Died 1 April 1965. Aged 58 years.*

F181 Sacred / to the memory of / a dear husband & father / Charles Victor / CHAMBERLAIN / born 1896 died 1965. / Also his dear wife / Daisy Lena / born 1897 died 1988. / Reunited in God's keeping / Also of Norman Victor, / son of the above, lost at sea / (H.M.S. REPULSE) Dec 1941, / aged 20 years. (E) *[see page 186]*

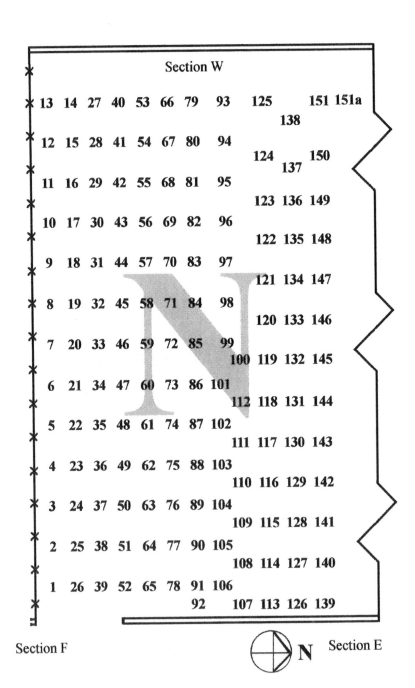

Section W

13 14 27 40 53 66 79   93   125   151 151a

                              138

12 15 28 41 54 67 80   94

                       124   150

                           137

11 16 29 42 55 68 81   95

                       123 136 149

10 17 30 43 56 69 82   96

                       122 135 148

 9 18 31 44 57 70 83   97

                      121 134 147

 8 19 32 45 58 71 84   98

                       120 133 146

 7 20 33 46 59 72 85   99

                    100 119 132 145

 6 21 34 47 60 73 86 101

                    112 118 131 144

 5 22 35 48 61 74 87 102

                  111 117 130 143

 4 23 36 49 62 75 88 103

                  110 116 129 142

 3 24 37 50 63 76 89 104

                  109 115 128 141

 2 25 38 51 64 77 90 105

                  108 114 127 140

 1 26 39 52 65 78 91 106

               92   107 113 126 139

Section F   N   Section E

Churchyard Plan - New Extension

Section W   Telegraph pole

164 177 190 203 216 229 242 255 268 281 294

163 176 189 202 215 228 241 254 267 280 293

162 175 188 201 214 227 240 253 266 279 292

161 174 187 200 213 226 239 252 265 278 291

160 173 186 199 212 225 238 251 264 277 290

159 172 185 198 211 224 237 250 263 276 289

158 171 184 197 210 223 236 249 262 275 288

157 170 183 196 209 222 235 248 261 274 287

156 169 182 195 208 221 234 247 260 273 286 299

155 168 181 194 207 220 233 246 259 272 285 298

154 167 180 193 206 219 232 245 258 271 284 297

153 166 179 192 205 218 231 244 257 270 283 296

152 165 178 191 204 217 230 243 256 269 282 295

Section D

 N

Churchyard Plan - New Extension

St. Andrew's Churchyard
New Extension

As described on page 49, the New Extension of the churchyard was consecrated in the late 1950s, with the first interment taking place in September 1960.   Burials began in the south-east corner, and continued along the allotment fence to the wall overlooking the road in Rotton Row, and then in rows northwards towards the church. The sequence was broken, however, when at the beginning of 1970 burials began to take place further north, in the area of the wall.   At the time this ran east to west across the site, but it was removed in 1985 when the 'Sancti' plot was purchased. By 1993 the original area was full and the siting of graves began in the 'Sancti' plot, and continues northwards today.

For three generations the Greedy family undertook the role of undertakers in the parish. They were succeeded in 1975 by one of their long term employees, Mr Stan Shopland, who ran the business until his retirement in 1983.   Through the continuing interest and close co-operation of his widow, Mrs Nesta Shopland, it has been possible to draw up a more detailed record of the burials in this section than in the remainder of the churchyard. Where plots have been identified, but no headstone was erected, the entry is given in *italic* script.

> All headstones in this Section
> face East,
> unless otherwise noted

N1   *Mr Chester ARTHURS. Died 19 September 1960. Aged 73 years.*

N2   (F/H) SLOCOMBE. *[Charles Leonard SLOCOMBE. Died 20 September 1960. Aged 61 years]*

N3   In / loving memory of / Hannah BARRINGTON / who died 2nd October 1960. / Aged 69 years. / and / Ernest James BARRINGTON / husband of the above / who died 22nd October 1960. / Aged 72 years. / At rest.

N4   *Henry William DARBY. Died 21 October 1960. Aged 66 years. Mrs Alice May DARBY. Died 1 Jan 1973. Aged 72 years.*

N5   *Arthur Thomas WHITE. Died 29 October 1960. Aged 59 years.*
N6   *Mrs Iris Ada GREEDY. Died 1 November 1960. Aged 50 years.*
N7   *Frederick James HINES. Died 8 November 1960. Aged 65 years.*

N8   In loving memory of / Arthur FURZE / Died 19. November 1960 / aged 60 years. / At rest.

N9   *Mrs Maria Ann DULBOROUGH. Died 31 December 1960. Aged 73 years. James DULBOROUGH. Died 6 January 1975. Aged 83 years.*

N10   In / loving memory / of / Mabel Constance, / beloved wife of / Robert DIBBLE, / passed away 3rd February 1961, / aged 79 years. / Also of / Robert DIBBLE, / passed away 6th March 1963, / Aged 80 years.

N11   Francis Joseph LAWRENCE. Died 15 February 1961. Aged 49 years.

N12 In / loving memory of / Annie Lee FURZE / who passed away 19th Feb. 1961, / Aged 76. / Also John / Beloved husband of the above / who passed away 23rd Nov. 1966. / Aged 77. / Re-united.

N13 *James Tuckfield WHITE. Died 23 February 1961. Aged 73 years.*

N14 *Mrs Minnie ARNOTT. Died 27 February 1961. Aged 70 years.*
George ARNOTT. Died 27 December 1968. Aged 77 years.

N15 In / loving memory of / a dear husband and father / Dr George Edward KELLY / born 1925 – died 1974. / Also his father / James Magee KELLY / born 1881 died 1961. / I know that my redeemer liveth.

N16 Fond memories / of / Edgar BARRINGTON / 9th April 1961 / aged 64. / And his wife / Elsie. / 24th Dec. 1968 / aged 70.

N17 (F/H) In loving / memory of / Alfred STONE / died / Sept 5 1961 / Aged 71 years

N18 *Mrs Emily Annie PRICE. Died 18 September 1961. Aged 71 years.*

N19 In / loving memory of / William Henry DUNN / Died Oct. 18th 1961. Aged 75. / Also his wife / Lucy Mary DUNN / died Oct 16th 1969. Aged 83.

N20 In / loving memory of / my dear wife / Mildred VAULTER / Fell asleep 28 Nov. 1961 / aged 69. / And of her beloved husband / Sydney VAULTER / fell asleep 19th Sep[t] 1967 / aged 77. / Blessed are the pure in the heart.

N21 *George QUICK. Died 4 December 1961. Aged 67 years.   Mrs Lillian Maud QUICK. Died 13 January 1968. Aged 69 years.*

N22 (F/H) Charles Lovell / Nelson PECK / died / 24th Dec 1961.

N23 *Allan PETTIT. Died 3 January 1962. Aged 48 years.*

N24 *Miss Ethel HEARD. Died 6 January 1962. Aged 80 years.*

N25 In / loving memory of / Arthur Horsford WILLIAMS / Died Jan 9th 1962 / Aged 74 / Also of his wife / Gwladys May WILLIAMS / Died May 6th 1978 / Aged 85.

N26 In loving memory of / my dear husband / Frank BAKER / died Jan. 14th 1962 / aged 65 / Also of his wife / Almina Elizabeth BAKER / died Feb 18th 1964. / At rest.

N27 In / loving memory / Ethel Kate Broughton KNIGHT / died January 1962 / aged 65. / Dorothy Gladys KNIGHT / died March 1962 / aged 63.

N28　In / loving memory / Edgar Ivan DEER / died 7th Feb. 1962 / aged 67. / Also his beloved wife / Violet May DEER / died 10th Dec. 1982 / aged 82. / Reunited.

N29　Foster Mothers / Auntie / Mabel BAKER / & / Louise SIBLEY / Our love from / the children.

N30　In / loving memory of / Edward　Morrison DRIVER / Died 30th Sept. 1962. / Aged 66. / And his wife / Gladys Gwendoline / Died 20th Sept. 1982. / Aged 87.

N31　*Edward James FERRIS. Died 30 September 1962. Aged 86 years.*

N32　In / loving memory / of my dear wife / Jean Elisabeth THORNE / beloved daughter of P J and H HAWKINS / died Oct 14th 1962. Aged 27 years.

N33　Charles / Andrew / BOWN. / Died / Jan 22. 1968. (E) Mabel / Annie / BOWN. / Died / Oct. 20 1962 (W)

N34　In / loving memory / of / Charles GADD, / who passed away / 10th November 1962. / Aged 79 years / And of his wife / Mary Anna GADD, / who passed away / 12th June 1965, / aged 81 years. / In God's keeping.

N35　*Sydney RIDGWAY. Died 11 December 1962. Aged 77 years.*

N36　*Mrs Annie Amelia NORMAN. Died 30 December 1962. Aged 68 years.*
John Walter NORMAN. Died 8 November 1972. Aged 88 years.

N37　(F/H)　At rest / William / WOODGATE / died / 5th April 1975 / Aged 82 /
Side　Sydney / John / WOODGATE / died　/ Jan 7 1963 / Aged 58.

N38　(F/H)　In loving / memory of / our daughter / Joyce *[SIMPSON]* / Died Jan 26 1963 / Aged 34.

N39　*Winifred Harriet. Wife of Fred BESLEY. Died 26 Feb 1963. Aged 60 years.*

N40　(F/H)　*Frank QUICK. Died 5 March 1963. Aged 73 years.*

N41　*Frank George STONE. Died 31 January 1968. Aged 62 years. Mrs Lily May STONE. Died 25 March 1963. Aged 57 years.*

N42　In / ever loving memory / of my dear wife / Gladys Mary WEILANDT / who died 13th May 1963. / aged 44. / Also our dear brother / William WEBBER / who died 6th May 1983 / aged 68. / R.I.P. / Alfred John WEBBER / who died 7th June 1980 / aged 75.

N43　In loving memory / of / Emily GRABHAM / 1890 - 1963 / Also Albert GRABHAM / 1900 – 1973.

N44 In / loving memory of / a dear mother and father / Sarah MORGAN / 1886 – 1981 / and / Thomas MORGAN / 1886 – 1963   *[Stooks]*   (F/H)   In / loving memory / of / Thomas Richard / MORGAN / Died 19-5-63 / Aged 77 years .

N45 In / treasured memory / of a devoted / husband and dad / Clifford Thomas / GREEDY / who fell asleep / May 27th 1963.   /   Also his wife / Margaret / Nov. 11th 1981. Treasured / memories of / Jim / August 1924 / March 1995.

N46 In / loving memory of / Mildred Emily FURZE / died June 15th 1963 / also Mabel FURZE / died February 11th 1965 / At rest.

N47 *William Henry LEE. Died 27 July 1963. Aged 75 years. Mrs Kate LEE. Died 8 September 1973. Aged 87 years.*

N48 In / ever loving memory of / a dear husband & father / William LASKEY, / died 22nd August 1963, / aged 76 years. / At rest / And his dear wife / Evelina, / a loving mother / died 27th January 1995, / aged 99 years, / R.I.P.

N49 (F/H) *Mrs Ada Elizabeth PERRIN. Died 26 September 1963. Aged 61 years.*

N50 Mizpah / Noel Gordon HARRIS / died 20th Oct. 1963 / Aged 65 years / Thelma Eirene HARRIS / died 29th Jan. 1995 / aged 92 years / The peace of God which passeth / all understanding.

N51 (F/H) In memory / Annie Irene / SALTER / Dec 29th 1963.

N52 In / loving memory of / our dear mother / Mary Ann DAVIES / passed away 24th Jan. 1964 / aged 85 / Also a dear daughter / Rose Helen HOOD / passed away 2nd April 1994 / aged 86 / Rest in peace. *[Manning & Knight]*

N53 *Wilfred Robert HOWELL. Died 26 January 1964. Aged 63 years.*

N54 (Base) *Walter Henry FURZE. Died 26 March 1964. Aged 81 years. Miss Edith Sarah DULBOROUGH. Died 23 February 1971. Aged 68 years.*

N55 (F/H) *Alice / HILL / died / 1st April / 1964/ Aged 73. Herbert HILL. Buried 25 August 1971. Aged 80 years.*

N56 (Cross) In ever / loving memory / of / my dear wife / Annie L BURKE, / Died 5th April 1964. Aged 80 years. / Rest in peace.

N57 *Frederick MITCHELL. Died 10 May 1964. Aged 66 years.*

N58 R.I.P. / Norman Frank WARREN / died 5th August 1964. / Aged 54.

N59   In / loving memory of / my dear husband / Capt. Harry L STEARS / who passed away / 23rd August 1964 / aged 76 years. / Also Alice Maud his wife / Died 30th October 1972 / aged 84 years.

N60   (F/H)   Clifford / James / HODGE / Died / Oct. 2nd 1964 / aged 65.
Mrs Ida F HODGE. Died 16 February 1967. Aged 64 years.

N61   *William ROWLEY. Died 18 January 1965. Aged 64 years.*

N62   In / loving memory of / a dear husband / Albert Edward TURNER / Died 19th Feb. 1965. Aged 61. / And / Violet Silvia TURNER / died 3rd Dec. 1987. Aged 82.

N63   (F/H)   In / loving memory of / William Charles / BAIGENT / Born July 11th 1901 / Died March 10th 1964.

N64   *Philip Paul TYLER. Died 25 March 1965. Aged 74 years.*

N65   William Fred / BARRINGTON / died 1st April 1965 / Aged 69.

N66   (Cross) In loving memory of / Eileen CHARLESWORTH / died April 26th 1965 / aged 74. / R.I.P. / and / John Caradoc CHARLESWORTH / died Dec. 18th 1968. Aged 81. / R.I.P.

N67   (F/H)   Harold MARGETTS / died 9th May 1965 / Aged 65.
Mrs Ruth Mary MARGETTS. Died 29 July 1968. Aged 74 years.

N68   Peace perfect peace / In loving memory of / a dear husband and father / Sidney YEANDLE, / died 12th June 1965, aged 89 / Also of Elizabeth / his dear wife / and our loving mother / died 7th Sept. 1965, aged 88 / Together still.   *[See page 168]*

N69   (F/H)   In / loving / memory   *Frederick William FOX. Died 14 September 1969. Aged 76 years. Mrs Annie FOX. Died 28 March 1970. Aged 78 years.*

N70   *Donald Louis MIRAMS. Died 17 January 1966. Aged 55 years.*

N71   (F/H) In loving memory / Major Elwin / EVERED, SLI / died / 3rd March 1966.

N72   To the / memory of / Ralph E. DYER / 1902 – 1966

N73   In / loving memory of / Mary Hester NURCOMBE / Died 4th August 1966 / Aged 57 years. / Also / her beloved husband / William John / Died 31st August 1989 / Aged 76 years / R.I.P.

N74   In / loving memory of / Ernest CUMMINS / died 6th August 1966 / aged 62 years

137

N75   In / loving memory of / Geoffrey James HOWELL / died 8th Oct. 1966 / Aged 72. / Also his wife / Sarah Jane / died 10th Sept. 1972 / aged 79.

N76   In / loving memory / of / Harold William VICKERY / died 27th October 1966 / aged 53 years.

N77   In / loving / memory of / a dear wife and mother / Emily Maud ANDREWS / who entered into rest / Dec. 12th 1966. Aged 72 years. / For me to live is Christ / And to die is gain. Phil. 1.21. / Also / William ANDREWS / Beloved husband of Emily Maud / And a devoted father / Called home Wednesday May 16th 1984 / Aged 90 years. / For ever with the Lord.

N78   (F/H)   In loving memory of / a dear husband and father / Percy BRISTOW / who passed away / 9th January 1967 / aged 55 years (W)

N79   Sidney ADAMS / 1900 – 1967.

N80   In / loving memory / of / William FURZE / died Jan 18 1967 / aged 86. / R.I.P. / Also / Minnie FURZE / died June. 14. 1984 / aged 88

N81   In / loving memory of / Zelie Eliza / KELLOW / 1893 – 1967 / Also her husband / Edwin KELLOW / 1889 – 1977 *[Stooks]*

N82   (F/H)   In memory / Alice May / MATTOCK / Died / March 1st 1967 / Aged 85.

N83   Mrs Alice WILSON. Died 27 March 1967. Aged 89 years.

N84   In loving memory of / William Thomas LANGDON / Died 5th April 1967 / aged 59. / and his wife / Mollie Lilian / died 14th June 1986 / aged 73.

N85   Miss Elizabeth Ann BURTON. Died 12 June 1967. Aged 85 years. Miss Rhoda BURTON. Died 12 October 1969. Aged 83 years.

N86   Harold Arthur Sidney HAYNES. Died 13 June 1967. Aged 72 years.

N87   In / loving memory of / Mortimer William TENNANT / died 7 August 1967 /aged 58 years / Also his beloved wife / Stella Mary / died 27 November 1982 / aged 76 years.

N88   In / loving memory / of / Edward C. LEWIS / 1899 – 1967 / and / Alice D. M. LEWIS / 1910 – 1997 *[Fine Memorials]*
(F/H)   In loving / memory of / Raymond / LEWIS / 7.5.1935. 6.9.1979.

N89   Cyril Edward WESTALL. Died 2 December 1967. Aged 65 years.

N90   In / loving memory of / Florence Elizabeth / WILMOTT / Died 13th December 1967 / Aged 70 years / Good night and God bless. /
Also of / Henry Thomas / husband of the above / Died 9th May 1970 / Aged 77 years

N91   In loving memory of / our parents / Lillian May SCOTT / died Dec. 15th. 1967 / aged 70 years / and / William George SCOTT / died Nov. 4th. 1975 / aged 76 years

N92   (Ground) In loving memory of / a dear husband & father / Eugene O'SULLIVAN / died April 24th 1990 / aged 66 years

N93   Beatrice Violet Ann TUCKFIELD. Died 20 January 1968. Aged 77 years.

N94   Stanley Alfred GRIDLEY. Died 21 April 1968. Aged 73 years.

N95   In / loving memory of / Kathleen Thelma Mary / VICKERY / died July 8th 1968 / Aged 41.

N96   In / loving / memory of / my dear wife / Annie MARTIN / who entered into rest / July 20th 1968. Aged 64 years. / Thanks be to God which giveth us / the victory through our Lord / Jesus Christ 1. Cor. 15,57. / Beloved husband of Annie / George Winchester MARTIN / March 24th 1899 – March 21st 1983 / Absent from the body / present with the Lord. 2 Cor.5.8.

N97   In / loving memory / of / Winifred Maud / JORDAN. / died 1st September 1968 / aged 62 years. / R.I.P. /
Also / Gilbert Henry / JORDAN / died 20th March 1994 / aged 97 years / R.I.P.

N98   *Miss Florence Edith SMITH. Died 11 September 1968. Aged 87 years.*

N99   *William Henry LANGDON. Died 28 September 1968. Aged 75 years.*

N100 *Miss Florence Edith MUSGRAVE. Died 6 December 1968. Aged 75 years.*

N101 (Cross) In / loving memory of / Eileen Mary / PEMBERTON (née BENISON) / April 3rd 1893. / December 11th 1968.

N102 *Josephine PONSFORD. Died 20 January 1969. Aged 75 years.*

N103 *Ernest HORE. Died 24 August 1969. Aged 68 years.*

N104 In / loving memory of / a dear husband & father / Charles WARREN / died 1st November 1969 / aged 83. / Rest in peace. / Also wife of the above / Sarah Elizabeth / WARREN / died 29th June 1973 / Aged 82. / Re-united.

N105 In / loving memory of / my dear husband / Frederick BRICE / Died Nov. 15th 1969 / Aged 66.

N106 In / loving memory of / our dear sister / Naomi PARKMAN / died 29th Dec 1969 / Aged 69.

N107 In loving memory / of / a dear husband / & father / Cecil H BARBER / died 5th June 1991 / aged 56

N108 *[Unmarked]*

N109 In / loving memory of / a dear Mother / Grandmother & Great Nan / Elsie Mary BOWDEN / died 9th Sept. 1993 / Aged 92 / God bless

N110 In / loving / memory of / a dear wife and / mother / Nora HAWKINS / 21st July 1921 / 16th Sept. 1993 / and a beloved / husband and father / Sydney HAWKINS / 8th May 1914 / 25th April 1997 / Together again

N111 *[Unmarked]*

N112 Treasured / memories of / a dear husband, dad / and grandad / Thomas Harold / CLAPP / died 16th Jan 1993 / aged 78 years / At rest. *[Manning & Knight]*
(F/H) THC.

N113 Treasured / memories of / a dear husband, father / and son / Derek Lambert HOOD / died 3rd April 1991 / aged 58 years. *[Manning & Knight]*

N114 In / loving memory of / a much loved husband and father / Robert Edward George / GREEDY / who died tragically / Oct. 10th 1987 Aged 30 years

N115 In / loving memory of / Edgar Charles QUICK / born 3rd Nov. 1913 / died 16th Dec. 1987 / And his beloved wife / Hilda Mary QUICK / born 25th Jan. 1920 / died 5th Sept. 1991 / Reunited   *[Manning & Knight]*

N116 In / loving memory of / a dear husband and father / William DAVEY / died 12. April 1988 / aged 95

N117 In / loving memory of / my dear wife / Ellen Emma GREGORY. / 27-12-1915 to 21-10-1990 / To live in the hearts of / those we love is not to die. / And her dear husband / Frederick Charles / GREGORY. / 13-2-1912 to 7-8-1998. / Reunited.

N118 Treasured memories / of a dear husband and father / Cecil SMITH / (Dennis) / Died 20th Sept. 1986 / aged 69 years. / And / a dear wife and mother / Nesta Effie SMITH / died 15th Feb 1999 / aged 82 years. / Together again.

N119 In affectionate memory / of / my caring wife / Patricia BELLAMY / loving mother and grandmother / tragically taken from us / 28th April 1988. Aged 53 years *[Manning & Knight]*

N120 In / loving memory of / Phillip David / JEFFS-MANSFIELD / aged 22 / Gone but not forgotten   *[Buried 14 June 1989]*

N121 In / loving memory of / Henry HOOPER / died 16th July 1989 / aged 73 years / Also/ Doris Lilian HOOPER / died 23rd Oct 1994 / aged 77 years / Rest in peace.*[G.F.S.]*

N122 (Metal label)   Elizabeth May / HODGE / Died Sept 18th 1989 / Aged 59 years.

N123 (F/H)   In loving memory / of our Beautiful Angel / Bethany Amber / 23rd Oct. 1993 – 3rd Mar 1995   *[Daughter of Samphire BARTHOLOMEW]*

N124 Treasured memories / of / Abigail Rose / BURTON / our dearly loved daughter / 7 Oct. 1993 / 31 July 1994.   *[Manning & Knight]*

N125 In / loving memory of / a dear / husband and father / Leslie Stuart Ralph / WILMOTT / died 21st August 1993 / aged 68 / Good night and God bless *[Manning & Knight]*
(F/H) LSRW.

N126 In / loving memory / of / Sidney James HILL M.B.E. / 1925 – 1991 / Also his beloved wife / Muriel Betty HILL / 1926 – 1994 / Jesus is alive   *[G.F.S.]*

N127 *Peggy Selina MILLS. Buried 22 March 1985. Aged 70 years.*

N128 In / memory of / John Dennis / WILSON / 1917 – 1985 / R.I.P.

N129 Ivan Bradley TAYLOR / Always lovingly remembered / 13th Oct 1949 – 28th Sep^t 1985 / R.I.P. *[Stooks]*

N130 In / loving memory of / our dear mother / Ellen Margaret TOVEY / died 28th Nov. 1985 / aged 88 years / Loved and remembered by us all / Also / in loving memory of / a dear wife and mother / "Dolly" BOARDMAN / died 24th March 1994 / aged 70 years / "Truly a star".

N131 In ever loving memory / of / Geoffrey John SMITH / who died / 27th December 1985 / aged 81 years / And his wife / Margery / who died / 23rd January 1988 / aged 76 years / Reunited.

N132 In loving memory / of / our dear son and brother / Kevin John STONE / who passed away 3 Jan. 1986 / aged 23 years. *[Manning & Knight]*

N133 In / loving memory of / Lilian May ADAMS / 1909 – 1986 / Also her husband / Albert James ADAMS / 1910 – 1988

N134 In / memory of / Lilian / Emily Theodora / BARRETT / 1912 – 1986 / Vera Grace FOSTER / 1916 – 1992 / Sydney Robert / FOSTER / 1913 – 1999

N135 *Thomas William NATION. Buried 21 January 1987. Aged 66 years.*

N136 Cherished / memories of / a dear / wife and mother / Margaret Nola / SWEETING / 27th January 1947 / 10th February 1987

N137 *Cecil Henry PARKIN. Buried 6 March 1987. Aged 74 years. Edward William PARKIN. Buried 8 February 1988. Aged 80 years.*

N138 (<u>Wood Cross</u>) Robert David / DAWE / 6th Sept 1986 - / 26th March 1987.

N139 In ever loving memory / of / Albert Edward HAYWARD / who passed away / June 7th 1991 aged 82 / Rest in peace. Also / his beloved wife / Rosa Evelyn HAYWARD / who passed away / August 31st 2000 Aged 87 / God Bless.

N140 In / loving memory / of / a dear husband and father / Geoffrey John / SAFFIN / 3rd Nov 1920 – 18th June 1983 / Always remembered

N141 In / loving memory of / Charles Thomas / ADAMS / of Harrow / 1908 – 1983 / A man of honour

N142 In / loving memory of / a dear husband and father / Reginald Arthur / SWEETING / Born 30th March 1914 / Died 19th August 1983 / aged 69.

/cont…………

N142 cont. Also / a dear wife and mother / Lucy Louisa / SWEETING / Born 25th August 1914 / Died 13 September / 1992 / aged 78

N143 In / loving memory of / Walter SEWELL / died 30 Aug 1983 / aged 64

N144 (Cross) In loving memory / Kathleen Alice / BEAUCHAMP / née BENISON / 13.2.88 – 13.10.83. / To know her / was to love her. (Reverse: 1888-1983)

N145 (F/H) In loving / memory of / Charles / Leonard / CORNISH / died / 21 Feb 1984. Doris / Annie / CORNISH / died / 9 June 1998

N146 Always / remembered / Veronica JOHNSON / Fell asleep / 24th April 1984 / In God's care

N147 In loving memory of / Lt. Colonel / F J WASOWICZ / 1897 – 1984 / Born in Lwow, Poland / for whose freedom he fought / in three wars, / died in exile in the country / he came also to love / "In His will is our peace"

N148 In loving memory / of / Evelyn THORNE / 17th June 1895 / 29th November 1984 / a devoted wife / mother and grandmother / and her husband / William Thomas / THORNE / 1st August 1894 / 28th March 1985

N149 In loving memory of / Cecil H W HOUKES / Died 15th March 1985 / Aged 77 years / and of his wife / Dorothy (Birdie) / Died 11th December 1997 / Aged 80 years / Forever in our thoughts

N150 Michael Edward Gerald HUNTLEY. Buried 19 April 1985. Aged 85 years.

N151 Precious / memories of / a dear mother / Jean May / BARRINGTON / passed peacefully away / 28th July 1987 / aged 42 / Missing you always / forgetting you never / Loved mother of / Mark, Paul, Carl and Claire

N151a Treasured / memories of / Carl Christopher / BARRINGTON / tragically taken from us / 26th October 1991 / aged 22 / In our hearts / you will always stay / because we loved you / in every way / Loved son of Ken and Jean / and brother of Mark, Paul and Claire *[Manning & Knight]*

N152 In / loving memory of / A Eric WOOD / 1906 – 1991 / He ministered with singing *[Manning & Knight]*

N153 In fondest memory of / a dear husband and father / Arthur BRADFORD / passed away 12th Jan. 1982 / aged 65 years.

N154 (F/H) Francis Henry NATION. Buried 11 March 1982. Aged 70 years.

N155 In / loving memory of / a dear husband and father / James DAVIES / who died 12th April 1982 / aged 68 years. / R.I.P.

N156 In / loving memory of / Frank THOMAS / who fell asleep / 28th April 1982 / aged 87.

N157 Peter George Noel / CARDNO / of Abbotsfield / Died in Sarawak / 1st February 1982 / Aged 51. / Buried here / 26th September 1983

N158 *George Albert GARMPS. Buried 1 November 1982. Aged 70 years.*

N159 In / loving memory / of / Mary JONES / née EDGAR / 15 June 1917 / 18 January 1983 / And / Horace John / JONES / 20 March 1912 / 10 February 1986

N160 (F/H) At rest / Reginald / Frank / WILLIAMS / 12th April 1901 / 17th Feb 1983

N161 In / loving memory of / Ethel Elizabeth / NATION / passed away / 24th Feb. 1983 / Aged 73. / Also / Henry Hector NATION / Died 11th April 1991 / Aged 88.

N162 *Jack LEAHY. Buried 30 April 1983. Aged 50 years.*

N163 *Dora POWER. Buried 25 May 1983. Aged 80 years.*

N164 *[unmarked]*

N165 Cherished memories of / Mary HALE / beloved mother and / grandmother / died 7th March 1991 / aged 71 years.*[C.W.S.]* (Tablet) Among Autumn's falling leaves / under the blue translucent sky / In the whispering of the breeze / God keeps a watchful eye.

N166 In loving memory / of / Ernest James / GAY / 1912 ◊ 1980.

N167 (Cross) In / loving memory of / Ella Violet CLAY / B. Burton-on-Trent / 8 July 1885 / D. Wiveliscombe / 23. Dec. 1980 / The Lord bless you and keep you (E)
Reverse   And of her / dearly loved husband / Gerard Arden CLAY / B. Burton / 17 Mar 1871 / D. Nkana, N. Rhodesia / 23 Feb 1955 / R.I.P.   (W)

N168 In / loving memory of / Kathleen WYATT / who died / 19th February 1981 / aged 79 years

N169 In / loving memory of / a very dear / husband and father / Arthur John Henry / HALE / died 18th April 1981 / aged 62 years

N170 *Fredrick Dennis LEAHY. Buried 5 June 1981. Aged 77 years.*

N171 Albert Edward / SMITH / died 26th July 1981 / aged 70. / Remembered always.

N172 Arthur James CREWS / "Dick" / died 28th Sept. 1981 / aged 80 / Also his wife / Maud Mildred CREWS / died 28th Sept. 2000 / aged 94

N173 In loving memory / of / a dear husband and father / Cyril John HEYWOOD / of Chorleys Farm, Whitefield. / 1909 – 1980 / At rest. / Also his beloved wife / Ena Emily HEYWOOD / 1916 – 1996 / United again *[Mang & Knt]*

N174 *[unmarked]*

N175 *Leonard SCULPHER.*
Buried 10 February 1982.
Aged 67 years.

N176 *[unmarked]*
N177 *[unmarked]*

N178 In / loving memory of / William Ernest / BRANFIELD / Bill / died 5th March 1991 / aged 86

[Manning & Knight]

N179 In loving memory of / Thomas John MORGAN / who died / 26th Aug. 1979 / Aged 69. / And his wife / Eleanor Maud MORGAN / who died 11th Nov. 1989 / Aged 73. / Reunited.

N180 In / loving memory of / a dear / husband and father / Raymond HILL / who died 1st Oct. 1979 / Aged 67 / Ever loving wife and mother / Renee HILL / née PASCOE / 3rd March 1912 / 21st March 1988 / At peace together again

N181 *Edgar WEBBER. Buried 4 December 1979. Aged 68 years.*

N182 In / loving memory / of / a dear husband & father / Clifford George / TUDBALL / died 29th February 1980 / aged 69 years

N182a (Brass) In loving memory / of / Paul TUDBALL / who died / 15th January 1982

N183 *[unmarked]*

N184 Kathleen / WARREN / 1912 – 1980 / R.I.P.

N185 *Mary Emma Margaret EASTMENT. Buried 26 August 1980. Aged 82 years.*

145

N186 (Wood Cross) Reserved. M. *Alison HEYWOOD. Buried 20 Feb 1986. Aged 48 years. Miss Olive Doreen MARTIN. Died 22 January 2001. Aged 77 years.*

N187 In loving / memory of / Frank GREEDY / Died / 24th Sept 1980 / Aged 79 years. / Emily GREEDY / died 14th May 1982 / aged 83 years.

N188 (Wood Cross) *Sally KER. Buried 12 November 1980. Aged 40 years. Mark Heathcote Menzies KER. Buried 7 November 1995. Aged 60 years.*

N189 (F/H) Mime Mills HANSEN / 1897 - 1980.

N190 *[unmarked]*

N191 *Gladys GRABHAM. Buried 2 January 1991. Aged 88 years.*

N192 Commander / Robert Alexander George / NESBITT / Royal Navy / Died 19th July 1979 Age 53 / Requiescat in pace

N193 *Mary GROVES. Buried 3 April 1979. Aged 90 years. Frederick Oliver GROVES. Buried 4 February 1980. Aged 84 years.*

N194 In fond memory / of / Leonard James / NURCOMBE / Died 16th Feb 1979 / Aged 61 / At rest.

N195 In / loving / memory of / Ronald Eric NATION / of this parish / 15th Feb 1915 – 21st July 1978

N196 In / loving memory of / Susan BROOM / who died 15th July 1978 / aged 66 years. / For ever in our thoughts.
(F/H) In loving memory

N197 In / loving memory of / our dear mother / Dorothy May REED / Died 22nd June 1978 / aged 55 / Rest in peace

N198 In loving memory / of / Elizabeth Jane VICKERY / (Betty) / Died June 9th 1978 / Aged 89 / also her husband / Frank Beamer VICKERY / Died Jan. 31st 1979 / Aged 84.

N199 In ever / loving memory of / our dear brother / William Henry MARTIN / of Grants Farm / who passed away / on 27th April 1978 / Aged 64 years / At rest
[Mang & Knt]

N200 In / loving memory of / my dear husband / John WALDRON / Died 17th April 1978 / Aged 75 years / Also / Elsie Clara / WALDRON / died 7th Nov 1989 / Aged 81 years / Together again

N201 *Alexandra Cornelius Annie BURT. Buried 17 April 1978. Aged 74 years.*

N202 In memory of / Stanley / NATION / died 25th Feb 1978 / aged 82 / And his wife / Gladys / died 10th Feb 1978 / Aged 77 / Reunited *[Carpenter, 53 Mary Street, Bridgwater, Som.]*

N203 In loving memory of / a dear wife & mother / Florence Maud JAMES / who died 16th November 1977 / aged 65 years /
Also John Patrick JAMES / a beloved husband & father / who died 11th October 1988 / aged 67 years / Reunited.

N204 In loving memory of / Nellie HAWKINS / died 1st Dec 1990 / aged 89 / dear wife of Joe / and mother to / Jean and Christine. *[Manning & Knight]*

N205 Herbert Francis / LEWIS / 1912 – 1975 / Sarah "Sally" / LEWIS / 1911 – 1998.

N206 *Emily Margaret GAINES.   Died 3 Aug 1975. Aged 57 years. William Ernest George GAINES. Died 4 January 1977. Aged 59 years.*

N207 In loving memory of / a dear wife & mother / Lilian Ethel Daisy / NORMAN / Died Jan 26th 1976 / Aged 69 /
Also / Francis John / NORMAN / Died Nov 19th 1982 / Aged 75.

N208 In / loving memory of / John HAYES / who passed peacefully away / 28th March 1976 / aged 59 years. *[Carpenter, 55 St Mary Street, Bridgwater]*

N209 In / loving memory of / Arthur George / SYMONS / 14th March 1911 / 4th Aug 1976. (F/H) In loving memory.

N210 In memory of / Cecil Ronald LEWIS / died 4 Dec 1976 / aged 66 / And his dear wife / Sybil Mary LEWIS / died 9 October 1987 / aged 75 / May they rest in peace.

N211 In / loving memory of / Edward John SELLICK / died 17th August 1979 / aged 72 years.

N212 *Ethel Mary BARRINGTON. Buried 16 December 1976. Aged 81 years.*

N213 (F/H) In / loving / memory of / Walter KING / died / 22 Feb 1977 / Aged 59 / Also / Amelia KING / beloved / wife and mother / Died / 20 July 1987 / Aged 78 years.

N214 In / loving memory of / Thomas Henry / DAVEY / died 21st March 1977 / aged 84 years / and his wife / Kathleen Mary / died 18th March 1978 / aged 74 years.

N215 *[unmarked]*

N216 Frank GREEDY. ("Bargo") Buried 2 August 1977. Aged 82 years.

N217 In loving memory of / Francis Ivor SMITH / who passed away / Oct 7th 1990 aged 82 / Rest in peace

N218 In / loving memory of / Thurston Ernest / BOWDEN / died 4 July 1975 / Aged 91 years / Also Emily his wife / died 26th Jan 1987 / Aged 91 years / Forever in our thoughts

N219 In / loving memory of / Ada Mary STEVENS / who died 25th Oct 1974 / aged 70 / At rest / Also of her husband / Cyril Thomas who died 5th June 1976 / aged 69 / Re-united

N220 Glyn DAVEY. Buried 3 July 1975. Aged 52 years.

N221 Joanna Mary Patricia SMITH. Buried 19 June 1975. Aged 15 years.

N222 In / loving memory of / a dear wife and mother / Lilian PEARCE / called to rest / 18th April 1975. / Also her husband / Herbert Samuel / PEARCE / devoted to his wife and family / who passed away / 26th November 1998 / aged 94 years / Together again *[Stooks, 48 Station Road, Taunton]*
N222a (Ground)   Mary / PEARCE / 1909 – 1989.

N223 In / memory of / our dear parents / Jessie ELMES / William ELMES / Both died Jan. 1975 / Aged 75.
N223a (F/H) In / memory of / Hilda / GUTTERIDGE / 1921 – 1993.

N224 In / loving memory / of / Olive Elizabeth / SELLICK / Died Oct 24. 1974 / aged 65. / RIP / Also her husband / Herbert Charles / SELLICK / Died Jan. 19. 1981 / Aged 75

N225 (Cross) Remembered with love / a dear husband, father and grandad / John MORAN / who died 13 June 1974 / aged 59 years.

N226 In / loving memory of / Lena FAIRHURST / died 25th March 1977 / Aged 83 years.

N227 (F/H) *[unmarked]*

N228 In / loving memory of / a dear husband, / father Grandfather / William SMITH / died 17th Feb. 1974 / Aged 66.

N229 In / loving memory of / a dear husband and father / Sidney Charles / GARDNER / died Jan 21st 1974. / Also his wife / May GARDNER / died May 31 1982 / aged 87 years.
N229a (Ground)   In memory of / Sheila Joyce GARDNER / April 17 1933 October 10 1995 / Dear wife, mum grandma / Always in our thoughts

N230 In / loving memory of / a dear husband & father / Cornelius Joseph / MASON / died 4th Aug 1990 / aged 84 years *[Manning & Knight]*

N231 *Sidney William DISNEY. Died 5 September 1973. Aged 77 years.*

N232 Remembering with love / Leonard James / NURCOMBE / who fell asleep / 23rd May 1973, aged 62. / At rest. / And his wife / Hilda May / NURCOMBE / who joined him on / 7th April 1998, aged 73.

N233 In/ loving memory of / Edward BABB /1892–1973/ Ellen Nell BABB /1904-1993

N234 *Dorothy Grace ROKER. Died 6 February 1973. Aged 72 years.*

N235 *Maurice Frank Surridge BARKER. Died 16 November 1973. Aged 70 years.*

N236 In / loving memory / of / Walter Frederick / PARKER / died 2nd Dec 1972 / aged 63 years
N236a In loving memory of / Doreen, Keith and / Patricia WHITE, / died 29th May 1976.

N237 To / the sacred memory / of my dear husband / Wilfred Matthias CHAMBERS / 1904 – 1972 / "Be kind". / and / his beloved wife / Ruby Ella / who died in Sussex / 1901–1989

N238 In memory / of / William Henry BAKER / died 19th. July 1972 / aged 75 years. / And of / his devoted wife / Beatrice Ellen BAKER / died 29th November 1988 / aged 89 years. / Reunited in God's keeping

N239 In loving memory / of / Annie GREENSLADE / (formerly PASSMORE) / 1900 –1972 / Lead kindly light.

N240 In / loving / memory of / William NORMAN / died June 4th 1927 / Aged 49. / Also / Elizabeth Alice his wife / died May 9th 1972 / aged 90. / Rest in peace.

N241 McCORMACK / In memory of / Alfred Ernest / 20.3.1901 – 12.3.1972 / Ellen Cecilia / 20.3.1901 – 10.11.1992.

N242 *[unmarked]*

N243 R. F. (Fred) BENNETT / Born 13th February 1942 / Died 25 February 1990 / In the happy anticipation / of the life to come.

N244 *[unmarked]*

N245 In loving memory / of / Yvonne Joan SULLY / died 17th. May 1973 / aged 22.

N246 (F/H) *Walter Henry JENKIN. Died 12 July 1971. Aged 69 years.*

N247 In loving memory of / my dear mother / Bessie VAULTER / who passed away / May 15th 1971 / aged 75 years. / Rest in peace. / And her son / Charlie VAULTER / who passed away / Sept. 30th 1996 / aged 78 years.

N248 (F/H) *Alan WHITE. Died 10 February 1971. Aged 27 years.*

N249 In memory of / my dear sister / Doris Alice KELLOW / died 26 December 1970 / aged 69 years

N250 In / loving memory of / Laura Emily MABBOTT / Mother of Joan & Lucy / Born 29th November 1903 / Died 16th December 1970 / With Christ.

N251 *William Henry SAFFIN. Died 4 September 1970. Aged 58 years.*

N252 In / loving / memory of / my dear wife / Muriel Rose WIGNEY / who entered into rest / 28th May 1970. Aged 68 years. / With Christ which is far better / Phil. 1.23.

N253 *Miss Lillian SAUNDERS. Died 21 February 1970. Aged 81 years.*

N254 (F/H) In loving memory of / William H HARTNELL / Died 24th Jan 1970 / aged 87. / And / Matilda HARTNELL / died 27th Jan 1972 / aged 86.

N255 Together / Mary Jane BARRINGTON / died Jan 3rd 1970 aged 82 / and / Clifford John BARRINGTON / died Feb 6th 1970 aged 80.

N256   *[Reserved]*

N257   In / loving / memory of / Arthur Williams / TARR / died 4th October 1993 / aged 81.   *[Manning & Knight]*
Ruby Mary TARR. Died 8 January 2001. Aged 81 years.

N258   (F/H)   Francis / C V / MACDONALD / 1913 – 1993.

N259   In / loving memory /of Rena Borwick / EDGAR / 28 March 1913 / 23 March 1994

N260   In / loving memory of / Juris REVICS / Born 20th April 1910 / in Latvia / died 6th April 1994   *[Manning & Knight]*

N261   In / ever loving memory / of / Libby PRISCOTT / born 22nd September 1944 / died 11th April 1994   *[Manning & Knight]*

N262   Treasured / memories of / a dear husband / William Gordon / WAYGOOD / 1923 – 1994 / Liebe dich   *[Manning & Knight]*

N263   In / loving memory / Frances Ambery SMITH / Born in India 1908 / Died 8th October 1994

N264   Beloved / husband, dad & / grandad / Clifford Francis / GAINES / 1913 – 1994 / Rest in peace *[Manning & Knight]*

N265   Though lovers be lost love shall not / and death shall have no dominion / Mary-Grace / 19th August 1934 / 16th December 1994 / Beloved wife of / David KEMBLE

N266   In   / loving memory of / Douglas Arthur VICKERY / who passed away / 8th September 1995 / aged 79 years / It broke our hearts to lose you / but you did not go alone / for part of us went with you / the day God called you home *[Manning & Knight]*

N267   In / loving memory of / Mary WEBBER / who passed away / 13th October 1995 / Aged 76 years *[Manning & Knight]*

N268   *Frances Amy PARKIN. Buried 3 November 1995. Aged 85 years.*
Rosa Mary PARKIN. Died 14 January 2001. Aged 91 years.

N269   *[Reserved]*

N270   In / loving memory of / a dear wife & mother / Beatrice May / MASON / Died 15th Dec. 1995 / Aged 90 years *[Manning & Knight]*

N271   (F/H)   In / loving / memory

N272   In loving memory of / David John TURNER / died 7 April 1996 / Aged 78 / also / his dearly loved wife / Gwyneth Doreen TURNER / "Gwen" / died 10 October 1999 / aged 77 / R.I.P. *[Manning & Knight]*
(F/H) In loving memory / of my darling / husband / David John / TURNER / 1917 – 1996. Aged 78 / "Love you forever".

N273   (Wood cross) (F/H) In loving memory   *Barry John ("Bull") REED. Buried 17 June 1996.   Aged 56 yrs*

N274   Happy / memories of / a beloved son & brother /   Luke McKINLEY / aged 18 years / 1977- 1996 / In our hearts forever

N275   In / loving memory / of / a dear husband & father / Eric Thomas WATTERS / died Aug. 24th 1996 / aged 67 years .

N276   Treasured memories of / Elsie DEER / 1918 – 1996 / Deeply loved / and always in our thoughts   *[Manning & Knight]*

N277   In / loving memory of / our dear mother / Winifred Edith / WALKER / who passed away on / the 21st January 1997 / aged 83 years / "Rest in God's keeping".
[Manning & Knight]

N278   In / loving memory of / Ronald George / ROWE / Born 27th May 1914 / Died 7th March 1997

N279   In / loving memory of / Edgar William (Bill) / BELLAMY / A loving Husband, Dad, / Grandad & Great-grandad / who passed away / 20th August 1997 / aged 84 years / Deeply loved and / always remembered
[Manning & Knight]

N280   Ann Gronau / WILSON / 23 September 1940 / 16 March 1998

N281   In loving memory of / Aunt Min / (Née STENNER) / 1910 –1998

N282   In / loving memory of / John Roy TIDBOALD / of Culverhay, Wiveliscombe / Who passed away on / 17th August 1998 / aged 77 years   *[Stooks]*

N283   In / loving remembrance of / Barbara Mercy Bicknell / BOND / died 17th December 1998 / aged 72 years   *[Manning & Knight]*

N284   Louise Nicola / BRANSCOMB / born 8th September 1972 / In / loving memory of / our precious / and courageous Daughter / and Sister / who left us suddenly / on the 6th April 1999 / aged 26 years / Lent by God and now / in his safe keeping / Always in our hearts / and thoughts

N285 In / loving memory of / Ernest William / VICKERY / Died 9th June 1999 / Aged 75 years   *[Manning & Knight]*

N286 In / loving memory of a dear / Mother and Grandmother / Dorothy Grace CROUCH / 3rd Dec. 1911 – 14th August 1999 / Beloved wife of / Edward G CROUCH / who died April 1979

N287 In loving memory of / James Leonard / CROCKER / beloved son, brother, grandson / and friend of many / died tragically 9th Jan 1997 / Aged 20 years / Voice of an angel / with a heart of gold *[Stooks]*

N288   (Wood Cross)

N289 Treasured / memories of / Sidney Ronald SEDGBEER / (Ron) / 1919-1999 / Dorothy Mary SEDGBEER / (Dot) / 1923-1999 / Much loved Mum and Dad

N290 In / loving memory / of / Kathleen Mary VICKERY / died 16th September 1999 / Aged 88

N291 In / loving memory of / Frederick Charles / O'BRIEN / Freddie /   1929 – 2000 / Dearly loved / never forgotten / Peace perfect peace

N292 In / loving memory of / Mark PUZEY / 2 Feb 1963 – 14 Feb 2000 / Much loved Husband, Father / Son & Brother / In our hearts you will always stay / loved and remembered every day

N293 Cherished / memories of / My dear son / Anthony / Michael Lloyd / TOWERS / Died 30th October 2000 / Aged 33 / Much loved Dad & Brother / We will always love you *[Manning & Knight]*

N294 David John Edward INGRAM, CBE. Died 15 January 2001. Aged 73 years.

N295 Frederick Reginald FOXWELL (Freddie). Died 22 January 2001. Aged 78 years.

N296 George Henry HAYES. Died 10 Febraury 2001. Aged 77 years.

N297 Anthony TOWERS (Tony). Died 14 February 2001. Aged 59 years.

N298 In loving memory of / Kathleen Lilian Generis / DIXON / Born 1916 - Died 4th March 2001 / Beloved Wife of JOHN / and Mother of / JEREMY & CAROMAY / So loving and so dearly loved. *[Manning & Knight]*

N299 Irene Joyce GEORGE. Died 5 April 2001. Aged 77 years.

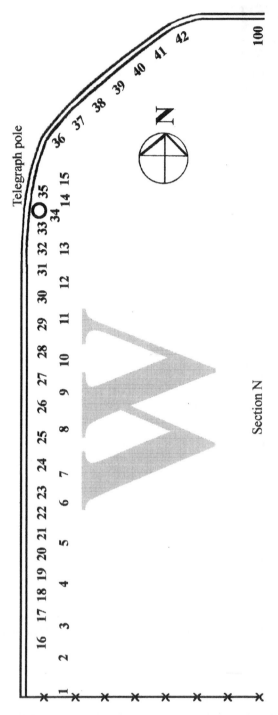

Churchyard Plan - Wall Section

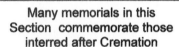

Churchyard
Wall Section

> Many memorials in this
> Section commemorate those
> interred after Cremation

W1   In loving memory of / Stella BARRINGTON / A dear wife, mother / and grandmother / Died 26th September 2000 / Aged 77 years.

W2   *[Reserved]*

W3   (Cross) In loving memory / of / Alfred Thomas MORANT / 20.12.1907 – 25.8.1987

W4   In precious memory of / our dear daughter / Nicola Anne PARNELL / Nikki / 1965 – 1989 / God has you in his keeping / we have you in our hearts. *[G.F.S.]*

W5   P. *[Reserved]*

W6   In / loving memory of / a dear wife and / devoted mother and granny / Pamela VALUKS / who fell asleep in the Lord / 1 June 1990 / aged 62 years / Not gone away / only in the next room. *[Manning & Knight]*

W7   In / loving memory of / a dear brave son / & brother / Marc Owen STEVENS / who died 25 April 1991 / Aged 5 years / Forever in our thoughts *[Manning & Knight]*

W8   S. *[Reserved]*

W9   P.B. *[Reserved]*

W10   In memoriam / John Bayard MORRIS / Died 2nd Jan. 1992 / Aged 88 / Queenie Gladys Longley / MORRIS / Died 11th Mar. 1992 / Aged 88 / Jack and Jill. *[G.F.S.]*

W11   *[unmarked]*

W12   In / loving / memory of / Major Harry VAULTER / who fell asleep / 9th June 1992 / aged 86 years / At the going down of the sun / and in the morning / we will remember him. / And of / Hilda VAULTER / who joined him on / 9th September 1993 / aged 73 years / "Love will never come to an end". *[G.F.S.]*

W13 Treasured / memories of / Francis John / PEARCE / died 28th Sept. 1992 / aged 84 years / Also his wife / Dora Frances PEARCE / died 6th May 1998 / aged 89 years / Reunited *[Manning & Knight]*

W14 Loving / memories of / a dear husband / Leslie Ronald / WESTERN / died 22nd Aug. 1993 / aged 80 / Forever with the Lord /
Also his loving wife / Phyllis Dorcas WESTERN / died 12th April 1998 / aged 75 / Together again *[Manning & Knight]*

W15 In / loving memory of / Stanley William / CLAPP / 1919 – 1998.
[Manning & Knight]

W16 In / loving memory of / Viola Nellie / JAMES / 1927 – 1999 / May God's peace / be with you Mum.

W17 William F HANNON / O.B.E. / 1921 – 1995

W18 In / loving memory of / Stella Jean GUSH / 24th Oct 1936 – 4th May 1998

W19 Michael O'DRISCOLL / "Jack" / 1905 – 1996

W20 D.W.H. / 1903 – 1996   *[Douglas Wilfred HADFIELD]*
Margaret Barbara HADFIELD. Buried 27 July 2000. Aged 90 years.

W21 (Wood cross & F/H) Dad / David TIER / 1938 – 1994 / Love you / Miss you

W22 In / memory of / Grace CHAPPLE / much loved mother and nanny / died 29th August 1991 / aged 83

W23 Horace / Edmund / HANNON / 1923 – 1991 / Loved by all / the family

W24 (F/H) In / loving / memory

W25 In / loving memory of / Harold George SPARKS / 1904 – 1992

W26 (F/H) In loving memory of / our baby daughters / Natalie and Stephanie / FAWCETT / died 22nd January / 1993

W27 In loving memory of / John (Jack) CARTER / 1923 – 1993

W28 Remembered with love / our dear Mum & Nan / Eileen STRICKLAND / died 29th April 1994 / aged 79.

W29 George Edward / TAPP / 4th Dec 1920 / 7th Dec 1994

W30 H.D.

W31 William Roy ROSS / 13.3.1914 – 30.9.1995 / "You have been taken from our sight / but never from our hearts"

W32 In / loving memory of / Leslie Webber LAND / 1908 – 1971 / Winifred Mary LAND / 1915 – 1995

W33 Loved and / always remembered / Guy HIGGINBOTTOM / "George" / died 22 April 1997 Aged 77

W34 In / loving memory / Reginald / Barry Lovaine / PERSSE / Brigadier K.S.L.I. / 1896 – 1985 / of / Whitefield Farm House / and of his wife / Sheeleh Patricia / PERSSE / née BATTERSBY / 1897 – 1979 *[A. Smith]*

W35 Jane ELLIS / 1951 – 1998.

W36 In loving memory of / William Henry GREEDY / Bill / Nov. 1927 – Sept. 1996 / and loving wife / Eileen Anna GREEDY / June 1930 – Aug. 2000 / Together forever.

W37 In / loving memory of / Stuart TOWLER / Sept. 3rd 1935 – May 4th 2000 / Forever in our thoughts

W38 Florence E HALES / 1914 – 1999.

W39 Peter MULLAN / 1936-2000 / "Forever in our hearts"

W40 In / loving memory of / Norman William EXCELL / 1912 – 1999 / Much loved and respected / by his family and friends

W41 Ashley MADDOCK / died 20 January 2000 / aged 21 / Always in our hearts dear / Mum, Jenny & family.

W42 *John WINTER. Died 16th April 2001. Aged 71 years.*

W100 In loving memory / of / Michael / Charles EDMED 1960 to 1996 / Stephen / James EDMED / 1957 to 1983 / Peter / John EDMED / 1952 to 1983.

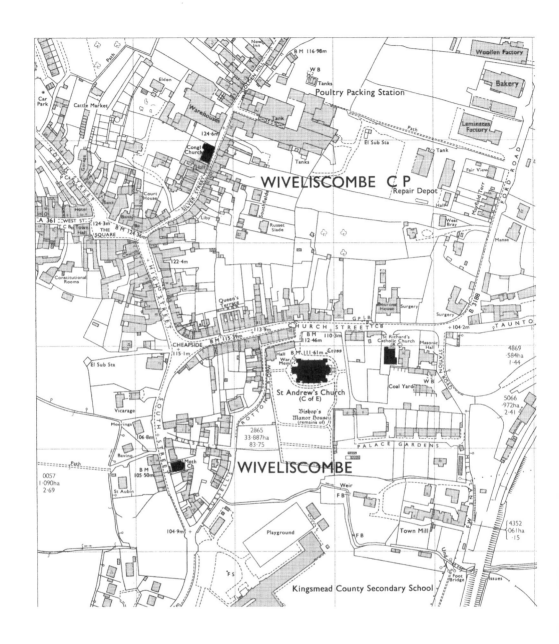

Wiveliscombe - 1970

Reproduced from the Ordnance Survey map with the permission of
Her Majesty's Stationery Office, © Crown Copyright, NC/01/097

Other Churches & Memorials

Other Churches & Memorials

Over the years other denominations have had a presence in Wiveliscombe. A note about each follows, together with the inscriptions recorded in their respective places of worship.

Roman Catholic Church

Roman Catholic parishioners met wherever they were able to find suitable premises until 1942, when regular services began at a property in Silver Street. Twenty years later the congregation sold some land in the town and with the proceeds a site in Church Street was purchased (once the Langdon egg processing plant). This became the first permanent Roman Catholic place of worship. Built by S Pearce & Sons, the church was designed by the Bristol architects Ivor Day & O'Brien. The unusual blue glass panels imbue the internal space with constant light. The church, dedicated to St. Richard of Chichester (1197-1253), is within the Diocese of Clifton, and was consecrated in 1967 by Bishop Rudderham. Mavis Amy Hind (parishioner 1949-1987) and James Upham (1848-1937) are remembered on two pieces of furniture near the altar. As there is no burial ground attached to the church, parishioners are buried in the St. Andrew's churchyard.

The Society of Friends

The earliest local references to the Society of Friends, or 'Quakers', appear in the late 17th Century. A site for a meeting house and graveyard half way between Wiveliscombe and Milverton, at the top of what is known as Quaking House Lane, was granted in 1679 by Edward Pole of Milverton. This was superseded by a more substantial meeting house being opened in Milverton in 1760, but the serene 'Friends' Burial Ground' survived, and is still in use. Prior to the mid 19th Century Friends' graves were unmarked, a custom which is reflected in the short length of the list of memorials (see following page).

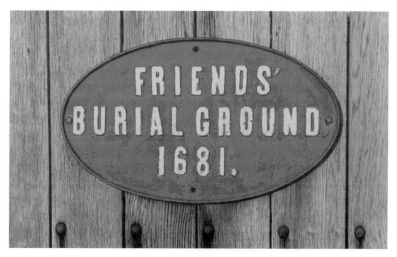

MEMORIALS IN THE FRIENDS' BURIAL GROUND

The Friends erected memorial footplates rather than headstones.
The earlier inscriptions also omitted the names of the months.

FB1   (Ground) In loving memory of / Emily / widow of Charles BROWN / of North Shields / who died at Wiveliscombe / the 23rd of 2nd M^{o}. 1904 / Aged 76 years.

FB2   (Ground)   Chris / WILLOUGHBY / 1947   2000.

FB3   (Ground) John Powell DAWSON / 1919 – 1998

FB4   (Ground) Helen Mary FEAR / Born / 12th June 1919 / Died / 17th August 1990

FB5   (Ground) John / PULLING / Shalom / 1920 – 1995

FB6   (Ground)   Stephen Francis / Bernard POYNTER / 10th November 1914 / 11th May 1996 / A beloved gentle / man / Madeleine POYNTER / 1st January 1910 / 11th May 1997 / His loving wife

FB7   (Ground) Mary Anna YOUNG / Born / 18th of 9th Month 1840 / Died / 3rd of 11th Month 1902

FB8   (Ground) Elizabeth Ann YOUNG / Born / 24th of 3rd Month 1844 / Died / 27th of 9th Month 1901

FB9   (Ground)   Mary Helen YOUNG / Born / 8th of 12th Month 1866 / Died / 28th of 10th Month 1868

FB10 (Ground) Ann John YOUNG / Born / 29th of 1st (?) Month 18... / Died / 14th (?) of 11th Month 1851

FB11 (Ground) John YOUNG / Born / 6th of 8th Month 1791 / Died / 26th of 11th Month 1862

FB12   (Ground) *[Blank]*

FB13   (Ground) Richard YOUNG / Born / 30th of ..../ Died ......

FB14 (Ground) Ann Richard YOUNG / Born / 17th of 6th Month 1810 / Died / 1st of 2nd Month 1871

FB15 (Ground) Ann YOUNG / Born / 14th of 6th Month 1784 / Died / 29th of 1st Month 1866

Evangelical Congregational Church

24th January 1660, GEORGE DAY, M.A., Hart Hall, Oxford Matriculated 28th March, 1655. B.A. 13th October 1657. MA. 3rd July, 1660. Resigned the living of Wiveliscombe in 1662, on being required to sign the Act of Uniformity. Became Pastor of a non-conforming congregation at Radcliff, London, where he died in 1697.

[ST. ANDREW'S VICARAGE – see page 35]

By his refusal to accept the Act of Uniformity, the Revd George Day was forced to resign from his living as Vicar of St Andrew's on 24th April 1662, and led the non-conformists in the town until the passing of the Toleration Act in 1689. At this time such congregations were legalised and their place of worship, the house of Joseph Stocker in North Street, became licensed as a preaching place. Finally freed from persecution, services took place in an outbuilding in the Old Court House in Silver Street until a chapel was built in North Street. In 1708 the first Independent Presbyterian chapel was inaugurated on the current site in Silver Street, and an original tablet is still visible in the wall over the entrance. It was enlarged in 1825 to accommodate 350. Further subsequent additions included two stained glass windows (1897), and electric light (1941). Rebuilt after a fire in 1976, the seating area was reduced but the two upper galleries remain. In 1787 an interdenominational Sunday School was set up. It became the Congregational Sunday School in 1810 and continues in the house built beside the chapel in 1890. The Evangelical Congregation Church and Wiveliscombe Christian Fellowship amalgamated in 1975.

CONGREGATIONAL CHURCH TABLETS

ECC1 [White Marble] In memory of / John WILLIAMS Esq[re] / who died April 7th 1853: / Aged 79 years / Also of Mary, his wife / who died Feby 27th 1855; / Aged 79 years / "Precious in the sight of the Lord / is the death of his saints. Ps. CXVI.15"

ECC2 [Black Slate] In Memoriam / Bessie Anne COURT / (nee DWELLY) / for 45 years the loving / and devoted wife of / Rev. Lewis H COURT / Methodist Minister / She entered into the larger life / on Feb. 4th 1944 aged 71 years / Her gracious spirit and winsome manner / endeared her to all the Lord's people / in the Exeter, Plymouth, Brighton / and Minehead Circuits where she / spent most of her life. She loved / this her home Church and her / husband gave this Memorial / in Dear and grateful / Remembrance of a / Beautiful life / Interred at Minehead

ECC3 [White Marble] The memory of / the just is / blessed / Proverbs X.7. / Be ye also ready / for in such an hour / as ye thinks not the / son of Man cometh / Matt. XXIV. 44. / Erected by the congregation / as a tribute / of their grateful and affectionate regard / to the memory of / The Rev[d]. Joseph BUCK / who for 30 years was their faithful and beloved pastor / He was suddenly called to enter into his rest / on the 2nd of April 1837 / Aged 58 years / Also of Anna his wife / who died July 15th 1851 / Aged 81 years

ECC4 [Brass] To the Glory of God / and in loving memory of Mildred Annie / only daughter of Frederick and Eva Anne THORNE / and grand-daughter of John and Lydia PRING / who died June 22nd 1900 / Aged 11 years

ECC5 [White Marble] In loving memory of / Thomas NEWTON. Born 1796: Died 1860 / More than a quarter of Century Deacon of / the Church and Superintendent of the / Sunday Schools / Harriett NEWTON wife of the above Born 1798: Died 1873 / IX. Acts XXXVI / Also the following sons and daughter / Rev John Foster NEWTON Born 1821: Died 1849 / James NEWTON Born 1827: Died 1832 / Harriett Eliza NEWTON Born 1834: Died 1835 / Robert Francis NEWTON Born 1843: Died 1849 / Thomas NEWTON Born 1824: Died 1858 / Alfred James NEWTON Born 1837: Died 1866 *[Manning]*

ECC6 [Brass] In loving remembrance of / Lydia PRING of Alpine House / for many years a Member of this Church / who entered into rest Jany 24th 1898 / This window is dedicated to her / cherished memory by her husband and daughter.

ECC7 [Brass] This window is erected by / John and Lydia PRING / in loving memory of their dear children / Lily Ann who died Feby 23rd 1855 / and Thomas Escott who died Dec 8th 1864

A picture hanging in the church records details about the organ in use there from 1829 to 1915. Originally built in London in 1796, it had at one time been on loan to the French Emperor, Napoleon Bonaparte, before the widow of its owner, the Chancellor of the Exchequer, sold it in 1827 to Mr Charles Bailey of Nynehead, from whom it was purchased by Mr John Lean for the Congregational Church. It was acquired by Dr C A Edwards in 1915 and transported to the Conservatorium of Music in Sydney, Australia. It was then used in a girls' school, before being moved to its current location in the Parish Church of St. Peter's, Watson's Bay. This remarkable provenance was found written on a paper inside the organ, a photograph of which accompanies the account.

CONGREGATIONAL CHURCHYARD MEMORIALS

No longer used for burials, the land for the Burial Ground was first purchased in 1810

ECY1 In affectionate remembrance of / Lily Ann / daughter of / John and Lydia PRING / who died Feb^{ry} 23rd 1855 / Aged nine months / Also of / Thomas Escott PRING / son of the above / who died Decr 8th 1864 / Aged 5 ½ years / "Not gone from memory, not gone from love / but gone to their Father's house above" / Also of / Lydia PRING / who entered into rest / January 24th 1898 / Aged 77 years / Also of / John PRING / of Alpine House / Husband of the above / who departed this life May 20th 1906 / Aged 85 years / Until the day break (E)

ECY2 I.H.S.   In loving memory of / Mary / the beloved wife of / Francis GREENSLADE / of Westbourne Villa / who died May 2nd 1897 / Aged 72 years / "Heaven is my home" / Also of Henry NEWTON / First husband of the / above / who died May 23rd 1864 / Aged 46 years (N)

ECY3   In affectionate remembrance of / Henry NEWTON died May 23rd 1864 aged 46 (W)   Henry Wensley NEWTON / died March 8th 1867 aged 21 / Frederick John Anthony NEWTON / died Dec 21, 1859. Aged 7. (E)

ECY4   In / affectionate remembrance of / Thomas NEWTON Junr / who sweetly slept in Jesus / June 17th 1858: aged 31 years / Resurgam / Also of Mary Ann / Widow of the above / who entered into rest / February 5th 1903 aged 80 years / A succourer of many (S)

ECY5   Sacred / to the memory of / Henry ROALS / who died August 5th 1825 / Aged 16 years / also of John ROALS. Father / of the above / who died June 27th 1857 / Aged 81 years. (N)

ECY6   Harriet NEWTON / buried in 1835 / + Revd. NEWTON....... (S)

ECY7   In / loving memory of / the Rev David EVANS / for 22 years Pastor of the / Independent Church Winsham / He died Dec 20, 1863(?5) / aged 69(?) years /......... (N)

ECY8   Sacred / to the memory of / Elizabeth SILVESTER / who departed this life / January the 4th 1877 / in the 77th year of her age / Also of John SILVESTER / husband of the above / who departed this life / November the 18th 1877 / in the 78th year of his age. *[Richards]* (E)

ECY9   In / loving memory / of / Mary Nurcombe THORNE / who entered into rest / May 17th 1933 / Aged .... Years / "And now I live afresh" / Also of Thomas THORNE, JP / dearly loved husband / of the above / died Oct. 6th 1944 / Aged 88 years / "Surely goodness and mercy have / followed me all the days of my life"(N)

ECY10   Dudley NURCOMBE / 1906 – 1984 / Deacon for 56 years / "A man greatly beloved" (E)

ECY11   Also his dear wife / Gladys / who passed away / 2nd September 1996 / Aged 81 / Sadly missed. (E)   *[NURCOMBE]*

ECY12   In / loving memory of / Mildred Annie / only daughter of / Frederick & Eva Anne THORNE / who fell asleep June 22, 1900 / Aged 11 years / Of such is the kingdom of heaven. (E)

ECY13   To / the dear memory of / Frederick THORNE J.P. / who passed to the homeland on Dec. 16, 1926 / Aged 72 years / A devoted husband, a loving father, and / a faithful servant of Jesus Christ / Not dead, but living unto thee /
Also of Eva Anne THORNE / beloved wife of the above / who died at Bexhill-on-Sea on Sep. 17 1936 / Aged 80 years / "The Fruit of the Spirit is love"

ECY14   In / memory of / Ann Collard GRIBBLE / the beloved daughter of / Charles & Ann GRIBBLE / who was removed by death / Feb^{ry} 7th 1829 / Aged 2 years and 10 months / Also of / Hannah COX, grandmother / of the above, / and widow of William COX, / (of this town) / who died Feb^{ry} 1st 1831 / aged 70 years / They sleep in Jesus and are blest. (W)

ECY15   In memory / of / Jane HAYS / who departed this life / the 14th of Sep^{tr} 1848 / Aged 33 years / Precious in the sight of the L*[ord]* (stone split in two) is the death of his saints / Also of Ann HAYS / who died March 21st 1885 (W)

ECY16   In memory of / James NEWTON / who died March 14th 1833 / aged ? years (W)

ECY17   In loving memory of / IHS / Albert Edward / son of Amos & Selina MARKS / who fell asleep in Jesus / Sunday Feb 25th 1883 / Aged 19 years / Not lost just gone before / Be ye also ready. (W)

ECY18   …… who died May 6th 1888 / Aged 62 years / "Absent from the body, / present with the Lord" / Also of / Maria JEWELL / widow of the above / who died January 17th 1900 / Aged 76 years / At Rest (W)

ECY19   E…. who died July 29 1849 / aged 38 years / and was interred in the / Wiveliscombe Churchyard / also of Ann / second wife of the above / who died Jany 21st 1870 / Aged 68 years (W)

ECY20   ………. Also William Broughton KNIGHT / grandson of the above / Died June 1st 1874 / Aged 36 years / Also Gertrude KNIGHT / daughter of the above W B KNIGHT / who died December 25th 1886(96?) / Aged 25 years /
Also Henry Edward KNIGHT / eldest son of the above W B KNIGHT / who died June 6th 1897 / aged 31 years (E)

ECY21   …. The beloved wife of / William KING / of Greenway in this Parish / who fell asleep in Jesus / October the 11th 1878 (?) / Aged 69 (?) years / Even so them also that sleep in / Jesus will God keep with him / also of William KING (E)

ECY22 In / memory of / Thomas C THORNE / who died June 3rd 1883 / aged 63 years / Also of Elizabeth /daughter of the above/ who died June 13th 1866 / Aged 13 years / Also of Ann K THORNE/ widow of the above /who died March 28th 1895 / Aged 73 years (E)

ECY23 I.H.S. / Sacred / to the memory of / Sarah ROBBINS / who died March 23rd 1879 / Aged 48 years / Thy will be done / Also of / Thomas ROBBINS / who fell asleep in Jesus / April 14th 1894 / Aged 64 years (E)

ECY24 In / memory of / Joseph ROGERS / who died Sept 29th 183?5 / aged 68 years / also of / Elizabeth / wife of the above / who died Dec. 1st 1865 / Aged 78 years / Also of / Edward / son of the above / who died Feby 8th 1835 / Aged 18 years (E)

ECY25 In / loving memory / of / Jane / the beloved wife of / E J THORNE / who entered into rest / September 6th 1902 / Aged 71 years / "Until the day break / and the shadows flee away" / Also of / Edward John THORNE / who entered into rest / December 18th 1918 / Aged 87 years / Leave we now thy servant sleeping. (S)

The Wesleyan Chapel

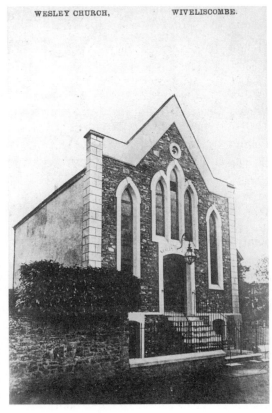

WESLEY CHURCH,   WIVELISCOMBE.

Prior to 1843, the Wesleyan Chapel was located in Golden Hill, below the now defunct New Inn.   The congregation outgrew the building, and in 1845 a new Chapel, seating 250, was erected by the Nurcombe family in South Street. Part of the Wellington Methodist Circuit, worship continued in the Chapel until 2nd June 1986 when, on account of the dwindling numbers and ageing congregation,   services ceased and the building was sold. The base of one tablet (by Jeboult) remains in the Chapel, and three others are stored within the Crypt of St. Andrew's *[see page 42]*. One (*V/G*), dating from 1849, is dedicated to George Duley and his young daughter.   Their gravestone was located in the grounds of the Chapel, on top of a disused well.   At a simple service on 26th June 1986, their remains were re-interred in the St. Andrew's churchyard.

167

Iron Mission Churches

At the present time, the clergy of Wiveliscombe are responsible for several churches in the nearby Brendon Hills: Chipstable, Clatworthy, Huish Champflower, Raddington and Langley Marsh.   As separate parishes, they are not included in this survey, with the exception of Langley Marsh, which is geographically within Wiveliscombe Parish and has one of a few surviving Iron Mission churches in the area.   Built at the end of the 19th Century, these tiny wood-lined churches were constructed of corrugated iron sheeting, hence their nomenclature. They catered for what was then a much larger rural community and, under their terms of reference, specifically included the religious education of the poor, particularly children. The initiator of these Mission Churches, the Reverend Howard McCririck (Vicar of Wiveliscombe 1891-1922 – *B22*), also wrote a guide to St. Andrew's *[page 197]*, and drew up the 'Succession of Vicars' *[page 35]*.

St. Luke's, Langley Marsh

St. Luke's is the only surviving Iron Mission Church in the Parish, and services continue to be held here each month. It began in 1888 as the Langley Mission Room, but on 14th October 1893 became a Mission Church, dedicated to St. Luke and seating 100. There being no accompanying burial ground, interments take place in Wiveliscombe. The organ was made by Jones and Company, 22 Bridge Street, Bristol.

MEMORIALS

[Wood]   In memory of the men connected / with Langley, Wiveliscombe who / gave their lives in the World War / 1939-1945 / William Stewart CAPPER, Major RA / Herbert Jack HANNON, Cpl. RAOC / Ernest Frederick MILLETT, Marine RMLI / Richard H WALSH, O/Tel. RNVR / R.I.P.

[Brass plate on Lectern]   To the Glory of God & in Memory of / Noel Clayton WOODHOUSE / Died Jan 9, 1902. Aged 6 years.

[Inscribed in Bible]   In loving memory of James LAND 1910 – 1973.

[Wood]   R.I.P. / In / remembrance of / Robert STONE / of Langley / in this parish who entered / into rest / July 4th 1921 / This tablet is placed to his memory by / his fellow parishioners with whom he / worshipped for 30 years.

[Brass] This window is dedicated to / the Glory of God / and in memory of his servant / Canon Harry FOWKE / 1906 – 1997 / Much loved in Langley.

[Brass plate on Table]   In memory of / Sidney and Elizabeth YEANDLE
[Sidney died 12 August 1965 aged 89. Elizabeth died 7 September 1965 aged 88 - N68]

Holy Trinity, Croford

Even smaller than St. Luke's, Langley Marsh (it was reputed to seat only 70), the Croford Iron Mission Church is first mentioned in the 1906 edition of the Bath & Wells Diocesan Kalendar: 'Mission Church erected at Croford Hamlet, cost £80'. While it was under construction, services were held in the old barn at Hillacre Farm, which dates from 1890. As with St. Luke's, the church was constructed of corrugated iron and lined with wood, but it fell into disrepair, and was dismantled in the spring of 1976. The 1932 photograph below shows the Mission Church and main road, with Castle Hill in the background.

Additional Memorials

The only other memorials in the Parish were several Hancock family tablets, which were known to have been moved to the garden of a private residence in the town at the time of the church rebuilding in 1829. They have not survived. The following story is less well authenticated.

Within his chapter on 'Traditions' in *Wifela's Combe*, Prebendary Hancock recounts the sad tale of Tytibye. He had committed suicide and, according to then prevailing custom which was abolished during the reign of George IV (1820-1830), was buried in unconsecrated ground with a stake driven through him. His grave is reputed to be in Jew's Lane at the junction with Greenway Lane just outside Wiveliscombe. Not surprisingly, there is no permanent memorial stone. In the past there were accounts of sightings of the ghost of Tytibye, most of them probably no more than pranks.

169

A Wiveliscombe Epitaph?

In the Somerset Studies Library, Taunton, is the following letter which appeared
with the above heading on 4th July 1942 in *THE SOMERSET COUNTY HERALD*.
No further correspondence appears to have taken place,
and no Pady headstone survives in the churchyard.
Bricks were produced, however, at Slape Moor near Wiveliscombe *[see page 7]*.

'A few days ago there came into my hands a copy of the third
edition "revised and enlarged" of a collection of curious
epitaphs compiled by Horatio Edward Norfolk, published in
1866. He arranged his epitaphs under the headings of the
counties in which they were supposed to have been found, and
I was sorry to see that he gave only three examples under the
heading of Somerset. I noticed, however, that under the
heading of Devon, Mr Norfolk gave the following example from
Wiveliscombe:

"Here lie the remains of James Pady, Brickmaker,
late of the parish, in hopes that his clay may be
remoulded in a workmanlike manner, far superior
to his former perishable materials.
Keep death and Judgement always in your eye,
    Or else the devil off with you will fly,
And in his kiln with brimstone ever fry,
    If you neglect the narrow road to seek,
Christ will reject you, like a half Burnt Brick."

I find it difficult to believe that such an inscription could ever
have appeared on the tombstone of a man at Wiveliscombe, or
anywhere else, although I am, of course, well aware that many
of the epitaphs which appeared to find favour a century or two
ago would be regarded to-day as being in extremely bad taste.
I wonder if any of your Wiveliscombe readers have met with
this epitaph before or can give any further information with
regard to it? – W.G.'

The War Memorials

The War Memorials

In Wiveliscombe the annual November wreath laying ceremony on Remembrance Day takes place at the War Memorial situated between the north and west doors of St. Andrew's Church. The Cornish granite cross with its three-tiered octagonal-shaped base *[see page 65]* commemorates those lost during the 1914-1918 war, the names of these casualties being listed on two plaques near the altar within the church *[T35 and T36]*. Overlooking the War Memorial is a bronze tablet on the church outer wall dedicated to, and listing, the fourteen who gave their lives during the 1939-1945 war *[see page 63]*. All denominations in the parish are included.

It is now possible to research war casualties on publicly available databases, and biographical details of all those on the Wiveliscombe memorials appear on page 179. However, researchers of the many memorials around the country have discovered how few can be regarded as entirely accurate, and Wiveliscombe is no exception. For example, the great losses suffered during the 1914-1919 war resulted in soldiers being transferred to other units, which may not appear on the memorial (likewise unrecorded promotions in rank, or even casualties being omitted altogether).

Minor inconsistencies appear on the church tablets and the Roll of Honour, the large wooden panel in the church, which is one of the town's two additional memorials. In the reproduction of this panel on page 175 the names have been rearranged alphabetically to enable easier study rather than being listed under each regiment. Commemorated are 238 parishioners and their sons 'who **are** serving their country ... in the Great War commenced August 1914'. The 1911 Census gives Wiveliscombe's population as 2,080. Within three years, therefore, over 11% of the total community (figures which included children and the elderly) were listed as 'serving their country', at least fifty-five of whom never returned. The 1921 Census reflected this loss, the population having dropped to 1,970. The wide variety of regiments in which parishioners served appears on page 187.

The impact on Wiveliscombe was considerable and a permanent amenity memorial was established in the town. Originally known as *Broad Meadow,* the land for the Recreation Ground was acquired by the townsfolk from John Tidboald to create a lasting tribute to those who fell. A time capsule is buried under the monument, which is situated on the north side of the 'Rec'. The drinking fountain on the north face is no longer operational, nor is that in the Second World War memorial fountain which was relocated to the east of the obelisk when the road was widened and the stream filled in.

TO
THE GLORIOUS
MEMORY OF THE
MEN OF
WIVELISCOMBE
WHO FELL IN
THE GREAT WAR
1914 – 1918

THIS
WAR MEMORIAL
RECREATION GROUND
OPENED ON 3RD JUNE 1920
WAS PROVIDED BY
PUBLIC SUBSCRIPTION
OF THE INHABITANTS OF
WIVELISCOMBE TO
THE GLORIOUS
MEMORY OF THE
MEN OF
WIVELISCOMBE
WHO FELL IN
THE GREAT WAR
1914-1918

There are two Commonwealth War Graves Commission headstones in St. Andrew's churchyard: Private T Besley who died on 16 February 1917 *[B20]* and Private G Rawle who died on 22 September 1915 *[D127].*

St. Luke's Church, Langley Marsh contains the following memorial:
In memory of the men connected / with Langley, Wiveliscombe who / gave their lives in the World War / 1939-1945: William Stewart Capper, Major, RA; Herbert Jack Hannon, Cpl. RAOC; Ernest Frederick Millett, Marine, RMLI; Richard H Walsh, O/Tel, RNVR.

ROLL
OF HONOUR :
PARISH OF WIVELISCOMBE

The unit titles are quoted as shown on the tablet.
The names of the men have been re-ordered alphabetically.
The numbers indicate the panel on which the name can be found. (lp = lower panel)

****

List of parishioners and parishioners' sons who are serving their
Country in the Army & Navy in the Great War commenced August 1914.

Walter ADAMS, Royal Garrison Art. *3ʳᵈ*
Frederick W ALLEN, R.N. Air Service *4ᵗʰ*
Edward BABB, Army Service Corps *4ᵗʰ*
Bernard BAILEY, 3ʳᵈ Can. O'seas Cont *4ᵗʰ*
William BAILEY, Somerset Yeomanry *2ⁿᵈ*
Albert BAKER, Somerset L.I. *1ˢᵗ*
Frank BAKER, Somerset L.I. *1ˢᵗ*
Frederick BAKER, Army Service Corp. *3ʳᵈ*
Thomas BAKER, R.E. *1ˢᵗlp*
Frank B BALMAN, Transvaal Scottish *3ʳᵈ*
William E BALMAN,
     Queen's Westminster Rifles *3ʳᵈ*
Joseph BANFIELD, Army Vet Corp. *4ᵗʰ*
Clifford BARRINGTON, Som L.I. *1ˢᵗ*
Edgar BARRINGTON, Army Med Corp *4ᵗʰ*
Edward BARRINGTON, SergᵗSom LI *1ˢᵗ*
Frederick BARRINGTON, Som L.I. *3ʳᵈlp*
Sidney BARRINGTON,
     Northumberland Fusiliers *3ʳᵈ*
Denis J BARTON, Major, Oxford L.I *2ⁿᵈ*
Froude BELLEW, H.M.S. New Zealand *1ˢᵗ*
Froude D BELLEW Capt. Som L.I. *1ˢᵗ*
Clifford BERRY, Somerset L.I. *4ᵗʰlp*
Frederick BERRY, Sergᵗ Somerset LI *1ˢᵗ*
Ernest BESLEY, 3ʳᵈ Hussars *3ʳᵈ*

Ernest BESLEY, Army Service Corp. *4ᵗʰ*
Frank BESLEY, Somerset L.I. *1ˢᵗ*
Thomas BESLEY, Somerset L.I. *1ˢᵗ*
Thomas BESLEY, Somerset L.I. *1ˢᵗ*
George H BOND, National Reserve *3ʳᵈ*
Charles B BOUCHER,
     Lieut, York & Lan. Regt. *2ⁿᵈ*
H. B. T. BOUCHER, 2ⁿᵈ Lieut
     Ceylon Planters Rifle Corp *2ⁿᵈlp*
Hilda M BOUCHER,
     Special Service V.A.D. *4ᵗʰ*
T. M. BOXALL, Lieut.
     Army Tank Corp. *3ʳᵈ*
Cyril BROOM, Somerset L.I. *1ˢᵗ*
William H BROOM, National Reserve *3ʳᵈ*
John S BROWN, 1ˢᵗ Can Overseas Cont *4ᵗʰ*
Percy BULL, Army Service Corp. *4ᵗʰ*
Frederick J L BUNT,
     Witwaterrand (sic) Rifles *4ᵗʰ*
George W BUNT, Army Ord. Corp. *4ᵗʰ*
Hedley E BUNT, Royal Marines *4ᵗʰ*
H J BURNETT, Som. L.I. *3ʳᵈlp*
William BURSTON, Som Yeomanry *2ⁿᵈ*
John BURTON, Somerset L.I *4ᵗʰlp*
Henry CHAPMAN, Army Service Corp *3ʳᵈ*

Thomas CHIPLIN, Somerset L.I. *1st*
Thomas CHORLEY, Somerset L.I. *1st*
Robert CHURCHILL, Somerset L.I. *1st*
Alexander CLAPP, West Som. Yeo^mry *4th*
Francis CLUBB, Oxfordshire . Yeo^mry *3rd*
Ernest COLES, Somerset L.I. *1st*
Ernest COLES, Devon Reg^t *4th*
William COLES, Seaforth Highlanders *3rd*
Cecil B COLLINGS, Major
    Dublin Fus. *2nd*
John CONIBEARE, Somerset L.I. *1st*
William CONIBERE, West Som. Yeo. *4th*
Edwin J COOK, Army Service Corp. *4th*
George COOK, Somerset Yeomanry *2nd*
William COOK, Somerset L.I. *1st*
Ernest COX, Somerset L.I. *2nd lp*
William COX, Somerset L.I. *1st*
Sidney CROCKER, Somerset L.I. *1st*
Albert CROSS, Lan.Corp^l,
    Somerset L.I. *1st*
Percy CRUMP, Somerset L.I. *3rd lp*
Arthur J CUMMINGS,
    Royal Flying Corps. *1st lp*
Albert CUMMINS, South Staff Reg^t *4th*
Henry CUMMINS, Somerset L.I. *1st*
Herbert DASCOMBE, Somerset L.I. *1st*
George DAY, Royal Engineers *4th*
John K DINHAM, R.A.M.C. *1st lp*
William DINHAM, R.N. *4th lp*
James DULBOROUGH, Somerset L.I. *1st*
John DULBOROUGH, Somerset L.I. *1st*
Thomas DULBOROUGH, Somerset LI *1st*
John C DUNN, 7th Hussars *3rd*
John DWELLY, Sportsman Battalion *4th*
Ernest EASTMENT, Somerset L.I. *1st*
Sidney EASTMENT, Royal Engineers *4th*
Arthur EDWARDS, Army Service Corp *3rd*
Ernest EDWARDS, Capt, 29th Punjabis *4th*
William F B EDWARDS, Capt,
    24th Punjabis *4th*
Harold G ELLIOTT,
    West Somerset Yeomanry *4th*
Frederick FERRIS, Somerset L.I. *4th*
Alfred C FROST, Wilts Reg^t (T) *2nd lp*
Arthur FURZE, Somerset L.I. *4th lp*

Charles FURZE, Labour Batt. *4th lp*
Edward FURZE, Somerset L.I. *1st*
John FURZE, Somerset Yeomanry *2nd*
John FURZE, Royal North Lancs *3rd lp*
William FURZE, Somerset L.I. *1st*
William FURZE, Somerset Yeomanry *2nd*
William FURZE, R.G.A. *3rd lp*
Robert GALE, Somerset Yeomanry *2nd*
William GAMLIN, Sergt. Somerset LI *4th*
Harold S GARNSEY, Somerset L.I. *1st*
Henry GILBERT, Serg^t
    Somerset L.I. *1st*
Theophilous GILBERT, Somerset L.I. *1st*
Albert E GILES, Royal Flying Corps *1st lp*
James GRAY, Somerset Yeomanry *2nd*
Benjamin GREEDY, Somerset L.I. *1st*
Ernest GREEDY, Somerset L.I. *1st*
Frank GREEDY, Somerset L.I. *1st*
Fred^k. GREEDY, Serj
    Canadian Cont *4th*
William GREEDY, Somerset L.I. *1st*
Ernest GUY, Somerset L.I. *1st*
Reginald GUY, H.M.S. Erin *1st*
F Willoughby HANCOCK R.F.C. *1st*
Ralph E HANCOCK, DSO Lieut,
    Devon Regt. *2nd*
Archibald HARRISON, Somerset L.I. *1st*
Thomas HARRISON, Serg^t
    Somerset L.I. *1st*
Thomas HARRISON, 1st Rifle Brigade *4th lp*
Ronald M D HARVEY , 2nd Lieut.
    N Staffordshire Reg. *2nd*
Allan M HATSWELL,
    Army Service Corp. *4th*
Harry HAWKINS, Dragoon Guards *3rd*
James HAWKINS, 2nd Lieut,
    20th Welsh *1st lp*
William HAWKINS, Bristol Yeo^mry *3rd*
Robert HEMBURROW, Somerset L.I. *4th*
Thomas HEMBURROW,
    Army Service Corp *3rd*
Florence S HILL, V.A.D. *2nd lp*
Frank HILL, Somerset L.I. *1st*
Frank HILL, 14th Gloucesters *4th*
William HILL, M.T. *4th lp*

Wilfred J HOLLEY, 2nd Lieut
9th Kings Shropshire L.I.   *1st lp*

Samuel KELLAND, Somerset L.I.   *4th*

Edwin KELLOW, Army Service Corp.   *3rd*

Thomas KELLOW, H.M.S. Exmouth   *1st*

William KELLOW, Somerst L.I.   *1st*

Sidney KNIGHT, Coldstream Guards   *3rd*

J LANGDON, 23rd London Batt   *4thlp*

Sidney C LANGFORD, R. Engineers   *3rd*

Cyril LEWIS, Army Service Corp.   *3rd*

Fred A LEWIS, R.F.A.   *1stlp*

William LEWIS, Somerset L.I.   *1st*

John LOCK, Devon Yeomanry   *4th*

Clement H LUXTON, Corpl, DCLI   *2nd*

Douglas H G McCRIRICK,
2nd Lieut., Somerset L.I.   *1st*

Alfred T MACGREGOR,
National Reserve   *3rd*

Mary G MAINWARING, Mrs, V.A.D.   *2ndlp*

Thomas MILLETT, National Reserve   *3rd*

Samuel MOGFORD, Somerset L.I.   *2nd*

Sidney MOODY, Somerset Yeomanry   *2nd*

Ernest MULLINS, Somerset L.I.   *2nd*

James E MULLINS, Worcestershire Reg   *3rd*

Thomas MULLINS, Somerset Yeomanry   *2nd*

Arthur NATION, Somerset L.I.   *2nd*

E R NATION, 17th Middlesex   *2ndlp*

Stanley NATION, Royal Horse Art.   *4th*

William NATION, National Reserve   *3rd*

Charles H W NEWNHAM,
Corpl, Army Medical Corp   *4th*

James F W NEWNHAM,
Corpl. Army Medical Corp   *2ndlp*

Jacob NORTH, Royal Navy   *2ndlp*

John H NORTH, Labour Batt.   *4th*

Edward NURCOMBE, Somerset L.I.   *2nd*

Harry OXENHAM, Somerset L.I.   *2nd*

Ernest PARSONS, Sportsman   *2ndlp*

Fred W PARSONS, Royal Marines   *3rdlp*

William J PARSONS, Royal Marines   *1st*

William PENBERTHY,
Dr. Army Medical Corp   *4th*

Ernest PERRY, Somerset L.I.   *2nd*

Ernest C PHILLIPS, Somerset L.I.   *2nd*

Harold PITCHER, 12th Batt.R.Fusiliers   *3rd*

Ernest L PONSFORD
Royal Flying Corps   *1st lp*

Reginald H PONSFORD,
Army Med. Corp.   *4th*

Archibald PROUT, Lance Corpl.,
Somerset L.I.   *2nd*

Charles PROUT, R.E.   *2ndlp*

Frederick PROUT, National Reserve   *3rd*

William PULSFORD, Junr.,
Somerset Yeomanry   *2nd*

George QUICK, Somerset L.I.   *2nd*

Ernest RANKMORE, Somerset L.I.   *2nd*

William H RAWLE, R.G.A.   *4thlp*

Seaburne RAYNER, Lieut., Lancs Fus.   *3rd*

Charles RICHARDS, Somerset L.I.   *2nd*

Clifford C RICHARDS, A.O.C.   *4th*

Frank RICHARDS, R.N.A.   *3rdlp*

Leonard RICHARDS, Somerset L.I.   *3rd*

Sidney RICHARDS, Army Service Corp   *3rd*

John P RISDON, Somerset L.I.   *2nd*

Ilbert G ROSS, Canadian Forces   *4th*

Ernest SALTER, Somerset L.I.   *2nd*

Fred^{k} SALTER, Boy Bugler,
Somerset L.I.   *1st lp*

William SALTER, Somerset L.I.   *2nd*

Ernest SEDGBEER, Somerset L.I.   *2nd*

Alexander V SHIRLEY,
14th Glou. Reg^{t}.   *4th*

William SHIRLEY, Somerset L.I.   *4th*

Henry SHOPLAND, H.M.S. Goliath   *3rd*

James SHOPLAND, Somerset L.I.   *4th*

Sidney SHOPLAND, Somerset L.I.   *2nd*

Walter SHOPLAND, Coldstream Grds   *4th*

William SHOPLAND, Grenadier Grds   *4th*

Frederick G H SIMS, Royal Field Art.   *4th*

George SLOCOMBE , Corpl,
Somerset L.I.   *2nd*

Philip E SLOCOMBE,
Lan. Corpl. National Reserve   *3rd*

Sidney SLOCOMBE, Somerset Yeo^{mry} *2nd*

Harry G SMITH, Corpl,
4th Dragoon Gds.   *3rd*

Tom SMITH,
H.M.S. Torpedo Boat No 99   *3rd*

Dr. W STEWART, Army Medical Corp   *2nd*

Alfred STONE, National Reserve 3rd
Frank STONE, Army Service Corp. 4th
Fred STONE,
        79th Cam. Highlanders. Canada $3^{rd}lp$
George W STONE, R.E. $3^{rd}lp$
Herbert STONE, Somerset L.I. 2nd
John STONE, Somerset L.I. 3rd
Sidney STONE, Somerset L.I. 2nd
William STONE, H.M.S. Brisk 1st
John R SULLY, Somerset L.I. 2nd
Alice THORNE, Special Service, VAD 4th
Arthur E THORNE, Hon Artillery Co. 3rd
Charles THORNE, Somerset Yeo^{mry} 2nd
Frederick J THORNE,
        Dr. Army Medical Corp. 2nd
Harold THORNE, Kent Buffs. 3rd
Kate THORNE, V.A.D. $2^{nd}lp$
Sidney R THORNE, Somerset Yeo^{mry} 2nd
William THORNE, South Africa Horse 4th
Clifford TREBLE,
        Central Force S. Africa 4th
Charles TUCKER, National Reserve 3rd
Henry TURNER, 2nd Dragoon Gds. 3rd
Robert UPHAM, Somerset L.I. $3^{rd}lp$
Sidney UPHAM, Somerset L.I. $4^{th}lp$
Chester VALLANCE, Somerset L.I. $3^{rd}lp$
William VALLANCE, Somerset L.I. 2nd
Amos VICKERY, Army Service Corp. 4th
Wilfred L VICKERY , Lance Corpl
        Seaforth Highlanders 3rd
William VICKERY, Somerset L.I. $4^{th}lp$
Archdale G WALKER ,
        2nd Lieut, N. Staffordshire Reg 3rd
Cecil WAREHAM, Army Service Corp. 4th
Benjamin WARMAN, National Reserve 3rd
Sidney WARREN, Somerset L.I. $3^{rd}lp$
Victor A WARREN, 9th Yorks $4^{th}lp$
William WARREN, Royal Engineers 4th
Frederick WEBBER, Somerset L.I. 2nd
Harold WEBBER, Royal Engineers 4th
Humphrey WEBBER, Somerset L.I. 2nd
Thomas WEBBER, Somerset L.I. 2nd
William J WEBBER, A.S.C. $4^{th}lp$
Frederick WILLIAMS, Somerset L.I. 2nd
Ernest WOODBERRY,
        Somerset Yeo^{mry} 2nd

Basil A WOODD, Capt.,
        National Reserve 3rd
Thomas WOODGATE,
        Somerset L.I. $1^{st}lp$
Herbert J WRIGHT, Somerset L.I. $1^{st}lp$
John YOUNG, *Royal Marines* 1st

Biographical Information

266852 Private Albert James ADAMS,   1st/6th Battalion, Devonshire Regiment
Husband of Annie Adams, of Langley Marsh. Died, cause unknown, Sunday 9th
February 1919. Age 40.   [At time of death, rank recorded as Lance Corporal]
Buried in St John's Cemetery, Bridgwater, Somerset
K/41836 Stoker Frank ARTHUR,   Royal Navy, H.M.S. "Vivid"
Son of William and M Arthur, Quaking House Farm, Milverton, husband of Maria
Elizabeth Arthur, Perry Green, Cheriton Fitzpaine. Died (shore base), cause unknown,
Wed 18th April 1917. Age 25. *Buried in Pennycomequick Cemetery, Plymouth, Devon*
41710 Private Thomas BAKER,   23rd Battalion, Welsh Regiment
Son of Martin L & Mary Baker of Wiveliscombe, husband of Mrs Baker of 4 Vale St.,
Barry, Glamorgan. Died, natural causes, Salonika campaign, Monday 2nd October 1916.
Age 34. [The Parish Memorial lists him as Sapper T Baker, RE.]
Buried in Lahana Military Cemetery, 56 kms NE of Thessalonika, Greece.
**550103 Lance Corporal William Ethelbert BALMAN,   2nd/16th Bn, London Regt
(Queen's Westminster Rifles)**   Born Watchet, Somerset. Son of W A and Jane
Balman, of High Street, Wiveliscombe. Resident in Taunton, and enlisted in London.
Died of wounds, Salonika campaign, Monday 26th March 1917. Age 26.
Buried in Sarigol Military Cemetery, Kriston, Greece
20206 Private Edward Sidney BARWICK,   11th Bn, Royal Warwickshire Regiment
Born Wiveliscombe. Only son of Mr & Mrs Barwick of Sidlescombe, Sussex, formerly
of Wiveliscombe. Enlisted at Coventry, Warwicks. Died of wounds, Battle of Arras,
Sat 14th April 1917. Age 30. *Buried in Etaples Military Cemetery, Pas de Calais, France*
Lieutenant Charles Bailey BOUCHER,   2nd Battalion, York & Lancaster Regiment
Son of Thomas and Elizabeth Boucher, of Greenway, Wiveliscombe. Killed in action,
near Ypres, Monday 9th August 1915, no known grave. Age 24.   *[T62]*
Commemorated on Menin Gate Memorial, Ypres, West-Vlaanderen, Belgium.
T4/071756 Private Percy BULL,   53rd (Gallipoli) Div. Train, Army Service Corps
Son of William Bull, Church Street, Wiveliscombe. Resident Wiveliscombe, enlisted
Leamington. Killed in action, Gallipoli campaign, Thursday 30th December 1915. Age
23.   *Buried in the Lancashire Landing Cemetery, near Sedd el Bahr Village, Turkey*
27255 Pte Harold James BURNETT,   7th Bn, Prince Albert's (Somerset Light Infantry)
Born Wiveliscombe. Son of James and Ellen BURNETT, Oakhampton Cottage, Wivelis-
combe. Resident of Wiveliscombe and enlisted in Taunton. Formerly No. 2017, West
Somerset Yeomanry. Wounded in action in France, died Sunday 31st December 1916.
Age 19.   *Buried in Towcester Road Cemetery, Northampton.*
**R4/140793 Private Jim BURSTON, "B" Sqdn, Remount Depot, (Swaythling)
Army Service Corps**   Born and resident in Milverton. Husband of Elizabeth M Slape
(formerly Burston), The New Inn, Wiveliscombe. Enlisted in Taunton.   Died, cause
unknown, Monday 1st May 1916. Age 42. *Buried in Netley Military Cemetery, Hants.*

240240 Private Robert CHURCHILL, 1st/5th Bn, Somerset Light Infantry
Born and resident in Wiveliscombe. Son of Walter and Eliza Churchill, Golden Hill,
Wiveliscombe. Enlisted in Wellington. Died, cause unknown, Palestine campaign,
Sunday 9th December 1917. Age 27. [At time of death, rank recorded as Lance
Corporal]   *Buried in Alexandria (Hadra) War Memorial Cemetery, Egypt*

32915 Private Charles Herbert COLLARD, 2nd Battalion, Hampshire Regiment
Born Wiveliscombe. Resident and enlisted in Bristol. Youngest son of Mrs Collard and
the late W. Collard of Town Mills, Wiveliscombe. Formerly No. 33878, Worcestershire
Regiment. Killed in action, Third Battle of Ypres, Wednesday 10th October 1917, no
known grave.
Commemorated on the Tyne Cot Memorial, Zonnebeke, Belgium

2nd Lieutenant Ernest COX, 3rd Bn, (attached 7th Bn), Somerset Light Infantry
Son of Florence Mary and the late William L Cox of The Alps, Wiveliscombe.
Formerly Army Service Corps. Died of wounds (in German field hospital), Saturday
8th December 1917. Age 21.
Buried in Quievy Communal Cemetery Extension, Nord, France. [E126]

21700 Private Lionel Percy CRUMP, 8th Battalion, Somerset Light Infantry
Born Wimbledon, Surrey. Resident at Wiveliscombe, and enlisted at Wellington. Son of
Percy Osborne and Mary Elizabeth Crump, 39 Alwyne Rd, Wimbledon. Died of wounds
received 18th/19th November, Saturday 9th December 1916. Age 23.
Buried in Etaples Military Cemetery, Pas de Calais, France

206886 Private John King DINHAM, 11th Battalion, Welsh Regiment
Born and resident in Wiveliscombe. Eldest son of John and Fanny Dinham, Northgate,
Wiveliscombe. Enlisted Swansea. Formerly Royal Army Medical Corps. Killed in
action, Salonika campaign, Wednesday 18th September 1918. Age 24.
Buried in the Doiran Military Cemetery, in the north of Greece

Captain William Francis Boucher EDWARDS, 24th Punjabis, Indian Army
Born 11 Mar 1880. Son of Mr F L Edwards, of Channel View, Burnham, Somerset.
Husband of Elsie Mabel (nee Greenway). 2nd Lieut, Bedfordshire Regt. 11th February
1899. Killed in action at Shaiba, Persian Gulf, Mesopotamia campaign, Wednesday
14th April 1915. Age 35. *Buried in Basra War Cemetery, Iraq*

27954 Private John FURZE, 8th Battalion, The Loyal North Lancashire Regiment
Born Wiveliscombe. Son of James Furze of Golden Hill, Wiveliscombe. Husband of Mrs
Furze of Ford Street, Wellington. Enlisted Taunton. Formerly No. T4/263677, Army
Service Corps. Killed in action, Sunday 5th August 1917, no known grave. Age 38.
Commemorated on the Menin Gate Memorial, Ypres, West-Vlaanderen, Belgium

982   Private William FURZE, 1st/1st West Somerset Yeomanry
Son of James Furze of Golden Hill, Wiveliscombe. Enlisted Taunton. Died from natural
causes, Alexandria Hospital, Cairo, Friday 5th November 1915. Age 30.
Buried in Alexandria (Chatby) Military Cemetery, Egypt.

3/7527 Coy Sergt Major William Henry GAMLIN, 6th Bn, Somerset Light Infantry
Born Wiveliscombe. Son of William & Elizabeth Gamlin of Golden Hill, Wiveliscombe, husband of Ellen Gamlin, of 55 Churchill Road, Brislington, Bristol. Served
in South Africa Campaign 1899-1902. Long Service & Good Conduct Medal. Re-
enlisted Taunton. Died of wounds, Monday 9th August 1915. Age 44.
Buried Boulogne Eastern Cemetery, France [A56]

466054 Pte Fred GREEDY, 72nd Bn, Canadian Infantry (British Columbia Regt)

Son of John and Jane Greedy, Taunton Road, Wiveliscombe. Went to Canada July 1913, and enlisted there. Died of wounds, Tuesday 14th November 1916. Age 24. Brother of Private W J Greedy. *Buried in Contay British Cemetery, Contay, Somme, France*

241282 Private William John GREEDY, 1st /5th Bn, Somerset Light Infantry

Born and resident in Wiveliscombe. Son of Mrs Sarah Jane Greedy and the late John Greedy, of Ford Road, Wiveliscombe. Enlisted in Taunton. Killed in action, Palestine campaign, Wednesday 10th April 1918. Age 26. Brother of Pte Fred Greedy. [At time of death, rank recorded as Lance Corporal]. *Buried in Ramleh War Cemetery, Israel.*

WR/256735 Sapper Walter John GREEDY, Royal Engineers

Son of Theophilus and Mary Greedy of Wiveliscombe, husband of J Greedy of Exbridge. Died in hospital, Exeter, natural causes, Sunday 22nd December 1918. Age 29. *Buried St. Nicholas Churchyard Extension, Brushford, Somerset. [CWGC headstone]*

20371 Private Ernest GUY,   2nd Battalion, Duke of Cornwall's Light Infantry

Born Wiveliscombe. Youngest son of Amelia and the late John Guy of Russell's Cottage, Wiveliscombe. Enlisted in Taunton. Formerly No. 6270, Somerset Light Infantry. Died of wounds, Salonika campaign, Saturday 9th December 1916. Age 24.
Buried in Mikra Cemetery, Kalamaria, Greece

The 1st/5th Somerset Light Infantry (Territorial Force) served in India from November 1914 to April 1917. Twenty-five of its soldiers hailed from Wiveliscombe. Known as the "Wivy Boys", they pose here at Dagshai, in the Simla Hills, India. [Photo: Richard Cornish and private collection]

Lieutenant Ralph Escott HANCOCK, DSO, 1st Battalion, Devonshire Regiment

Son of Frank E and Mariquita Hancock, of Ford House, Wiveliscombe, husband of Mary Hamilton Hancock. Killed in action, Battle of Festubert, Thursday 29th October 1914, no known grave. Age 26. *[See page 13 for memorial window, and T27]*
Commemorated on Le Touret Memorial, Pas de Calais, France

9596   Lance Corpl Archibald HARRISON, 1st Battalion, Somerset Light Infantry
Born and resident in Wiveliscombe. Son of Thomas and Ellen Jane Harrison, Queen's
Terrace, Wiveliscombe. Enlisted in Taunton. Formerly No. 38569, Royal Garrison
Artillery. Killed in action, Tuesday 6th July 1915. Age 24. *[E119]*
Buried in Talana Farm Cemetery, Ypres, West-Vlaanderen, Belgium

2nd Lieut Ronald Marmaduke Dawnay HARVEY, 4th Bn, North Staffordshire Regt
[Att. 1st Bn, Bedfordshire Regt] Son of the late Revd. Frederick Mortimer Harvey,
Rector of Bolnhurst, Beds, and his late wife Katherine Dorothea Harvey. Nephew of Mrs
Gertrude Mary Mainwaring of The Cottage, Wiveliscombe. Killed in action at Hill 60,
near Ypres, Tuesday 20th April 1915. Age 27. *[T50]*
Buried in Sanctuary Wood Cemetery, Ypres, Belgium.

145339 Sapper Frank Philip HOWELL, 102nd Field Company, Royal Engineers
Son of Mr Howell, Church St, Wiveliscombe. Resident Wiveliscombe. Enlisted Taunton.
Died of wounds, Saturday 13th October 1917, no known grave.
Commemorated on the Tyne Cot Memorial, Zonnebeke, Belgium

1081351 Private Walter James HYETT, 2nd Battalion, Canadian Railway Troops
Husband of Eva Agnes Hyett, formerly of Church St.,Wiveliscombe. Enlisted Canada.
Killed in action by a shell, Thursday 8th November 1917. Age 37.
[At time of death, rank recorded as Corporal]
Buried in Nine Elms British Cemetery, Poperinge, Belgium

16577 Private Samuel KELLAND,   6th Battalion, Somerset Light Infantry
Born and resident at Wiveliscombe.   Son of John and Maria Kelland. Killed in action,
Wednesday 22nd August 1917. Age 39. [At time of death, rank recorded as Lance
Corporal] *Buried in Tyne Cot Cemetery, Zonnebeke, West-Vlaanderen, Belgium*

72396 Private Geoffrey Walter KELLOW, 1st/6th Battalion, Cheshire Regt
Born and resident in Wiveliscombe.   Youngest son of Walter and Annie Kellow, Golden
Hill, Wiveliscombe. Enlisted in Wellington. Formerly No: 2745, West Somerset
Yeomanry. Killed in action, Thursday 22nd August 1918, no known grave. Age 19.
Commemorated on the Tyne Cot Memorial, Zonnebeke, Belgium

234247 1st Class Petty Officer Thomas KELLOW, R.N., H.M.S. "Exmouth"
Born Wiveliscombe. Son of Walter and Annie Kellow, Golden Hill, Wiveliscombe.
Accidentally drowned, Tuesday 16th February 1915. Age 26.
Commemorated on the Naval Memorial, Plymouth, Devon

31315 Private William Edward KING, 1st Battalion, Devonshire Regiment
Born at Bridgwater, and resident at Wiveliscombe. Second son of William Robert and
Emma Jane King, of Tor Cottage, Wiveliscombe. Enlisted in Taunton. Killed in action,
Third Battle of Ypres, Tuesday 30th October 1917. Age 19.
Commemorated on the Tyne Cot Memorial, Zonnebeke, Belgium

20788 Private William KING, 8th Battalion, Somerset Light Infantry
Born Langley Marsh, Somerset. Resident Wiveliscombe. Enlisted Taunton. Killed in
action, the first day of the Battle of the Somme, Saturday 1st July 1916, no known grave.
Commemorated on the Thiepval Memorial, Somme, France

9396   Private Sidney James KNIGHT, 2nd Battalion, Coldstream Guards
Born and resident in Bishops Lydeard. Enlisted in Taunton. Died of wounds,
Monday 1st January 1917.
Buried in St Sever Cemetery Extension, Rouen, Seine-Maritime, France

700783 Private Ernest LEWIS, 23rd (County of London) Bn, London Regiment
Born in Wiveliscombe. Resident in Peckham. Enlisted at Clapham Junction. Killed in action, Thursday 15th March 1917. *Buried in Chester Farm Cemetery, Ypres, Belgium*

15336 Private Edwin James MULLINS, 2nd/8th Bn, Worcestershire Regiment
Born Wiveliscombe. Son of James and Eva Mullins of Wiveliscombe. Resident in Leavesden, Herts. Enlisted at St Pancras, London. Killed in action, Thursday 21st March 1918, no known grave. Age 29.
Commemorated on the Pozieres Memorial, Somme, France

F/1558 Private Edwin Richard NATION, 2nd Battalion, Middlesex Regt
Born Somerset. Eldest son of William and Elizabeth Nation, Style Road, Wiveliscombe. Enlisted Fulham. Killed in action, Tuesday 31st July 1917, no known grave. Age 25.
Commemorated on the Menin Gate Memorial, Ypres, West-Vlaanderen, Belgium

2nd Lieut Alfred Ernest PARSONS, 4th Bn, Royal Fusiliers (City of London Regt)
Son of Octavia L Parsons, of Wiveliscombe and the late Alfred E Parsons. Killed in action Thursday 3rd May, 1917, no known grave. Age 22.
Commemorated on the Arras Memorial, Pas de Calais, France

PLY/1478 L/Corpl Frederick William PARSONS, Royal Marine Light Infantry, 2nd RM Bn, RN Division Born Newton Abbot, Devon. Son of William J and Annie Parsons, husband of Annie Parsons, of Langley Cross. Died of wounds (in German field hospital), Tuesday 9th April 1918. Age 28.
Buried Denain Communal Cemetery, Nord, France [E86]

7478 Private Charles RICHARDS, 6th Battalion, Somerset Light Infantry
Born and enlisted in Taunton, Somerset. Killed in action, Saturday 25th September 1915, no known grave.
Commemorated on Panel 21 on the Menin Gate Memorial, Ypres, Belgium

210960 Flt Sgt Frank RICHARDS, No 1 Aeroplane Supply Depot, Royal Air Force
Son of Annie & the late Charles Richards, of Wiveliscombe. Died, cause unknown, Thursday 24th July 1919. Age 32.
Buried in Terlincthun British Cemetery, Wimille, Pas de Calais, France

42458 Private Sydney Alfred RICHARDS, 2nd/8th Battalion, Manchester Regiment
Born Wiveliscombe. Enlisted at Tredegar, Monmouthshire. Formerly No. 147088, Royal Army Service Corps. Killed in action, Monday 8th October 1917, no known grave.
Commemorated on the Tyne Cot Memorial, Zonnebeke, Belgium

PLY/13492 Pte Henry SHOPLAND, Royal Marine Light Infantry, H.M.S."Goliath"
Son of James and Emily Shopland, Golden Hill, Wiveliscombe. Killed in action, off Gallipoli, Thursday 13th May 1915, no known grave. Age 26.
Commemorated on the Naval Memorial, Plymouth, Devon

201546 Gunner Harold Frederick STEVENS, Royal Field Artillery
Enlisted Wiveliscombe. Resident Honicknowle, Devon. Son of Joshua & Elizabeth Ann Stevens, of Holly Park, Tamerton Foliot, Devon. Nephew of William and James Dunn of Jews Farm, Wiveliscombe. Died of wounds, 24th October 1917. Age 20.
Buried in Etaples Military Cemetery, Pas de Calais, France

16247 Private Jack STONE, 6th Battalion, Somerset Light Infantry
Born Chipstable, Somerset. Enlisted at Wiveliscombe. Son of Mrs M A Stone, High Street, Wiveliscombe. Killed in action, Thursday 23rd August 1917, no known grave. Age 44. *Commemorated on the Tyne Cot Memorial, Zonnebeke, Belgium*

R4/139898 Private Walter STRICKLAND, Royal Army Service Corps
Born Pitminster, Somerset. Resident and enlisted at Wiveliscombe. Died in England, cause unknown, Wednesday 28th February 1917. Age 27.
Buried All Saints Churchyard, Norton Fitzwarren, Somerset [CWGC headstone]

26071 Private Albert John TROAKE, 10th Battalion, Devonshire Regiment
Born Hockworthy, Devon. Son of John & Mary Troake, husband of Elizabeth Troake of Russells, Wiveliscombe. Killed in action, Salonika campaign, Wed 25th April 1917, no known grave. Age 35. *Commemorated on the Doiran Memorial, North Greece.*

24881 Private Walter George TUCKER, 2nd Battalion, Devonshire Regiment
Born Harberton, Devon. Resident at Starcross, Devon, enlisted Exeter. Son of William George & Charlotte Tucker, 1 Mayfield Terrace, Wiveliscombe. Killed in action, Sunday 26th May 1918, no known grave. Age 20.   [At time of death, rank recorded as Acting Corporal]   *Commemorated on the Soissons Memorial, Aisne, France*

25460 Private Frank Chester VALLANCE,   7th Battalion, Somerset Light Infantry
Born and resident Wiveliscombe. Son of Mr & Mrs Vallance of West Road, Wiveliscombe. Enlisted Wellington. Died of wounds, Battle of the Somme, Tuesday 3rd October 1916. Age 19.   *Buried in Grove Town Cemetery, Meaulte, Somme, France*

240875 Private William Robert VALLANCE, 1st /5th Bn, Somerset Light Infantry
Born and enlisted Wiveliscombe. Son of William Edward and Annie Jane Vallance, West Road, Wiveliscombe. Killed in action, Palestine campaign, Friday 23rd November 1917, no known grave. Age 22. *Commemorated on Panel 17 of the Jerusalem Memorial, Israel*

R/357030 Private Amos VICKERY, Royal Army Service Corps
Born Bishops Lydeard. Enlisted Taunton. Husband of Alice Maud Vickery, Pond Cottage, Fitzhead. Died Bristol Hospital, after an accident, Wednesday 29th August 1917. Age 31. *Buried St Mary's Churchyard, Bishops Lydeard, Somerset [CWGC headstone]*

1009   Lance Corporal Wilfred Llewellyn VICKERY, 1st Bn, Seaforth Highlanders
Born Wiveliscombe. Son of John and Lucy Vickery of Wiveliscombe. Enlisted Taunton. Died of wounds, Monday 21st December 1914. Age 27 (One of 'the Old Contemptibles')
Buried in Lillers Communal Cemetery, Pas de Calais, France

2nd Lieut Archdale Gillam WALKER, 4th Battalion, North Staffordshire Regiment [Att. 2nd Bn Royal Scots Fusiliers]   Son of the late Henry John Cureton and Catherine Jane Walker of Woking. Killed in action near Festubert, Monday 17th May 1915. Age 26.   *Commemorated on Panel 35, Le Touret Memorial, Pas de Calais, France [T50]*

42526 Private Albert Victor WARREN, D Coy, 9th Battalion, Yorkshire Regiment
Born Cardiff. Second son of James and Emily Warren, The Anchor Inn, Church Street, Wiveliscombe. Resident in Wiveliscombe. Enlisted at Hilsea. Killed in action, Third Battle of Ypres, Thursday 7th June 1917, no known grave. Age 20.
Commemorated on Panel 33 of the Menin Gate Memorial, Ypres, Belgium

31978 Private Edgar WEBBER, 1st Battalion, Somerset Light Infantry
Born and resident Wiveliscombe. Second son of Charles Hayes and Mary Ann Webber, East Weare, West Road, Wiveliscombe. Killed in action, Monday 15th April 1918, no known grave. *Commemorated on the Ploegsteert Memorial, Comines-Warneton, Belgium*

20410 Private William John WEBBER, 6th Battalion, Somerset Light Infantry
Born and resident in Wiveliscombe. Son of William and Charlotte Webber, of Croford, Wiveliscombe. Enlisted Taunton. Killed in action, 22nd August 1917, no known grave. Age 21.   *Commemorated on the Tyne Cot Memorial, Zonnebeke, Belgium*

THE WAR OF 1939 - 1945

63502 Major William Stewart CAPPER, Royal Artillery
Born in India. The son of Alfred Stewart and Nora Janet Capper, of Langley House, Wiveliscombe. Died and buried at sea off Tobruk, Wed 3rd November 1943. Age 29.
Commemorated on Panel 2/Column 1 of the Brookwood Memorial, Surrey. [T34]

T/14273518 Driver Philip Charles GREEDY, Royal Army Service Corps
Son of William John and Florence Jane Greedy, husband of Helen Mary Greedy, of Croford, Wiveliscombe. Killed in action, Normandy, Wednesday 19th July 1944. Age 37.
Buried in the Ranville War Cemetery, Normandy.

14579943 Corpl Herbert John HANNON, 17 Vehicle Company, Royal Army Ordnance Corps Born Langley, Wiveliscombe. Son of W T and Evelyn Thorne of Wiveliscombe. Killed in action, Normandy, Thursday 3rd August 1944. Age 20.
Buried in the Bayeux War Cemetery, Normandy.

5675576 Pte Maurice Charles Clifford HAWKINS, 7th Bn, Somerset Light Infantry
Son of Thomas and Elizabeth Hawkins, husband of Dorothy May Hawkins of Wiveliscombe. Died in England, cause unknown, Thursday 30th October 1941. Age 24.
Buried privately in St. Andrew's Churchyard, Wiveliscombe [F152]

PLY/X 698 Marine Dudley John HEMBURROW, Royal Marines, H.M.S. "Glorious"
Born Wiveliscombe. Son of Thomas and Florence Amy Hemburrow, husband of Doris Jacobs Lenman Hemburrow, of Plymouth. Killed in action, North Sea, Sunday 9th June 1940. Age 27.
Commemorated on Panel 43/Column 2 of the Naval Memorial, Plymouth, Devon

Paymaster Sub Lieut Joseph Anthony HEWLETT, Royal Naval Volunteer Reserve, H.M.S. "Vernon" Son of Beatrice Hewlett, of Wiveliscombe. Killed in an air raid while on duty (Portsmouth 'blitz'), Tuesday 11th March 1941. Age 24.
Buried privately in St. Andrew's Churchyard, Wiveliscombe [F138]

14396098 Pte Wilfred John Dennis LEWIS, 1st Battalion, Somerset Light Infantry
Born Wiveliscombe. Killed in action, North Arakan, Burma, Thurs 27th January 1944, no known grave. Age 31. *Commemorated Face 7, the Rangoon Memorial, Myanmar [F173]*

170457 Flying Officer Victor Francis Dobell MEADE, Royal Air Force Volunteer Reserve, Air Bomber, 630 Sqdn. Son of Francis and Edith Meade, husband of Margaret Joan Meade, of Wiveliscombe. Killed in an aircraft accident, Thursday 17th May, 1945. Age 23. *Buried privately in St Andrew's Churchyard, Wiveliscombe [F151]*

PO/X 103643 Marine Ernest Frederick MILLETT, Royal Marines
Born Langley, Wiveliscombe. Son of Thomas and Elizabeth Millett. Husband of Ethel Millett, of Oake, Somerset. Died ashore (natural causes), Thursday 2nd September 1943. Age 31. *Buried in Syracuse War Cemetery, Sicily.*

D/J 58600 Able Seaman William Arthur PROLL, Royal Navy, H.M.S. "Diamond"
Son of Margaret Proll of Stogumber, Somerset. Killed in action, off Greece, Sunday 27th April 1941. Age 41. *Commemorated on the Naval Memorial, Plymouth, Devon*

1646008 Gunner Ernest John STONE, 239 Battery, 77 H.A.A. Regiment, R. A.
Born Somerset. Son of James and Edith Stone, husband of Lilian Agnes Stone, of Wiveliscombe. Died in Japanese captivity, Monday 29th November 1943, no known grave. Age 29. *Commemorated on Column 31 of the Singapore Memorial, Singapore*

930352 Flight Sergeant Hilgrove Pridgin TEALE, R.A.F. Volunteer Reserve, 233 Squadron Born Derbyshire. Son of Revd. Kenneth W Pridgin and Laura Mary Teale, of Cullompton. *[see page 39]* Lost in action, off Gibraltar, Sun 8th Nov 1942, no known grave. Age 29. *Commemorated on Panel 4/Column 2 of the Malta Memorial, Malta*

D/JX 262898 Ord/Telegraphist Richard Hector WALSH, R.N., H.M.S. "Mourne" Son of Richard and Florence Alberta Walsh, husband of Mary Cecilia Walsh of Langley, Somerset. Killed in action, off the Lizard, Thursday 15th June 1944, no known grave. Age 37. *Commemorated on Panel 89/Column 1 of the Naval Memorial, Plymouth, Devon*

62289 Flying Officer Robert WHELDON, Royal Air Force Volunteer Reserve, 501 Squadron History Degree, Hons. (Balliol College, Oxford). Son of John David and Margaret Louise Wheldon of Wiveliscombe. Born 4th May 1916. Killed in action, over Northern France, Saturday 25th April 1942, no known grave. Age 25. *Commemorated on Panel 68 of the Runnymede Memorial, Surrey*

BORN OR RESIDENT IN WIVELISCOMBE, BUT NOT COMMEMORATED ON PARISH WAR MEMORIALS

17415   Pte John Uppington BETTY, Duke of Cornwall's Lt. Inf. Killed in action 10 June 1915

32227   Pte Charles William BLACKMORE, Somerset Light Infantry. Died 27 October 1917

27155   Pte William Thomas BRANFIELD, Somerset Lt. Inf. Killed in action 30 Nov 1917

295169   Pte William BROADRIBB, Somerset Light Infantry. Killed in action 27 Dec 1917

15526   Pte Robert BURSTON, Somerset Light Infantry. Died 14 March 1916

-   Norman V CHAMBERLAIN. Lost at sea, HMS Repulse, 10 December 1941. *[F181]*

29764   Pte George CHILCOTT, Wiltshire Regiment. Killed in action 13 September 1918

T/437281 Dvr Henry GIBBS, Royal Army Service Corps. Died 1 September 1918

32185   Pte Robert Gooding HENSON, Somerset Light Infantry. Died of wounds 22 Apr 1917

3/8539   Pte William HODGE, Dorset Regt. Killed in action 5 May 1915. *[E90]*

S/37638 Pte Sydney JEWEL, Royal Army Service Corps. Died 13 January 1917

273339 Gunner William Charles MEAD, Royal Field Artillery. Died 12 October 1918

4839   Pte Samuel PENGILLEY, Somerset Light Infantry. Died in India 4 June 1918.

14497   Pte Arthur PERROTT, Devonshire Regt. Killed in action 25 September 1915

260482 Pte William John PRING, Gloucestershire Regt. Died of wounds 14 April 1918

7845   Pte Gilbert ROCKETT, Somerset Light Infantry. Died of wounds 12 May 1915

201437   Pte George SYMONS, Somerset Light Infantry. Died 23 June 1918.

22503   Pte James TARR, Somerset Light Infantry. Killed in action 24 August 1916

10061 Pte William VICKERY, MM, Somerset L.I. Died of wounds 28 September 1917

Private Samuel PENGILLEY's headstone photographed by the author in Peshawar, NWFP, Pakistan - May AD. 2000.

186

UNITS IN WHICH THE MEN AND WOMEN OF WIVELISCOMBE SERVED DURING THE 1914-1918 WAR

(Taken from the Roll of Honour, but listed here with their official titles)

NAVAL FORCES
HMS Brisk, HMS Erin, HMS Exmouth,
HMS Goliath, HMS New Zealand,
H.M. Torpedo Boat No. 99.
Royal Marine Light Infantry
Royal Naval Air Service

MILITARY FORCES
2nd Dragoon Guards (Queen's Bays)
3rd (King's Own) Hussars
4th (Royal Irish) Dragoon Guards
7th (Queen's Own) Hussars
Army Ordnance Corps
 Army Service Corps
Army Veterinary Corps
Bristol Yeomanry *[as listed]*
Coldstream Guards
Corps of Royal Engineers
Devonshire Regiment
Devon Yeomanry *[as listed]*
Duke of Cornwall's Light Infantry
The Buffs (East Kent) Regiment
Gloucestershire Regiment
Grenadier Guards
Honourable Artillery Company
King's Shropshire Light Infantry
Labour Corps
Lancashire Fusiliers
Loyal North Lancashire Regiment
Middlesex Regiment (Duke of
        Cambridge's Own)
National Reserve *[as listed]*
N. Staffordshire Regt (Prince of Wales's)
Northumberland Fusiliers
Oxfordshire and Buckinghamshire
        Light Infantry
Oxfordshire Yeomanry (Queens'
        Own Oxfordshire Hussars)

Princess of Wales's Own Yorkshire Regt
Queen's Westminster Rifles
        (London Regt)
Rifle Brigade
        (The Prince Consort's Own)
Royal Army Medical Corps
Royal Dublin Fusiliers
Royal Field Artillery
Royal Fusiliers (City of London Regt)
Royal Garrison Artillery
Royal Horse Artillery
Seaforth Highlanders (Ross-shire Buffs,
        The Duke of Albany's)
Somerset Light Infantry
        (Prince Albert's)
South Staffordshire Regiment
Tank Corps
Voluntary Aid Detachment
Welsh Regiment
West Somerset (Hussars) Yeomanry
Wiltshire Regiment (The Duke
        of Edinburgh's)
Worcestershire Regiment
York and Lancaster Regiment

AIR FORCE
Royal Flying Corps

OVERSEAS FORCES
24th Punjabis, Indian Army
29th Punjabis, Indian Army
79th Cameron Highlanders of Canada
British Columbia Regiment
Canadian Railway Troops
Ceylon Planters Rifle Corps
Transvaal Scottish Regiment
Witwatersrand Rifles

Annexes and Indexes

Annexes and Indexes

Memorials are a valuable source of information for local research. To illustrate this, various lists have been drawn up from the headstones in the St. Andrew's churchyard. All could be the subject of further study, but the following annexes highlight some of the material available:

♦♦SYMBOLS OF REMEMBRANCE ♦♦BURIALS BY AGE
♦♦ BURIALS BY MONTH ♦♦ENGRAVERS/STONE MASONS
♦♦ LOCATIONS ♦♦OCCUPATIONS

Many biblical epitaphs, poems and extracts from hymns can also be found within the inscription lists.

Annex A: *SYMBOLS OF REMEMBRANCE*

In addition to the factual information about the deceased, headstones sometimes include symbols of remembrance. Though less popular nowadays, these symbols were once subject to fashion, and pattern books were kept by the stonemasons to help with selection. One of the most common are the letters: **I.H.S.** Sometimes erroneously believed to mean 'In His Service', this symbol in fact represents the first three letters of the name Jesus (= Saviour of Mankind) in Greek - *IHΣΥΣ*. It also happens to be the most prevalent image in the Wiveliscombe churchyard. Drawings of other motifs appear as illustrations throughout the text. A brief description of some of the more common examples follow:

> *DOVE :* The Holy Ghost. The Dove with a sprig of olive is the dove of the Ark, and indicates good tidings and peace.
> *FLOWERS:* Several flowers were used and were very popular. The lily and lily of the valley indicate the purified soul. A rose signifies the Virgin Mary. A rose without thorns depicts perfection/without faults.
> *GRAPES / VINE:* These two symbols were interchangeable. The vine becomes wine, which symbolises man's spiritual transformation.
> *HANDSHAKE:* A sharing/joint partnership: a temporary separation between man and wife.
> *'MIZPAH':* Hebrew – 'May the Lord watch between me and thee when we are absent from one another' *[Gen. 31. 48-50]*.

Many of the motifs found in the large 19th Century cemeteries are absent from the St. Andrew's churchyard where there are no mausolea or elaborate memorials. These include, for example, the *upturned torch* (love is dead), *skull and crossbones* (death and the transitory nature of life on earth), or *draped urns* (token of respect in the presence of Christ), amongst many others.

191

Annex B: *SUMMARY OF BURIALS BY AGE GROUP*

*Wiveliscombe 'lies in a valley, almost at the foot of some lofty hills, and is
itself raised on an eminence, which adds much to its salubrity and cleanli-
ness; indeed, its inhabitants are noted for their longevity.'*
General Directory for the County of Somerset Wm. Bragg (1840)

As the current churchyard dates from 1829, the above quotation from 1840 refers to only
eleven years of the period of the burials covered in the following chart (1829-2000). It
appears, however, that the 'salubrity' continued, as longevity is still graphically evident.
As already noted, the presence of the Infirmary may be relevant. *[see page 68]*

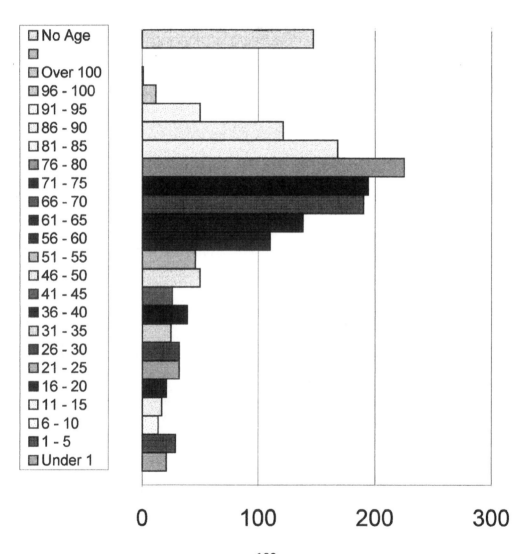

Annex C: *SUMMARY OF BURIALS BY MONTH*

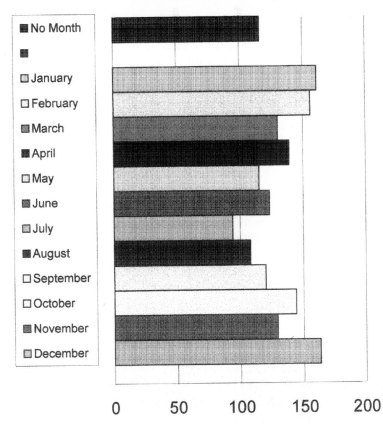

Legend:
- No Month
- ■
- January
- February
- March
- April
- May
- June
- July
- August
- September
- October
- November
- December

(x-axis: 0, 50, 100, 150, 200)

Annex D: *ENGRAVERS AND STONEMASONS*

The undertaker was an important member of the local community, usually known to all and well respected. Often, as with Wiveliscombe, the business was run by a local family, who passed it on from father to son. They worked closely with the stonemasons, who supplied and/or engraved the headstones and were responsible for moving memorials and kerbs when additional interments were to take place. Their names can sometimes be found engraved or embossed upon the reverse face of the headstone. Where recorded during the survey, the names have been added in *[italic script]*.

Carpenter, 55 St Mary Street,
                 Bridgwater
Collard, Taunton
Fine Memorials
Glenhaven Funeral Services
[G.F.S.]
Hart, Son, Peard & Co., London
Manning & Son, Taunton
Manning & Knight

Morgan, Taunton
F. Osborne & Co. Ltd, London
Phippard
Pollard, Taunton
S. Richards
R. Shout, London
A. Smith
Stooks, 48 Station Road, Taunton
Thatcher

Annex E: *LOCATIONS*

Farms or houses in the local area are mentioned in some of the inscriptions. These are listed alphabetically below, together with the name of the family concerned (and section / plot number). Other locations further afield follow.

WEST SOMERSET

Abbotsfield	N157	Cardno	Grants Farm	F48	Martin
Billey Farm	A2	Payne		N199	Martin
	A3	Brice		E33	Takle
	A5	Howe	Greenway	D91	Boucher
Bournes House	C33	Edwards	Hartswell	C14	Back
Castle	A42	Walker		D166	Lutley
Challick Farm	E97	Windsor		C44-5	Wood
Chorleys Farm,	N173	Heywood	Huish Champflower	D214	Turner
Whitefield			Jews Farm	A13	Thorne
Clatworthy	D129	Bailey		A14	Thorne
	D134	Cock		E48	Dunn
Clerkspool	A40	North	Jews House	C1-4	Boucher
	E84	Merchant	Kingsmead	C29	Pulsford
Cotcombe	C35	Stevens	Lambrook	C4	Boucher
Court House	E65	Hancock		D37	Boucher
Croford	F53	Bennett		D85	Coombs
	D167	Edbrooke		D55	Snape
	D40	Stone	Langley	D18	Arscott
	D42	Wyatt		D20	Arscott
Crowcombe	D41	Robbins		D33	Arscott
Culverhay	E76	Tidboald		D34	Arscott
	N282	Tidboald		D107	North
Culverhead	C46a	Taylor		E7	Stone
Fleed	A7-8	Hill	Langley Marsh	A12	Westcott
Ford	D35	Arscott		E18	Kellow
	A49	Boucher	Lion Hotel	D109	Hawkins
	E42	Jones	Manor	E68	Williams
	E30	Tyler	Manor Farm	C51	Dyer
Ford, Higher	F80	Thomas		D86	Lutley
Fries Farm (Frys)	B14-15	Lutley	Manor House	E67	Williams
	E62	Saunders	Minehead	E101	Balman

194

Oakhampton House	E51	Dyke
Oakhampton Manor	D82	Bellew
	D81	Norton
Old Cleeve	D170	Edbrooke
Perry's Farm	F172	Clapp
Pitt Farm	E32	Addicott
Prospect House	C2-3	Boucher
	D10	Poole
Pyncombe	D159	Bennett
Quaking House	E155	Arthur
Rodhuish	A27	Boucher
Sharpe House	B7	Chorley
	D30	Hancock
	D30	Haydon
	D29	Lutley
Storey's Close	E28	Risdon
Taunton	D93	Chorley
Tiverton	D30	Haydon
Upingtons	D185	Treliving
Vicarage	C40	Llewellin
Wellington	D170	Edbrooke
Whitefield	A15	Clapp
	A50	Tyler
	B2	Lyddon
	D24	North
	D191	Pugsley
	F12	Heywood
	W34	Persse
Withycombe	D156	Hill

OTHER LOCATIONS

Alford, Cheshire	D55	Edwards
Auckland	D160	Burton
Australia	C42	Nurcombe
	D174	Middleton
Bath	D6	Tuckfield
Bolnhurst, Beds	C47	Harvey
Boulogne, France	A56	Gamlin
Brazil	E54	Hancock

Burma	F173	Lewis
Burton-on-Trent	N167	Clay
Cardiff	D214	Turner
Clayhanger	F13	Heywood
Clifton, Bristol	D188	Lean
Coly River	D206	Bellew
Damerham, Wilts	D85	Coombs
Exeter	D170	Edbrooke
Fulham Cemetery	E18	Kellow
Great Holland, Essex	C46	Jefferys-Taylor
Harrow	N141	Adams
Haslebury Plucknett	D80	Hancock
Herts	A42	Walker
India	N263	Smith
Langport	D167	Blake
Latvia	F39	Calis
	N260	Revics
	F37	Sakne
London	D65	Coller
	D47	Moore
Argyle Sq	A48	Martin
Tower Hamlets	B12	Hatswell
Northern Rhodesia	N167	Clay
Orlandin, Pembroke	C37	Laugharne
Poland	N147	Wasowicz
Quievy	E126	Cox
Ratcliffe, Leics	C46	Jefferys-Taylor
Redruth	C50	Penberthy
Rio de Janiero	E54	Hancock
Sarawak	N157	Cardno
Shirley, Southampton	E85	White
Stockleigh Court, Devon	D88	Bellew
Stoke, Coventry	B2	Lyddon
Sussex	N237	Chambers
Uganda	E54	Hancock
Walcot, Bath	D6	Tuckfield
West Hatch	E50	Reece
Weston-super-Mare	A49	Boucher
Whitmore Hall, Staffs	E35	Mainwaring
Winsham Cemetery	C1	Boucher

Annex F: *RECORDED OCCUPATIONS*

Occupations as recorded on headstones:

MILITARY

Navy
C14	Back	D31	Back
B18	Burston	B4	Hewlett
D87	Keats	N192	Nesbitt
B4	Proll	B4	Walsh

R.N.V.R. — F138 Hewlett

Royal Marines
A42	Fischer	B4	Hemburrow
B4	Millett	E86	Parsons

Master Mariner — E153 Varney

Army
5th Inniskilling Drg.	C46	O'Neal
15th Hussars	D81	Norton
40th Regt of Foot	E148	Fox
93rd Highlanders	D71	Russell
Durham Light Inf.	C46a	Jefferys-Taylor
Kings Shropshire L.I.	W34	Persse
N. Devon Militia	A44	Bruton
R.A.O.C.	B4	Hannon

R.A.S.C.
B4	Greedy	D127	Rawle

Royal Artillery
B4	Stone	B4	Capper

Somerset Militia — F42 Strong, D93 Chorley

Somerset L.I.
		B20	Besley
N71	Evered	E119	Harrison
B4	Hawkins	F152	Hawkins
B4	Lewis	F173	Lewis
		B4	Meade
		E144	Parsons

Air Force
F151	Meade	B4	Wheldon
B4	Teale		

Latvian Officers
F39	Calis	F37	Sakne

War Grave
B20	Besley	D127	Rawle

Waterloo Veteran — D174 Bale

Ecclesiastical

Churchwardens
F106	Webb	C16	Sellick

Clergy
D80	Hancock	E54	Hancock
C47	Harvey	C40	Llewellin
B22	McCririck	E50	Reece

Sexton
D21	Tuckfield	D23	Tuckfield

Wesleyan Preacher — A45 Thresher

Medical

Doctor	C33	Edwards
Surgeon	E71	Hancock
State Registered Nurse	D115	Carr

Other Professions

Foster Mothers
N29	Baker	N29	Sibley

Indian Woods & Forests — E35 Mainwaring

Inland Revenue	A41	Holborow
Painter	D94	Vickery
Sadler	D143	Burston
Tradesman	C31	Cooksley
Tutor & Biologist	E54	Hancock

Sources and Bibliography

BATH & WELLS DIOCESAN KALENDAR 1891-1906 (Somerset Studies Library)
BRAGG'S DIRECTORY (1840)
BRITISH BIOGRAPHICAL INDEX edited by David Bank & Anthony Esposito
    (K G Saur, University of Glasgow, 1990)
BRITISH CEMETERIES (National Federation of Cemetery Friends Leaflet, 1999)
COMMONWEALTH WAR GRAVES COMMISSION, MAIDENHEAD
DEBRETT'S PEERAGE AND TITLES OF COURTESY 1928
DICTIONARY OF CHRISTIAN LORE & LEGEND J C J Metford (Thames
    & Hudson, 1983) ISBN 0-500-27373-1
THE DISTINGUISHED SERVICE ORDER O'Moore Creagh
AN EXCAVATION AT NUNNINGTON PARK (West Somerset Archaeological and
    Natural History Proceedings. Vol. 103. 1958/59)
*A GENERAL ACCOUNT OF WEST SOMERSET: DESCRIPTION OF THE TONE AND
    THE HISTORY OF THE TOWN OF TAUNTON* Edward Jeboult (1873)
GENERAL DIRECTORY FOR THE COUNTY OF SOMERSET Wm. Bragg (1840)
*THE GREAT WAR 1914-1918 - SOMERSET COUNTY MEMORIAL BOOK IN WELLS
    CATHEDRAL* 2 Vols. (E Goodman & Son, The Phoenix Press, 1923)
A GUIDE TO THE PARISH CHURCH OF ST ANDREWS, WIVELISCOMBE
    Compiled by W J Lyddon, 1955 (Somerset Studies Library ref: S 726.5)
HISTORIC TOWNS IN SOMERSET M Aston and R Leech. (1977)
A HISTORY OF MILVERTON Frank E Farley & Don F Ekless
    (The Milverton and Fitzhead Society, 1986) ISBN 0-9511087-0-0
THE HISTORY AND ANTIQUITIES OF SOMERSET John Collinson (1791)
KELLY'S DIRECTORY OF SOMERSET
LECTURE BY DON BIANCO OF ENGLISH HERITAGE
    (Friends of Kensal Green Cemetery, November 2000)
*LIST OF BUILDINGS OF SPECIAL ARCHITECTURAL OR HISTORIC INTEREST :
    DISTRICT OF TAUNTON DEANE*
    Department of the Environment (March 1984)(ref 33)
MORRIS' DIRECTORY OF SOMERSET AND BRISTOL (1872)
OFFICERS DIED IN THE GREAT WAR, 1914-1919 (HMSO, 1919)
OFFICIAL GUIDE – WIVELISCOMBE 1927
*THE PARISH CHURCHES OF WELLINGTON AND WIVELISCOMBE, SOMERSET
    AD 1910* The Rev. Howard McCririck, Vicar. (May 1910)
    (Somerset Studies Library ref: S 726-5 (0086823))
A POPULAR HISTORY OF WEST SOMERSET Edward Jeboult (1893)
THE PROVIDENT SOCIETY OF 1810 S Batey (1981)
QUAKERS IN WELLINGTON : 1689-1989 Doris Flatt
RECORDING AND ANALYSING GRAVEYARDS Harold Mytum
    (Council for British Archaeology, 2000) ISBN 1-902771-09-5.
A SHORT GUIDE TO THE PARISH CHURCH OF ST ANDREW, WIVELISCOMBE
    D H Luxton (Wiveliscombe Parochial Church Council, 2000)

SOLDIERS DIED IN THE GREAT WAR, 1914-1919 (HMSO, 1919)

*SOME ACCOUNT OF THE TOWN AND PARISH OF WIVELISCOMBE
[READ AT THE MEETING OF THE SOMERSETSHIRE ARCHAEOLOGICAL
SOCIETY]* William Lewis, Cardiff (1883)

SOMERSET G W Wade, DD and J H Wade, MA (Methuen & Co, Ltd, 1912)

SOMERSET COUNTY GAZETTE (Various Editions)

SOMERSET COUNTY HERALD (Various Editions)

*STUDIES IN SOMERSET HISTORY (For the Defence of the Community :
The Wiveliscombe Corps of Volunteers 1803-1805)* J H Hamer (1971)

TAUNTON DEANE: PARISH MAPS PROJECT
(Leaflets on Wiveliscombe and walks in the surrounding area)

WELLINGTON WEEKLY NEWS (Various Editions)

WIFELA'S COMBE: A HISTORY OF THE PARISH OF WIVELISCOMBE F Hancock,
MA, SCL, FSA (Barnicott & Pearce, 1911, reprint ISBN 1-86241-009-7)

WIVELISCOMBE "BITS AND PIECES" : 1920'S – 1980'S Ivor Burston. (1983)

WIVELISCOMBE CONGREGATIONAL CHURCH: A BRIEF HISTORY

WIVELISCOMBE : DISPENSARY AND INFIRMARY 1804 C Waldron

WIVELISCOMBE: DRAFT ARCHAEOLOGICAL ASSESSMENT
(Somerset County Council Environment and Property Department,
Architectural and Historic Heritage Group, 1998)

WIVELISCOMBE : THE GATEWAY TO EXMOOR Edited by Charles Mann and
published by The Wiveliscombe Parish Council (1980)

****

Illustrations

Drawings by *Diana Farrington:*

**Cover 4 14 17 35 53 55 71 72 93 108 118 123
132 145 175 178 188 196 218 220 Back Cover**

Plans by *Frances Dransfield* and *Michael Austin:*

14 42 52 54 62 66 73 96 114 130 131 154

Old maps and photographs provided by *Richard Cornish, Harry Farrington,
William Hancock, Dixon Luxton, Nesta Peppard,
John Whitmarsh* and *Wesley Wyatt*:

15 46 50 158 167 169 181

Permission has kindly been granted for the reproduction of the pictures
on pages **6, 8** and **12** by:

The Somerset Archaeological and Natural History Society

and for the Ordnance Survey Map on page **158** by:

Her Majesty's Stationery Office.

All other photographs by the author.

Index of Inscriptions

BALE, W	26 Apr 1872	D125	BENNETT, J	14 Jan 1893	D159
BALMAN, C	5 Jan 1868	D141	BENNETT, J	1986	D84
BALMAN, F L	8 Feb 1909	E101	BENNETT, L	11 Jan 1869	D159
BALMAN, J	8 Mar 1867	D141	BENNETT, M E	15 Jul 1926	E46
BALMAN, J	12 May 1931	E121	BENNETT, R F	25 Feb 1990	N243
BALMAN, W	27 Oct 1869	D141	BENNETT, W L	27 Jul 1932	E46
BALMAN, W A	7 Dec 1908	E121	BERRY, A	-	A53
BALMAN, W E	[1914-1919] T35	p179	BERRY, C	-	A53
BANFIELD, E	21 Sep 1953	F11	BERRY, E I	25 Jan 1933	E128
BANFIELD, J	26 Jan 1947	F11	BERRY, M A	1 Aug 1907	A53
BARBER, C H	5 Jun 1991	N107	BERRY, W	2 Jul 1892	A53
BARKER, M F S	*16 Nov 1973*	*N235*	BERRY, W	16 Mar 1927	E128
BARRETT, L E T	1986	N134	*BESLEY, W H*	*26 Feb 1963*	*N39*
BARRINGTON, A	3 Jan 1949	E160	BESLEY, T	16 Feb 1917	B20
BARRINGTON, C	7 Jul 1922	E160	BICKNELL, F	8 Jan 1900	E146
BARRINGTON, C C	26 Oct 1991	N151a	BIRD, C	29 Jun 1879	D58
BARRINGTON, C J	6 Feb 1970	N255	BIRD, L A	1 Jul 1991	D117
BARRINGTON, E	1 Dec 1926	E3	BIRD, M E	20 Nov 1957	F59
BARRINGTON, E	9 Apr 1961	N16	BISHOP, E H	20 May 1965	E15
BARRINGTON, E	24 Dec 1968	N16	BISHOP, T	18 Dec 1924	E15
BARRINGTON, E	15 Sep 1981	F19	BLAKE, M	19 Oct 1850	D167
BARRINGTON, E J	22 Oct 1960	N3	BOARDMAN, D	24 Mar 1994	N130
BARRINGTON, E M	*B/16 Dec1976*	*N212*	BOND, B M B	17 Dec 1998	N283
BARRINGTON, H	2 Oct 1960	N3	BOND, E	27 Dec 1931	E142
BARRINGTON, J M	28 Jul 1987	N151	BOND, G H	30 May 1883	D102
BARRINGTON, K	4 Dec 1904	E3	BOND, H C	16 Aug 1928	E89
BARRINGTON, L M	18 Jan 1950	F19	BOND, M E J	26 Apr 1920	E89
BARRINGTON, M A	11 Feb 1940	E3	BOND, S	17 Jan 1898	D102
BARRINGTON, M J	3 Jan 1970	N255	BOND, W	27 Dec 1940	E142
BARRINGTON, R	30 Mar 1932	E2	BOND, W D	April 1912	D102
BARRINGTON, S	*26 Sep 2000*	*W1*	BOOKER, M B	8 Oct 1944	F32
BARRINGTON, W F	1 Apr 1965	N65	BOUCHER, A	7 Apr 1838	T8
BARRY, V A	9 Feb 1920	E86	BOUCHER, A	10 Aug 1862	A27
BARTHOLOMEW, B A	3 Mar 1995	N123	BOUCHER, A	14 Jan 1873	C3
BARWICK, C	2 Nov 1945	E25	BOUCHER, A	14 Jan 1873	T25
BARWICK, S	[1914-1919] T36	p179	BOUCHER, A	28 Nov 1888	A49
BARWICK, W	28 Dec 1937	E25	BOUCHER, A	2 Apr 1913	C1
BATTERSBY, S P	1979	W34	BOUCHER, A	5 Jan 1925	D91
BEAUCHAMP, K A	13 Oct 1983	N144	BOUCHER, A	5 Jan 1925	T13
BELLAMY, C H	14 Jan 1956	F9	BOUCHER, B	29 Feb 1812	T7
BELLAMY, E	30 Aug 1948	F149	BOUCHER, B	26 Aug 1838	T8
BELLAMY, E	2 Mar 1989	F9	BOUCHER, B	8 Feb 1844	A27
BELLAMY, E W	20 Aug 1997	N279	BOUCHER, B	9 Dec 1874	T9
BELLAMY, H	12 Dec 1949	F149	BOUCHER, B H	8 Jan 1928	T10
BELLAMY, P	28 Apr 1988	N119	BOUCHER, B H L	1947	D38
BELLEW, A M	16 Feb 1882	T21	BOUCHER, C	16 Aug 1886	D91
BELLEW, B	27 Mar 1906	D206	BOUCHER, C	16 Aug 1886	T13
BELLEW, H	19 Apr 1894	T21	BOUCHER, C B	9 Aug 1915	T62
BELLEW, H B	17 Sep 1904	D82	BOUCHER, C B	[1914-1919] T36	p179
BELLEW, H J	20 Jun 1891	D206	BOUCHER, C E	29 Jan 1863	D90
BELLEW, L P	16 Nov 1909	D88	BOUCHER, C M	23 Oct 1824	T7
BELLEW, M F	12 Apr 1902	T21	BOUCHER, C M	9 Oct 1858	T8
BELLEW, T	3 Feb 1924	T52	BOUCHER, E	20 Dec 1805	T7
BENISON, E M	11 Dec 1968	N101	BOUCHER, E	4 Jul 1823	T7
BENISON, K A	13 Oct 1983	N144	BOUCHER, E	23 Oct 1835	T8
BENNETT, A	23 Jan 1945	F53	BOUCHER, E	20 Feb 1877	C3
BENNETT, E H	1988	D84	BOUCHER, E	20 Feb 1877	T25
BENNETT, G E	1988	D84	BOUCHER, E	26 Oct 1878	D83

BOUCHER, E	19 May 1880	T25	BROWN, E	4 Nov 1848		D198
BOUCHER, E	31 Mar 1881	C2	BROWN, E	23 Feb 1904		p166
BOUCHER, E	31 Mar 1881	T24	BROWN, E	27 Oct 1968		F110
BOUCHER, E	9 Mar 1885	C1	BROWN, E C	12 Nov 1954		F110
BOUCHER, E	9 Mar 1885	T25	BROWN, J	18 Oct 1864		D198
BOUCHER, E	20 Mar 1898	D38	BRUTON, G	22 Jul 1862		A44
BOUCHER, E A	27 Nov 1824	T7	BRUTON, Lt Col	20 Apr 1846		A44
BOUCHER, E G	7 Jan 1860	T8	BUCK, A	15 Jul 1851		p163
BOUCHER, E M	1945	D37	BUCK, J	2 Apr 1837		p163
BOUCHER, G G	13 Jul 1818	T7	BULL, J	31 Dec 1890		D120
BOUCHER, H	27 Nov 1904	T10	BULL, P	[1914-1919]	T35	p179
BOUCHER, H L	5 May 1891	T40	BULL, S	6 Dec 1886		D120
BOUCHER, L	24 Jun 1883	T25	BUNT, F	17 Feb 1937		E94
BOUCHER, M	22 Dec 1777	T4	BURFITT, R	27 Jan 1871		A22
BOUCHER, M A	24 Dec 1858	C4	BURFITT, T	1 Aug 1875		A22
BOUCHER, M A	24 Dec 1858	T23	BURGE, R B	21 Nov 1942		F170
BOUCHER, M T	27 Dec 1888	C2	BURGE, R T	7 Jan 1968		F170
BOUCHER, M T	27 Dec 1888	T24	BURKE, A L	5 Apr 1964		N56
BOUCHER, S	9 Jun 1862	A49	BURNETT, H J	[1914-1919]	T36	p179
BOUCHER, T	28 Aug 1811	T4	BURSTON, I R	29 Jan 1988		B18
BOUCHER, T	23 Sep 1858	C4	BURSTON, J	[1914-1919]	T35	p179
BOUCHER, T	23 Sep 1858	T23	BURSTON, L	5 Jan 1996		B18
BOUCHER, W	25 Sep 1881	D37	BURSTON, N	5 Feb 1825		D142
BOWDAGE, E	1893	T26	BURSTON, W	30 Apr 1823		D142
BOWDEN, E	26 Jan 1987	N218	BURSTON, W	27 Jun 1860		D143
BOWDEN, E M	9 Sep 1993	N109	BURTON, A R	31 Jul 1994		N124
BOWDEN, T E	4 Jul 1975	N218	BURTON, C	14 Apr 1908		D160
BOWERING, V M	1991	T65	BURTON, E	29 Oct 1894		D160
BOWN, C A	22 Jan 1968	N33	*BURTON, E A*	*12 Jun 1967*		*N85*
BOWN, M A	20 Oct 1962	N33	BURTON, G A	1983		D116
BOXALL, A	25 Dec 1930	D17	BURTON, J	9 Aug 1886		D160
BOXALL, B H	26 Feb 1985	E8	BURTON, M	12 Jul 1938		A17
BOXALL, G	26 May 1927	D17	*BURTON, R*	*12 Oct 1969*		*N85*
BOXALL, G A	Easter Mon 1910	D16	BURTON, W	16 May 1933		A17
BOXALL, G G	18 Mar 1991	E8	BURTON, W A	1990		D116
BOXALL, L E	23 Oct 1933	E8	*BURT, A C A*	*B/17 Apr1978*		*N201*
BRADFORD, A	12 Jan 1982	N153				
BRANFIELD, H	Nov 1871	D219				
BRANFIELD, W	1878	D219	**C**			
BRANFIELD, W E	5 Mar 1991	N178	T. C.	1889		D106
BRANSCOMB, L N	6 April 1999	N284	W. C.	-		A36
BRANSTON, G	12 Feb 1919	E123	CALIS, J	5 Nov 1953		F39
BRELEY, M	15 Aug 1933	E118	CAPPER, A S	1966		T29
BRICE, F	15 Nov 1969	N105	CAPPER, N J	1971		T29
BRICE, H	29 Mar 1917	A3	CAPPER, W S	1943		T28
BRICE, J	17 Feb 1915	A3	CAPPER, W S	3 Nov 1943		T34
BRICE, M A	7 Oct 1959	F24	CAPPER, W S	[1939-1945]		p168
BRICE, W T	24 Nov 1958	F24	CAPPER, W S	[1939-1945]		p174
BRIDGES, G D	16 Sep 1996	D92	CAPPER, W S	[1939-1945]	B4	p185
BRIGGS, F	15 Sep 1899	T22	CARDNO, P G N	1 Feb 1982		N157
BRIGGS, L E	20 Nov 1928	T22	CARR, K M	23 May 1989		D115
BRISTOW, J H	2 Oct 1948	F157	CARTER, J	1993		W27
BRISTOW, P	9 Jan 1967	N78	CASLEY, F J	19 Jun 1985		E117
BROOK, E	7? 1909?	A23	CATFORD, B	21 Jun 1929		E63
BROOM, S	15 Jul 1978	N196	CATFORD, E F	24 May 1935		E63
BROOM, W H	29 Mar 1951	F123	CAUSLEY, E D	1 Apr 1909		D118
BROWN, C H	5 Mar 185?	D197	CAUSLEY, W L W	16 Feb 1909		D118
BROWN, C H	3 May 1856	D197	CHALKLEY, C	5 May 1957		F162

CHAMBERLAIN, C V	1965	F181	COCKS, C L	2 Apr 1949	F113
CHAMBERLAIN, D L	1988	F181	COCKS, E M	16 Aug 1964	F113
CHAMBERLAIN, N V	Dec 1941	F181	COLDREY, F T W	14 Dec 1946	F16
CHAMBERS, R E	1989	N237	COLE, C	25 Jan 1935	E74
CHAMBERS, W M	1972	N237	COLE, J	12 May 1930	E74
CHANIN, D A	17 Jul 1944	C52	COLES, L C	22 Aug 1965	F55
CHANIN, M	14 Nov 1956	C52	COLES, S	14 Mar 1952	F55
CHAPMAN, E	22 Jan 1985	F44	COLLARD, A	19 Aug 1942	F52
CHAPMAN, T E	12 Jul 1957	F44	COLLARD, B	1 Nov 1855	D46
CHAPPLE, G	29 Aug 1991	W22	COLLARD, B	18 Jun 1917	E101
CHARLESWORTH, E	26 Apr 1965	N66	COLLARD, C	[1914-1919] T36	p180
CHARLESWORTH, J C	18 Dec 1968	N66	COLLARD, E	Jul 1839	A62
CHEDZEY, E A	9 Apr 1938	E75	COLLARD, E J	23 Sep 1932	E101
CHEEK, E	6 Jul 1902	E109	COLLARD, F	12 Dec 1922	E82
CHEEK, W	13 Feb 1913	E109	COLLARD, F L	8 Feb 1909	E101
CHIDGEY, A	1 Dec 1973	C22	COLLARD, J	Jul 1834	A61
CHIDGEY, C G	22 Oct 1952	E98	COLLARD, M	7 Nov 1897	D48
CHIDGEY, E	24 May 1930	E98	COLLARD, P	Feb 1855	A60
CHIDGEY, W C	19 May 1970	C22	COLLARD, S	Aug 1859	A61
CHIPLIN, B	1932	E158	COLLARD, S	2 May 1909	E107
CHIPLIN, W	1944	E158	COLLARD, S A	28 Oct 1885	D89
CHORLEY, A	25 Feb 1845?	D93	COLLARD, T	Jun 1804	A62
CHORLEY, E	1833	V/C	COLLARD, W	Jan 1829	A62
CHORLEY, E	1854	T42	COLLARD, W	Sep 1843	A60
CHORLEY, E	23 Feb 1891	T14	COLLARD, W	22 Apr 1879	D48
CHORLEY, E	1891	V/C	COLLARD, W	9 Nov 1898	E107
CHORLEY, J	22 Feb 1839	D93	COLLARD, W	18 Mar 1912	E82
CHORLEY, J	18 Dec 1988	E115	COLLARD, W	16 May 1951	F52
CHORLEY, W	9 Feb 1870	A52	COLLER, E	10 Jul 1889	D65
CHORLEY {family}	-	B7	COLLES, (inf)	?	T44
CHUBB, L	26 Jul 1950	F150	CONIBERE, A J	1 Jul 1955	F40
CHUBB, R	8 Sep 1933	D122	CONIBERE, E	20 May 1973	F41
CHUBB, R	31 Aug 1995	D122	CONIBERE, F H	10 Jun 1966	F40
CHURCHILL, R	[1914-1919] T36	p180	CONIBERE, W H	27 Apr 1956	F41
CLAPP, A	23 Jun 1909	A15	CONIBERE, W J	19 Aug 1982	C28
CLAPP, E	11 Mar 1940	F172	COOK, E M	1970	E122
CLAPP, E M	20 Jun 1969	F92	COOK, F H	1962	E122
CLAPP, J	11 Nov 1880	A15	COOK, F R	1907	E122
CLAPP, J	25 Feb 1890	A15	COOK, M A	1927	E122
CLAPP, J	8 Oct 1957	F92	COOKSLEY, A	24 Aug 1882	D7
CLAPP, S W	1998	W15	COOKSLEY, S	9 Apr 1851	C31
CLAPP, T H	16 Jan 1993	N112	COOKSLEY, T	30 Jan 1839	C31
CLAPP, W B	13 Oct 1953	F172	COOKSLEY, W	9 Jan 1877	D7
CLAPP, W R B	29 Apr 1991	F172	COOMBS, C S	2? Sep 1906	D85
CLARKE, J	29 Feb 1988	D119	CORNISH, A	6 Apr 1939	F67
CLATWORTHY, A	9 Aug 1865	B17	CORNISH, A L	28 Jun 1981	F67
CLATWORTHY, E	5 May 1804	B17	CORNISH, C L	21 Feb 1984	N145
CLATWORTHY, J	5 Nov 1831	B17	CORNISH, D A	9 Jun 1998	N145
CLATWORTHY, J	4 Dec 1865	D199	CORNISH, W J	23 Jun 1946	F67
CLATWORTHY, J	4 Jun 1873	B17	COTES, L	24 Jun 1883	T25
CLAY, E V	23 Dec 1980	N167	COURT, B A	4 Feb 1944	p163
CLAY, G A	23 Feb 1955	N167	COWLING, E	27 Oct 1900	D164
CLEEVE, J	9 Oct 1904	E103	COWLING, E	26 Jan 1901	D164
CLEEVE, R	12 Jan 1915	E103	COWLING, E	1 May 1931	D164
CLUTTERBUCK, M	25 Jan 1985	C20	COWLING, M A	14 Nov 1909	D164
COCK, J R	17 Apr 1895	D134	COWLING, T	25 Oct 1885	D164
COCK, L	1895	V/H	COX, E	[1914-1919] T36	p180
COCK, P	1889	V/H	COX, E	8 Dec 1917	E126

COX, E L	27 Feb 1942	F101	CUMMINS, L M	6 Dec 1905	E150
COX, E M	31 Jul 1936	E60	CUMMINS, S	21 Jun 1931	E154
COX, E M L	25 Apr 1945	F101			
COX, E R D(?)	12 Oct 1878	D222			
COX, F M	1 Jan 1946	E126	**D**		
COX, H	1 Feb 1831	p166	H. D.	-	W30
COX, J	3 Feb 1867	A31	*DARBY, A M*	*1 Jan 1973*	*N4*
COX, J	28 Apr 1889	D31a	*DARBY, H W*	*21 Oct 1960*	*N4*
COX, J C	10 Feb 1942	E60	DASCOMBE, D M	1999	C30
COX, M	20 Aug 1867	A31	DASCOMBE, H C	1974	C30
COX, M	12 Feb 1933	D31a	DAVEY, B	20 Jan 1933	E91
COX, M H	22 Oct 1899	D31a	DAVEY, E	26 Feb 1939	E91
COX, N E	22 Jul 1989	D13	*DAVEY, G*	*B/3 Jul 1975*	*N220*
COX, R N	18 Oct 1991	D13	DAVEY, K M	18 Mar 1978	N214
COX, W L	5 Jul 1915	E126	DAVEY, T	14 Jul 1946	E91
CRANMER, B	9 Apr 1831	C9	DAVEY, T H	21 Mar 1977	N214
CREWS, A J	28 Sep 1981	N172	DAVEY, W	12 Apr 1988	N116
CREWS, M M	28 Sep 2000	N172	DAVIES, J	12 Apr 1982	N155
CRIDDLE, M	23 Dec 1950	E96	DAVIES, M A	24 Jan 1964	N52
CRIDDLE, T	14 May 1935	E96	DAVIS, E	1 Feb 1889	D215
CROCKER, J L	9 Jan 1997	N287	DAVIS, G	26 Dec 1923	D215
CROSS, B E	3 Mar 1925	D15	DAVIS, G	26 Dec 1923	T52
CROSS, C L P	16 Apr 1944	F103	DAVY, H	Nov 1872	A59
CROSS, F M	2 May 1895	D15	DAVY, M	Jan 1872	A59
CROSS, H	23 Aug 1924	D133	DAVY, W C	Nov 1851	A59
CROSS, L M	13 Jul 1874	C37	DAWE, J B	5 Sep 1960	F8
CROSS, L P	29 May 1868	C37	DAWE, M	27 Jun 1986	F8
CROSS, P G	16 Nov 1928	D15	DAWE, R D	26 Mar 1987	N138
CROSS, R K	19 Feb 1895	D15	DAWSON, J P	1998	p162
CROSS, T C	3 Mar 1898	D133	DEER, E	1996	N276
CROUCH, D G	14 Aug 1999	N286	DEER, E I	7 Feb 1962	N28
CROUCH, E G	April 1979	N286	DEER, P R	1990	E173
CROWCOMBE, M	27 Jul 1938	E58	DEER, V M	10 Dec 1982	N28
CROWCOMBE, T	5 May 1954	E58	DIBBLE, M C	3 Feb 1961	N10
CROWTER, W	23 Jun 1617	T53	DIBBLE, R	6 Mar 1963	N10
CRUMP, P	[1914-1919] T36	p180	DINHAM, F B	23 Nov 1943	E57
CRUWYS, E	26 May 1874	D181	DINHAM, J K	[1914-1919] T36	p180
CRUWYS, J	25 Feb 1878	D181	DINHAM, S F	14 Apr 1920	D85
CRUWYS, S	13 Feb 1867	D181	DINHAM, T	16 Apr 1891	D85
CRUWYS, S	23 Jun 1874	D181	DINHAM, T	6 Sep 1898	D154a
CULLIFORD, B	9 Nov 1851	D193	DINHAM, W	4 Jun 1941	F33
CULLIFORD, C	16 Sep 1878	D194	*DISNEY, S W*	*5 Sep 1973*	*N231*
CULLIFORD, T	19 Mar 1846	D193	DIXON, K L G	4 Mar 2001	N298
CULLIFORD, T	17 May 1855	D194	*DOBLE, C F*	*B/7 Sep 1938*	*E24a*
CULLIFORD, T	18 Oct 1861	D194	DOBSON, T A	10 Oct 1990	C55
CULVERWELL, B	11 Feb 1848	C6	DOWN, A H	23 Jul 1947	D111
CULVERWELL, E	16 Apr 1876	C7	DOWN, M A	2 Oct 1928	D111
CULVERWELL, J	15 Aug 1860?	C5	DRISCOLL, J	1 Jun 1955	F45
CULVERWELL, M	23 Apr 1824	C39	DRISCOLL, J	1984	F45
CULVERWELL, R	21 Mar 1827	C39	DRIVER, E M	30 Sep 1962	N30
CULVERWELL, R	16 Jan 1848	C6	DRIVER, G G	20 Sep 1982	N30
CUMMINS, A J	30 Nov 1985	E154	DRURY, M A	22 Feb 1881	D130
CUMMINS, E	6 Aug 1966	N74	DULBOROUGH, E	13 Jan 1951	A4
CUMMINS, E A	19 Sep 1935	E26	*DULBOROUGH, E S*	*23 Feb 1971*	*N54*
CUMMINS, E M	20 Nov 1926	E38	DULBOROUGH, J	2 Dec 1916	A4
CUMMINS, H	21 Dec 1951	E26	*DULBOROUGH, J*	*6 Jan 1975*	*N9*
CUMMINS, I A	20 Nov 1984	E154	DULBOROUGH, J	3 May 1992	F147
CUMMINS, J	4 Jan 1938	E154	*DULBOROUGH, M A*	*31 Dec 1960*	*N9*

DULEY, G	6 Jul 1849	V/G	ELLIS, J	1998	W35
DULEY, G E	31 Oct 1849	V/G	ELMES, J	Jan 1975	N223
DUNN, A	16 Nov 1824	C38	ELMES, W	Jan 1975	N223
DUNN, H J	23 Dec 1874	D161	EVANS, D	20 Dec 1863/5?	p165
DUNN, J	11 Nov 1912	E48	EVELYN, S E	1926	V/C
DUNN, J C	12 Oct 1938	A18	EVERED E	3 Mar 1966	N71
DUNN, L M	16 Oct 1969	N19	EXCELL, N W	1999	W40
DUNN, M A	3 Sep 1928	D135			
DUNN, S	23 Oct 1924	E48			
DUNN, T	2 Dec 1829	C38	**F**		
DUNN, W H	18 Oct 1961	N19	M. E. H. F.	-	T48
DWELLY, B A	4 Feb 1944	p163	FAIRHURST, L	25 Mar 1977	N226
DWELLY, H	27 Oct 1926	A46	FAWCETT, N	22 Jan 1993	W26
DWELLY, M A	27 May 1944	F49	FAWCETT, S	22 Jan 1993	W26
DWELLY, W	21 Jul 1924	A46	FEAR, H M	17 Aug 1990	p162
DYER, E S	18 May 1934	C51	FEATHERSTONE, A	30 Jun 1918	T22
DYER, R E	1966	N72	FEATHERSTONE, E A	8 May 1934	E29
DYKE, G	10 Apr 1900	E51	FEATHERSTONE, E	1852	V/E
DYNEVOR, A S	1939	E54	FEATHERSTONE, E	19 Jan 1852	T22
			FEATHERSTONE, E	1897	V/E
			FEATHERSTONE, E	2 Feb 1897	T22
E			FEATHERSTONE, E	29 Nov 1920	T22
EASTMENT, A	31 Oct 1972	F140	FEATHERSTONE, E A	4 Jul 1849	T22
EASTMENT, A R	13 Mar 1973	F141	FEATHERSTONE, E J	1871	V/E
EASTMENT, F C	6 May 1947	F140	FEATHERSTONE, E J	17 Mar 1871	T22
EASTMENT, F C	30 Nov 1975	F141	FEATHERSTONE, F	1853	V/E
EASTMENT, J F	5 Feb 1938	E113	FEATHERSTONE, F	17 Jul 1853	T22
EASTMENT, M	12 Dec 1933	E113	FEATHERSTONE, F	15 Sep 1899	T22
EASTMENT, M E M	*B/26 Aug 1980*	*N185*	FEATHERSTONE, F M	6 Dec 1916	E29
EASTMENT, R J	16 May 1949	F141	FEATHERSTONE, F M	6 Dec 1916	T22
EDBROOKE, A	9 Oct 1905	D170	FEATHERSTONE, J	1833	V/E
EDBROOKE, B	26 Dec 1828	D168	FEATHERSTONE, J T	1866	V/E
EDBROOKE, G	13 Mar 1815	D168	FEATHERSTONE, J T	27 Feb 1866	T22
EDBROOKE, M	19 Oct 1850	D167	FEATHERSTONE, L	1849	V/E
EDBROOKE, T	9 Sep 1873	D170	FEATHERSTONE, L	8 May 1934	T22
EDGAR, M	18 Jan 1983	N159	FEATHERSTONE, L A	30 Nov 1879	T22
EDGAR, R B	23 Mar 1994	N259	FEATHERSTONE, M	1837	V/E
EDMED, M C	1996	W100	FELLOWES, Y	1993	T57
EDMED, P J	1983	W100	*FERRIS, E J*	*30 Sep 1962*	*N31*
EDMED, S J	1983	W100	FERRIS, F	14 Oct 1952	F47
EDWARDS, A	27 Mar 1895	D55	FERRIS, S J	9 Nov 1950	F47
EDWARDS, A F	-	C33	FIELD, C C	7 Jan 1875	A9
EDWARDS, A F	18 Aug 1876	T3	FIELD, J	3 Nov 1837	A9
EDWARDS, A M	13 Oct 1887	C33	FIELD, M	29 Mar 1847	A9
EDWARDS, F H	1 Dec 1911	C34	FIELD, S	15 Sep 1866	A9
EDWARDS, M	10 May 1891	D59	FIELD, S C	10 Sep 1847	A9
EDWARDS, W F B	[1914-1919] T36	p180	FISCHER, E M	29 Jun 1870	A42
ELFORD, J	-	V/A	FISCHER, I N	8 Nov 185?	A42
ELFORD, J	27 Mar 1832	T15	FLEMING, N M W	19 Nov 1950	F167
ELFORD, M	3 Sep 1822	T15	FLOOD, D	24 Apr 1999	T31
ELLIOTT, E E	1967	F168	FLOOD, D A	24 Apr 1999	F83
ELLIOTT, F J	1958	F165	FLOOD, E L	27 Apr 1958	F83
ELLIOTT, G H	19 Mar 1942	E138	FLOOD, F W	26 Apr 1944	F83
ELLIOTT, G R	29 Jul 1992	F97	FOLLETT, L	27 May 1927	E99
ELLIOTT, H G	1973	F168	FOSTER, J	12 Jun 1887	D56
ELLIOTT, H G	1973	T41	FOSTER, S R	1999	N134
ELLIOTT, M	8 Jan 1913	E138	FOSTER, V G	1992	N134
ELLIOTT, S M	1976	F165	FOWKE, H	1997	p168

FOX, A	*28 Mar 1970*	*N69*	
FOX, F W	*14 Sep 1969*	*N69*	
FOX, J	17 Mar 1904	E148	
FOXWELL, F R	*22 Jan 2001*	*N295*	
FRANCE, E	3 Jan 1930	E14	
FRANCE, J C	30 Sep 1928	E14	
FROST, E	3 Feb 1900	D154	
FROST, M E	12 Dec 1936	C36	
FROST, W	23 Jun 1887	D154	
FRY, E	19 Nov 1941	F135	
FRY, J	24 Jul 1950	F135	
FUDGE, G C	8 Dec 1996	D179	
FUDGE, P R	30 Apr 1979	F67	
FURZE, A	19 Nov 1960	N8	
FURZE, A L	19 Feb 1961	N12	
FURZE, C	31 May 1944	F153	
FURZE, E	10 Apr 1964	E114	
FURZE, E J	31 Jan 1950	A16	
FURZE, J	[1914-1919]	T36	p180
FURZE, J	17 Aug 1934	E169	
FURZE, J	23 Nov 1966	N12	
FURZE, M	11 Feb 1965	N46	
FURZE, M	14 Jun 1984	N80	
FURZE, M E	15 Jun 1963	N46	
FURZE, M J	22 Jan 1939	E169	
FURZE, R	31 Jan 1941	F153	
FURZE, S J	30 Apr 1938	E114	
FURZE, W	[1914-1919]	T36	p180
FURZE, W	18 Jan 1967	N80	
FURZE, W H	*26 Mar 1964*	*N54*	

G

GADD, C	10 Nov 1962	N34	
GADD, E E	27 Apr 1961	F70	
GADD, F	27 Jun 1997	D131	
GADD, J	8 Jun 1948	F70	
GADD, M A	12 Jun 1965	N34	
GADD, W J	19 Oct 1987	D131	
GAINES, C F	1994	N264	
GAINES, E M	*3 Aug 1975*	*N206*	
GAINES, W E G	*4 Jan 1977*	*N206*	
GAMLIN, E	3 Sep 1907	A56	
GAMLIN, J	14 Dec 1861	D165	
GAMLIN, J	21 Jun 1864	D165	
GAMLIN, J	5 Nov 1874	D165	
GAMLIN, L	6 Mar 1879	A52	
GAMLIN, T	22 Nov 1877	A52	
GAMLIN, W	8 Feb 1882	A56	
GAMLIN, W	[1914-1919]	T36	p180
GAMLIN, W H	9 Aug 1915	A56	
GARDNER, M	31 May 1982	N229	
GARDNER, S C	21 Jan 1974	N229	
GARDNER, S J	10 Oct 1995	N229a	
GARMPS, G A	*B/1Nov 1982*	*N158*	
GAY, E J	1980	N166	
GENREY, A R	1985	E172	
GENREY, E	1994	E172	

GEORGE, I J	*5 Apr 2001*	*N299*	
GERRARD, K	28 Sep 1925	E27	
GIBBS, B	2 Feb 1960	F20	
GIBBS, E L	18 Aug 1988	E34	
GIBBS, J	19 Feb 1950	F122	
GIBBS, L B	28 Mar 1969	F122	
GIBBS, W	7 Aug 1962	F20	
GODDARD, J	25 Sep 1885	A19	
GODDARD, J	? Mar ?	A19	
GOVIER, B	24 Apr 1908	D192	
GRABHAM, A	1973	N43	
GRABHAM, E	1963	N43	
GRABHAM, G	*B/2 Jan 1991*	*N191*	
GREED, B H	20 Feb 1900	E136	
GREED, J	25 Dec 1943	E136	
GREEDY, C T	27 May 1963	N45	
GREEDY, D	13 Feb 1957	F133	
GREEDY, E	10 Jul 1889	D65	
GREEDY, E	30 Oct 1944	F176	
GREEDY, E	18 Jan 1958	F143	
GREEDY, E	14 May 1982	N187	
GREEDY, E A	*5 Aug 2000*	*W36*	
GREEDY, E J	10 Oct 1927	E22	
GREEDY, F	[1914-1919]	T36	p181
GREEDY, F	3 Mar 1940	F171	
GREEDY, F	24 Sep 1980	N187	
GREEDY, F	*B/2 Aug 1977*	*N216*	
GREEDY, F C	19 Jan 1949	F133	
GREEDY, G	1989	F106	
GREEDY, H	19 May 1950	F88	
GREEDY, I A	*1 Nov 1960*	*N6*	
GREEDY, J	1888	D65	
GREEDY, J	1 Feb 1897	A6	
GREEDY, J	March 1995	N45	
GREEDY, L	5 Jan 1996	B18	
GREEDY, M	29 Jun 1880	D65	
GREEDY, M	18 May 1919	E127	
GREEDY, M	11 Nov 1981	N45	
GREEDY, M E	4 Feb 1959	F88	
GREEDY, P C	[1939-1945]	B4	p185
GREEDY, R E G	10 Oct 1987	N114	
GREEDY, W	19 Jul 1895	A6	
GREEDY, W	[1914-1919]	T35	p181
GREEDY, W	[1914-1919]	T36	p181
GREEDY, W	11 Feb 1955	F89	
GREEDY, W	19 Mar 1961	F176	
GREEDY, W	30 Dec 1968	F143	
GREEDY, W	19 Jun 1981	F106	
GREEDY, W H	*11 Sep 1996*	*W36*	
GREEN, E	1987	D178	
GREENSLADE, A	1972	N239	
GREENSLADE, F	20 Dec 1912	E17	
GREENSLADE, M	2 May 1897	p164	
GREENWAY, V M	1991	T65	
GREGORY, E E	21 Oct 1990	N117	
GREGORY, F C	7 Aug 1998	N117	
GRIBBLE, A C	7 Feb 1829	p166	
GRIDLEY, S A	*21 Apr 1968*	*N94*	

GROVES, F O	B/4 Feb 1980	N193	HANCOCK, S	1861	V/D
GROVES, M	B/3 Apr 1979	N193	HANCOCK, W	1813	D30
GUNNINGHAM, E	1978	C15	HANCOCK, W	19 Jan 1849	T38
GUNNINGHAM, E J	1976	C15	HANCOCK, W	2 Dec 1896	D78
GUSH, S J	4 May 1998	W18	HANCOCK, W	2 Dec 1896	T61
GUTTERIDGE, H	1993	N223a	HANCOCK, W I	26 Jan 1910	E71
GUY, E	[1914-1919] T36	p181	HANCOCK, W J	7 Mar 1878	D30
GUY, H	7 Aug 1959	F107	HANCOCK, W M	1838	V/D
GUY, L P	28 Apr 1971	F107	HANNON, H E	1991	W23
			HANNON, H J	[1939-1945] B4	p185
			HANNON, H J	[1939-1945]	p168
H			HANNON, H J	(1939-1945)	p174
D. W. H.	1996	W20	HANNON, J	13 Jul 1927	E73
W. H.	1881	D97	HANNON, W F	1995	W17
HADFIELD, D W	*see DWH*	*W20*	HANSEN, M M	1980	N189
HADFIELD, M B	*B/27 Jul 2000*	*W20*	HARGREAVES, G M	2 Feb 1960	F31
HAINES, C G	17 Apr 1946	F82	HARGREAVES, J	13 Feb 1948	F31
HAINES, J	8 Apr 1960	F82	HARRIS, N G	20 Oct 1963	N50
HALE, A J H	18 Apr 1981	N169	HARRIS, T E	29 Jan 1995	N50
HALE, M	7 Mar 1991	N165	HARRISON, A	[1914-1919] T36	p182
HALES, F E	1999	W38	HARRISON, A	6 Jul 1915	E119
HANCOCK, A	1851	V/D	HARRISON, E J	16 Dec 1938	E119
HANCOCK, A B	1883	V/D	HARRISON, J T	13 Jul 1926	E119
HANCOCK, A S	1939	E54	HARTNELL, B M	29 Jun 1969	F26
HANCOCK, B	1 Sep 1784	T55	HARTNELL, C W	4 Nov 1952	F61
HANCOCK, E	21 Apr 1910	D30	HARTNELL, H J	7 Apr 1911	A29
HANCOCK, E	1925	V/D	HARTNELL, M	27 Jan 1972	N254
HANCOCK, E B	1874	V/D	HARTNELL, M A	29 Apr 1939	A29
HANCOCK, E D	29 Dec 1925	E65	HARTNELL, O	10 Dec 1971	F26
HANCOCK, F	1858	V/D	HARTNELL, W H	24 Jan 1970	N254
HANCOCK, F	17 May 1858	T37	HARVEY, E	23 Feb 1797	T43
HANCOCK, F	1920	V/D	HARVEY, E	14 Apr 1819	T43
HANCOCK, F C	11 Dec 1959	E65	HARVEY, E D	16 Jan 1816	T43
HANCOCK, F E	29 Oct 1943	E64	HARVEY, F M	8 Oct 1912	C47
HANCOCK, F J	1844	V/D	HARVEY, J	17 Jul 1792	T43
HANCOCK, F M	1864	V/D	HARVEY, J	4 Apr 1821	T43
HANCOCK, G	1864	V/D	HARVEY, J D	23 Mar 1823	T43
HANCOCK, G L R	22 Jun 1940	E54	HARVEY, R M D	[1914-1919] T35	p182
HANCOCK, G W	17 Sep 1937	E53	HARVEY, R M D	20 Apr 1915	T50
HANCOCK, J	1860	D30	HATSWELL, A	7 Oct 1937	E140
HANCOCK, J	5 Sep 1881	D80	HATSWELL, E	20 Feb 1861	B12
HANCOCK, J V	12 Dec 1959	E72	HATSWELL, E J	15 Oct 1903	B11
HANCOCK, L R	26 May 1943	E54	HATSWELL, H J	9 Feb 1878	B12
HANCOCK, M	22 Aug 1909	D78	HATSWELL, J	10 Aug 1891	B11
HANCOCK, M A	28 Jul 1828	D30	HATSWELL, K	15 Jun 1935	E140
HANCOCK, M E	24 Jun 1958	E64	HAWKINS, D M	22 Sep 1972	E43
HANCOCK, M F	1917	V/D	HAWKINS, E A	7 May 1927	E45
HANCOCK, M G	1844	V/D	HAWKINS, E I	4 Jun 1901	E105
HANCOCK, P	1838	V/D	HAWKINS, E J	3 Mar 1957	E43
HANCOCK, P	19 Apr 1838	T37	HAWKINS, F J	28 Jan 1936	E43
HANCOCK, P	1870	V/D	HAWKINS, J	17 Apr 1870	D109
HANCOCK, P F	16 Oct 1933	E72	HAWKINS, J E	14 Oct 1962	N32
HANCOCK, P F	16 Oct 1933	T39	HAWKINS, M C C	30 Oct 1941	F152
HANCOCK, P K	1832	V/D	HAWKINS, M C C	[1939-1945] B4	p185
HANCOCK, P K	1868	V/D	HAWKINS, N	1 Dec 1990	N204
HANCOCK, R E	[1914-1919] T35	p181	HAWKINS, N	16 Sep 1993	N110
HANCOCK, R E	29 Oct 1914	T27	HAWKINS, R	7 Oct 1956	E105
HANCOCK, R I	1908	V/D	HAWKINS, R F	29 Mar 1982	E43

Name	Date	Ref
HAWKINS, S	25 Apr 1997	N110
HAWKINS, W	31 Dec 1881	D109
HAYDON, E	21 Apr 1910	D30
HAYDON, M A	19 May 1939	D30
HAYES, C J	12 Oct 1950	F178
HAYES, G H	*10 Feb 2001*	*N296*
HAYES, J	12 Oct 1864	D158
HAYES, J	17 Jan 1883	D158
HAYES, J	28 Mar 1976	N208
HAYNES, H A S	*13 Jun 1967*	*N86*
HAYS, A	21 Mar 1885	p166
HAYS, J	14 Sep1848	p166
HAYWARD, A E	7 Jun 1991	N139
HAYWARD, R E	31 Aug 2000	N139
HEARD, E	*6 Jan 1962*	*N24*
HEMBURROW, D J	[1939-1945] B4	p185
HERBERT, D M	29 Jun 1999	B21
HEWLETT, A B	14 Feb 1967	F138
HEWLETT, F G	4 Dec 1944	F138
HEWLETT, J A	[1939-1945] B4	p185
HEWLETT, J A	11 Mar 1941	F138
HEYWOOD, A	*B/20 Feb 1986*	*N186*
HEYWOOD, C J	1980	N173
HEYWOOD, E	14 May 1941	F12
HEYWOOD, E E	1996	N173
HEYWOOD, J H	-	F13
HEYWOOD, R	5 Feb 1940	F13
HEYWOOD, W	26 Jun 1966	F12
HIGGINBOTTOM, G	22 Apr 1997	W33
HILL, A	8 Dec 1841	D121
HILL, A	1 Apr 1964	N55
HILL, A V	14 May 1950	C53
HILL, B	8 May 1831	D45
HILL, C H	24 Sep 1954	F130
HILL, E	20 May 1809	D45
HILL, E	28 Sep 1853	A8
HILL, E	13 Mar 1868	A8
HILL, E	10 Jul 1891	A7
HILL, E	10 Jul 1954	E79
HILL, F W	3 Jun 1942	F84
HILL, H	12 Apr 1877	A7
HILL, H	*B/25 Aug 1971*	*N55*
HILL, J	15 Jan 1923	D156
HILL, K	16 Dec 1963	F130
HILL, M	20 Oct 1894	D180
HILL, M B	1994	N126
HILL, O M	16 Jun 1983	E37
HILL, P B	2 Jul 1862	D145
HILL, R	1 Oct 1979	N180
HILL, R	21 Mar 1988	N180
HILL, S A	30 Oct 1892	D156
HILL, S E	15 Sep 1932	D150
HILL, S J	18 Jul 1969	C53
HILL, S J	1991	N126
HILL, S J M	14 Nov 1938	D16
HILL, T R	25 May 1935	E79
HILL, W	8 Oct 1858	D121
HILL, W	21 Dec 1898	D180

Name	Date	Ref
HIND, M A	1987	p161
HINES, F J	*8 Nov 1960*	*N7*
HITCHCOCK, H	12 Jan 1893	D60
HOBBS, A W	31 Dec 1953	F110
HODGE, C	-	F111
HODGE, C J	2 Oct 1964	N60
HODGE, E	2 Aug 1929	E90
HODGE, E M	18 Sep 1989	N122
HODGE, G	16 Apr 1917	D32
HODGE, H J	19 Apr 1950	F105
HODGE, I F	*16 Feb 1967*	*N60*
HODGE, M A	10 Apr 1915	D32
HODGE, M A	20 Oct 1952	F105
HODGE, W G	5 May 1915	E90
HODGES, E	14 Jun 1867	D223
HOLBOROW, W	24 Apr 1869	A41
HOLE, A C	15 Feb 1985	F6
HOLE, J A	30 Jan 1960	F6
HOLLEY, A M	31 Mar 1905	F139
HOLLEY, E	4 Jan 1944	F139
HOLLEY, W	16 Dec 1949	F139
HOLLEY, W J	2 Feb 1961	F23
HOOD, D L	3 Apr 1991	N113
HOOD, R H	2 Apr 1994	N52
HOOPER, D L	23 Oct 1994	N121
HOOPER, H	16 Jul 1989	N121
HORE, E	*24 Aug 1969*	*N103*
HOUKES, C H W	15 Mar 1985	N149
HOUKES, D	11 Dec 1997	N149
HOWE, R	7 Jul 1888	A5
HOWE, W	14 Feb 1951	F148
HOWELL, F	[1914-1919] T35	p182
HOWELL, G J	8 Oct 1966	N75
HOWELL, J	10 Oct 1931	E130
HOWELL, S A	26 Feb 1953	E130
HOWELL, S J	10 Sep 1972	N75
HOWELL, W R	*26 Jan 1964*	*N53*
HOYLE, J	25 Oct 1930	E12
HOYLE, J	6 Aug 1935	E12
HUMPHRIES, E J	3 Feb 1950	F132
HUNTLEY, M E G	*B/19 Apr 1985*	*N150*
HURFORD, M	27 Aug 1878	D128
HURLEY, C A	28 Oct 1928	E5
HURLEY, J	9 Feb 1950	E5
HURST, S B	5 Mar 1952	F62
HYETT, W J	[1914-1919] T36	p182

I

Name	Date	Ref
INGRAM, D J E	15 Jan 2001	N294
IRISH, E	19 Jul 1919	C49
IRISH, H	1 Jun 1923	C48

J

Name	Date	Ref
JAMES, F M	16 Nov 1977	N203
JAMES, J P	11 Oct 1988	N203
JAMES, V N	1999	W16

JEFFERYS-TAYLOR, E	27 Oct 1949	C46	KING, C	5 Jan 1906	C36
JEFFERYS-TAYLOR, H	24 Jan 1962	C46a	KING, E	28 Jul 1865	C36
JEFFS-MANSFIELD, P D	*B/14 Jun 1989*	N120	KING, E	30 Jan 1960	F128
JENKIN, W H	*12 Jul 1971*	*N246*	KING, E E	30 Jun 1975	F128
JENKINS, A	16 Jul 1926	D176	KING, F	Nov 1893	D61
JENKINS, E C	10 Apr 1896	D176	KING, H	27 Oct 1926	A46
JENKINS, J	11 Oct 1896	D176	KING, I M	16 Mar 1907	E124
JENKINS, L	7 Feb 1894	D176	KING, J	15 Sep 1828	A28
[JEWELL]	6 May 1888	p170	KING, J	21 Sep 1873	A46
JEWELL, B H	19 Oct 1951	E11a	KING, M A	13 Dec 1890	A46
JEWELL, M	17 Jan 1900	p172	KING, M E	12 Dec 1936	C36
JEWELL, R	12 Nov 1937	E11a	KING, V D	20 Mar 1914	E124
JOHNSON, M	30 Nov 1887	D9	KING, W	24 Jun 1865	C36
JOHNSON, V	24 Apr 1984	N146	KING	11 Oct 1878?	p166
JONES, H J	10 Feb 1986	N159	KING, W	22 Aug 1902	D175
JONES, M	18 Jan 1983	N159	KING, W	[1914-1919] T35	p182
JONES, M H	27 Jul 1938	E42	KING, W	[1914-1919] T36	p182
JONES, T	20 Aug1958	E42	KING, W	22 Feb 1977	N213
JONES, W	15 Jan 1889	A26	KIRK, A H	1977	E69
JORDAN, G H	20 Mar 1994	N97	KIRK, J J	1988	E69
JORDAN, W M	1 Sep 1968	N97	KNIGHT, D G	Mar 1962	N27
Joyce [SIMPSON]	26 Jan 1963	N38	KNIGHT, E K B	Jan 1962	N27
			KNIGHT, G	25 Dec 1886?	p166
			KNIGHT, G B	20 Feb 1905	E134
K			KNIGHT, G B	24 May 1913	E134
KEATS, F	4 Feb 1898	D87	KNIGHT, H E	6 Jun 1897	p166
KEATS, M E	5 Dec 1901	E164	KNIGHT, S	[1914-1919] T35	p182
KEEVIL, E	19 May 1880	T25	KNIGHT, W B	1 Jun 1874	p166
KELLAND, E	19 Dec 1871	D207	KUHN, R	14 Jun 1957	F25
KELLAND, J	27 Nov 1883	D162			
KELLAND, M A	17 May 1871	D162			
KELLAND, M A	20 Mar 1875	D162	**L**		
KELLAND, S	8 Jun 1888	D213	E. L.	1893	D183
KELLAND, S	26 Aug 1899	D213	LAND, H E	1958	E93
KELLAND, S	[1914-1919] T35	p182	LAND, J	1937	E93
KELLOCK, M E	18 Nov 1952	F56	LAND, J	1973	E93
KELLOW, A	15 Aug 1959	E13	LAND, J	1973	p168
KELLOW, D A	26 Dec 1970	N249	LAND, L W	1971	W32
KELLOW, E	9 Jul 1905	E18	LAND, W M	1995	W32
KELLOW, E	1977	N81	LANE, H A	31 Dec 1875	D1
KELLOW, F	15 Dec 1928	E13	LANE, W H	27 Feb 1870	D1
KELLOW, G	[1914-1919] T36	p182	LANG, J	1986	E162
KELLOW, J	9 Nov 1862	D163	*LANG, M M*	*1 Apr 1965*	*F180*
KELLOW, M A	24 Feb 1909	E18	LANGDON, B A	5 Mar 1959	F75
KELLOW, M E	21 Feb 1935	E1	LANGDON, M L	14 Jun 1986	N84
KELLOW, T	9 Mar 1895	D14	*LANGDON, W H*	*28 Sep 1968*	*N99*
KELLOW, T	5 Sep 1898	E18	LANGDON, W T	5 Apr 1967	N84
KELLOW, T	[1914-1919] T36	p182	LANGLEY, C A M	27 Oct 1837	C41
KELLOW, W	18 Aug 1898	D14	LANSDOWN, H	8 Dec 1864	D217
KELLOW, Z E	1967	N81	LANSDOWN, L	9 Nov 1876	D217
KELLY, G E	1974	N15	LANSDOWN, M	6 Sep 1870	D217
KELLY, J M	1961	N15	LANSDOWN, S	4 Dec 1864	D217
KEMBLE, M-G	16 Dec 1994	N265	LANSDOWN, T	4 Nov 1876	D217
KER, M H M	*B/7 Nov1995*	*N188*	LANSDOWN, W	5 Dec 1864	D217
KER, S	*B/12 Nov 1980*	*N188*	LARCOMBE, A	25 Aug 1869	D2
KETTLEWELL, G K	24 May 1936	E92	LARCOMBE, E	17 Nov 1879	D26
KIMBER, M A	14 Nov 1918	A21	LARCOMBE, F	26 Dec 1876	D3
KING, A	20 Jul 1987	N213	LARCOMBE, H	25 Apr 1916	E100

LARCOMBE, M J	24 Dec 1919	E100	LOVELL, H	14 Jan 1979	F7	
LARCOMBE, W	25 Dec 1921	D26	LOVELL, M	29 May 1955	C43	
LASKEY, E	27 Jan 1995	N48	LUCAS, B M	8 Feb 1943	F114	
LASKEY, W	22 Aug 1963	N48	LUCAS, C J	29 Apr 1926	D211	
LAUGHARNE, L P	29 May 1868	C37	LUCAS, E	4 May 1893	D210	
LAWRENCE, A	1993	F65	LUCAS, E	10 Nov 1901	D210	
LAWRENCE, F J	*15 Feb 1961*	*N11*	LUCAS, F	15 Sep 1902	E66	
LAWRENCE, M	1998	F65	LUCAS, H H	18 Mar 1936	E66	
LEAHY, F D	*B/5 Jun 1981*	*N170*	LUMBER, J	1963	F179	
LEAHY, J	*B/30 Apr 1983*	*N162*	LUTLEY, A C	1889	V/C	
LEAN, E S	8 Jul 1878	D188	LUTLEY, A M	14 Mar 1917	B14	
LEAN, E S	-	T59	LUTLEY, E	1853	V/C	
LEAN, J	3 Jan 1887	D186	LUTLEY, E	1864	V/C	
LEAN, L	29 Aug 1866	D188	LUTLEY, E	1854/1865?	T42	
LEAN, L	-	T59	LUTLEY, E	24 Dec 1876	D166	
LEE, H	22 Aug 1904	E31	LUTLEY, E	20 Mar 1898	D38	
LEE, K	*8 Sep 1973*	*N47*	LUTLEY, E	10 Mar 1906	V/C	
LEE, M	21 Mar 1937	E31	LUTLEY, E J	2 Feb 1881	B14	
LEE, W H	*27 Jul 1963*	*N47*	LUTLEY, F	13 Aug 1886	D86	
LEGGE, F L	10 Dec 1860	D147	LUTLEY, H H	1926	V/C	
LEMPRIERE, F A	25 Dec 1880	D104	LUTLEY, J	1852	V/C	
LEMPRIERE, T L	14 Oct 1908	D104	LUTLEY, J	1854/1865?	T42	
LEMPRIERE, W H	2 Feb 1882	D104	LUTLEY, J	2 Feb 1860	T5	
LEWIS, A	6 Mar 1962	F173	LUTLEY, J	-	V/C	
LEWIS, A D M	1997	N88	LUTLEY, J E	18 Mar 1928	E50	
[L]EWIS, C	May 1926	E20	LUTLEY, J M	-	V/C	
LEWIS, C R	4 Dec 1976	N210	LUTLEY, L	-	V/C	
LEWIS, E	[1914-1919] T35	p183	LUTLEY, M	25 Oct 1862	T5	
LEWIS, E C	1967	N88	LUTLEY, M	11 Apr 1869	B15	
[L]EWIS, F	May 1926	E20	LUTLEY, M	-	V/C	
LEWIS, H F	1975	N205	LUTLEY, M A	3 Jun 1901	D86	
LEWIS, R	6 Sep 1979	N88	LUTLEY, M A	19 May 1939	D30	
LEWIS, S	1998	N205	LUTLEY, M H	1872	V/C	
LEWIS, S M	9 Oct 1987	N210	LUTLEY, M J	23 Feb 1914	B14	
LEWIS, W	13 Apr 1941	F173	LUTLEY, M P	11 Aug 1863	T5	
LEWIS, W J D	26/27 Jan 1944	F173	LUTLEY, R J	-	V/C	
LEWIS, W J D	[1939- 1945] B4	p185	LUTLEY, R W	13 Dec 1959	D29	
LIGHT, A M	13 Aug 1878	D195	LUTLEY, S B	1872	V/C	
LIGHT, J	22 May 1871	D195	LUTLEY, S J	29 Apr 1901	E50	
LILLEY, W H	17 Jul 1983	C26	LUTLEY, W	25 Dec 1837	B15	
LLEWELLIN, E W	31 Mar 1872	T54	LUTLEY, W C	-	V/C	
LLEWELLIN, E W M	22 Oct 1928	T54	LUXMOORE, M	3 Sep 1822	T15	
LLEWELLIN, J	28 Dec 1869	C40	*LUXTON, A*	*11 Oct 1960*	*E149*	
LLEWELLIN, J	28 Dec 1869	T54	LUXTON, C H	5 Jun 1957	E149	
LOCK, E L	13 Dec 1963	F160	*LUXTON, C M*	*17 Apr 1962*	*E149*	
LOCK, G	13 Oct 1877	D64	*LUXTON, F H*	*5 Sep 1938*	*E11*	
LOCK, H	6 Feb 1933	A10	LUXTON, H E A	9 Mar 2000	C56	
LOCK, J	1940	A10a	LUXTON, L	11 Jan 1905	E149	
LOCK, R W	1 Feb 1951	F159	LUXTON, L	17 Feb 1918	E149	
LOCK, T	17 Oct 1933	A10	*LUXTON, L*	*12 Oct 1960*	*E149*	
LOCK, W	20 Sep 1973	F160	LUXTON, M E	28 Apr 1973	E149	
LORD, H	24 Dec 1855	A33	*LUXTON, W K*	*27 Nov 1885*	*B23*	
LORD, H	19 Nov 1863	A33	LYDDON, A L	1933	B2	
LOVELL, C	15 Feb 1917	C43	LYDDON, A R	17 May 1967	B19	
LOVELL, C	14 Apr 1955	F58	LYDDON, M	26 Mar 1906	B2	
LOVELL, E P	8 Feb 1993	C43	LYDDON, W J	10 Mar 1958	B19	
LOVELL, E S	31 May 1984	F58				
LOVELL, F M	27 Oct 1988	F7				

NESBITT, R A G	19 Jul 1979	N192				
NEWCOMBE, A J	7 Sep 1976	F81	O'BRIEN, F C	6 Feb 2000	N291
NEWCOMBE, E A	16 Jan 1987	F81	O'DRISCOLL, M	1996	W19
NEWTON, A	16 Nov 1909	E125	O'NEAL, E	27 Oct 1949	C46
NEWTON, A A	30 Oct 1947	F17	ORCHARD, M	8 Jun 1960	F89
NEWTON, A J	1866	p164	ORCHARD, S J	14 Apr 1953	F89
NEWTON, B	5 Aug 1882	D113	O'SULLIVAN, E	24 Apr 1990	N92
NEWTON, F J	24 Jul 1953	E125	OVERTON, E W	31 Mar 1872	T54
NEWTON, F J A	21 Dec 1859	p165	OXENHAM, C	12 Feb 1927	E87
NEWTON, H	1835	p165	OXENHAM, C H	4 Jun 1940	E87
NEWTON, H	23 May 1864	p165	OXENHAM, H	22 Apr 1950	E87
NEWTON, H	23 May 1864	p165	OXENHAM, M H	7 Jan 1910	E87
NEWTON, H	1873	p164			

O

P

NEWTON, H E	1835	p165			
NEWTON, H W	8 Mar 1867	p165	P.	-	W5
NEWTON, J	1832	p164	PAIN, W & E	-	F98
NEWTON, J	14 Mar 1833	p166	PARKER, W F	2 Dec 1972	N236
NEWTON, J	28 Mar 1858	D113	*PARKIN, C H*	*B/6 Mar 1987*	*N137*
NEWTON, J F	1849	p164	*PARKIN, E W*	*B/8 Feb 1988*	*N137*
NEWTON, M	18 Feb 1911	E125	*PARKIN, F A*	*B/3 Nov 1995*	*N268*
NEWTON, M A	5 Feb 1903	p165	PARKIN, R M	14 Jan 2001	N268
NEWTON, Revd.	-	p165	PARKMAN, H	23 May 1912	D43
NEWTON, R F	1849	p164	PARKMAN, J	-	D43
NEWTON, T	1858	p164	PARKMAN, J	-	D43
NEWTON, T	17 Jun 1858	p165	PARKMAN, J	21 Apr 1882	D43
NEWTON, T	1860	p164	PARKMAN, J	29 Jul 1935	E40
NORMAN, A A	*30 Dec 1962*	*N36*	PARKMAN, N	29 Dec 1969	N106
NORMAN, E A	9 May 1972	N240	PARKMAN, R	-	D43
NORMAN, E D	12 Mar 1822	V/B	PARKMAN, W	4 Feb 1935	D43
NORMAN, F J	19 Nov 1982	N207	PARNELL, N A	1989	W4
NORMAN, J T	20 Mar 1825	V/B	PARROTT, F J	?19 Jan 1944	E156
NORMAN, J W	*8 Nov 1972*	*N36*	PARROTT, W	2 Jan 1937?	E156
NORMAN, L E D	26 Jan 1976	N207	PARSONS, A E	[1914-1919] T35	p183
NORMAN, M J	6 Aug 1831	V/B	PARSONS, A E	9 Jun 1951	F112
NORMAN, W	4 Jun 1927	N240	PARSONS, D E	3 May 1907	E86
NORTH, D	5 Apr 1807?	D24	PARSONS, F G	19 Nov 1910	E86
NORTH, E J	14 Apr 1878?	B1	PARSONS, F W	[1914-1919] T36	p183
NORTH, E W	15 Apr 1820	D24	PARSONS, F W	9 Apr 1918	E86
NORTH, F	5 Dec 1928	A39	PARSONS, G H	2 Dec 1921	E144
NORTH, J	22 Apr 1887	D107	PARSONS, S	13 Dec 1989	F112
NORTH, J	24 Jun 1891	A40	PARSONS, V A	9 Feb 1920	E86
NORTH, W	19 Feb 1891	D107	PARSONS, W G	13 Feb 1946	E144
NORTON, H E	14 Aug 1950	D81	PASCOE, R	21 Mar 1988	N180
NORTON, M F L B	4 Dec 1962	D81	PASSMORE, A	1972	N239
NURCOMBE, A	28 Feb 1872	D100	PAYNE, E	9 Apr 1934	D172
NURCOMBE, C	20 Dec 1827	D99	PAYNE, J	22 Oct 1848	A25
NURCOMBE, D	1984	p165	PAYNE, J	17 Feb 1911	A2
NURCOMBE, E	27 Oct 1882	D100	PAYNE, J E	10 Nov 1906	D110
NURCOMBE, G	2 Sep 1996	p166	PAYNE, W	9 Aug 1928	D171
NURCOMBE, H M	7 Apr 1998	N232	PEAKE, E M	1945	D37
NURCOMBE, J	17 Jun 1871	D98	PEAPLE, N A	21 Jul 1985	E171
NURCOMBE, L J	23 May 1973	N232	PEARCE, D F	6 May 1998	W13
NURCOMBE, L J	16 Feb 1979	N194	PEARCE, F J	28 Sep 1992	W13
NURCOMBE, M	28 Jan 1863	D98	PEARCE, H S	26 Nov 1998	N222
NURCOMBE, M	11 Oct 1870	C42	PEARCE, L	18 Apr 1975	N222
NURCOMBE, M H	4 Aug 1966	N73	PEARCE, M	1989	N222a
NURCOMBE, P	2 Jun 1839	D99	PEARSE, E B	18 Nov 1880	D57
NURCOMBE, W J	31 Aug 1989	N73			

PEARSE, F	27 Jun 1859	D57	PUGSLEY, S R	23 Mar 1909	D189
PEARSE, M P	2 Apr 1878	D4	PULLING, J	1995	p162
PEARSE, W	26 Apr 1874	D4	PULSFORD, A	24 Oct 1936	E95
PECK, B	1970	C24	PULSFORD, L M	8 Aug 1933	E80
PECK, C L N	24 Dec 1961	N22	PULSFORD, S	19 Jul 1969	C29
PEMBERTON, E M	11 Dec 1968	N101	PULSFORD, W	2 Oct 1959	E80
PENBERTHY, M	21 Oct 1928	C50	PULSFORD, W E	21 Oct 1974	C29
Penelope	182?	C8	PULSFORD, W G	27 May 1947	E95
PERRIN, A E	*26 Sep 1963*	*N49*	PURDUE, E S	1857	V/E
PERSSE, R B L	1985	W34	PUZEY, M	14 Feb 2000	N292
PERSSE, S P	1979	W34			
PETTIT, A	*3 Jan 1962*	*N23*	**Q**		
POCOCK, C	7 May 1887	D201	QUICK, C C	6 Jun 1918	D184
POCOCK, J	7 Jan 1862	D201	QUICK, E	25 May 1921	D182
POCOCK, J	-	T6	QUICK, E C	16 Dec 1987	N115
POCOCK, T	12 Mar 1867	D201	*QUICK, F*	*5 Mar 1963*	*N40*
POCOCK, T	-	T6	QUICK, G	4 Dec 1915	D182
PONSFORD, J	*20 Jan 1969*	*N102*	*QUICK, G*	*4 Dec 1961*	*N21*
POOLE, E M	29 Oct 1899	D10	QUICK, G H	1982	E93
POOLE, E P	5 Nov 1894	D10	QUICK, G M	1996	E93
POOLE, M J	*4 May 2001*	*F70*	QUICK, H M	5 Sep 1991	N115
POPE, O M	25 Jan 1993	F3	*QUICK, L M*	*13 Jan 1968*	*N21*
POWELL, S F	9 Mar 1938	E57	QUICK, L J	4 Jan 1925	D184
POWER, D	*B/25 May 1983*	*N163*			
POWLESLAND, G E	20 Dec 1895	B6			
POYNTER, M	11 May 1997	p162	**R**		
POYNTER, S F B	11 May 1996	p162	A. R.	1866	D72
PRATT, J E	27 Nov 1940	F116	J. R.	1891	D63
PRATT, J W	23 May 1943	F116	S. R.	1862	D75
PRESCOTT, F M	2 May 1955	F77	RAPPS, C	13 Feb 1975	F144
PRESCOTT, T H	15 Jun 1973	F77	RAPPS, W G	25 Apr 1960	F144
PRICE, E A	*18 Sep 1961*	*N18*	RAWLE, G	22 Sep 1915	D127
PRICE, M	14 Jun 1917	D192	RAWLE, H	16 Mar 1941	F154
PRIDDLE, R	18 Feb 1958	F2	RAWLE, H	31 Jan 1952	E161
PRING, J	20 May 1906	p164	RAWLE, J	17 Dec 1920	E161
PRING, L	24 Jan 1898	p164	RAWLE, J	19 Nov 1947	F154
PRING, L	24 Jan 1898	p164	RAWLE, M A	27 Feb 1941	E24
PRING, L A	23 Feb 1855	p164	RAYSON, W D J	12 Feb 1985	C54
PRING, L A	23 Feb 1855	p164	REECE, A D	20 Nov 1904	E50
PRING, T E	8 Dec 1864	p164	REECE, A E	21 Feb 1940	E50
PRING, T E	8 Dec 1864	p164	*REED, B J*	*B/17 Jun 1996*	*N273*
PRIOR, C	12 Aug 1953	F74	REED, A	1954	F45a
PRIOR, E K	14 Jan 2000	F74	REED, D M	22 Jun 1978	N197
PRISCOTT, L	11 Apr 1994	N261	REED, E	19 Dec 1952	F29
PROLL, W A	[1939-1945] B4	p185	REED, M	2000	F45a
PROUT, A M	8 Oct 1940	F100	REED, T	27 Jul 1953	F29
PROUT, E L	8 Apr 1951	F100	REEVES, E	28 Apr 1938	E24
PROUT, E M	20 Nov 1926	E38	REVICS, J	6 Apr 1994	N260
PROUT, F E	22 Nov 1952	F46	RICHARDS, A	14 Jan 1862	D77
PROUT, G	8 Jun 1917	E36	RICHARDS, A	30 Jun 1866	D73
PROUT, G	6 May 1933	E36	RICHARDS, C	[1914-1919] T35	p183
PROUT, L	17 Apr 1953	F28	RICHARDS, C C	6 Sep 1965	F69
PROUT, M	22 Oct 1935	E38	RICHARDS, E	14 Dec 1892	D153
PROUT, M A	17 Jul 1975	F46	RICHARDS, E D	17 Jan 1983	F68
PUGSLEY, E	12 Dec 1868	D187	RICHARDS, E H	15 Dec 1912	E83
PUGSLEY, J F	3 Aug 1880	D187	RICHARDS, E J	8 Oct 1910	E83
PUGSLEY, L	5 May 1882	D191	RICHARDS, E M	15 Nov 1891	D152
PUGSLEY, M F	10 Oct 1868	D190	RICHARDS, F	[1914-1919] T35	p183

RICHARDS, H	20 Dec 1915	D132	SAKNE, V	24 Jan 1952	F37
RICHARDS, J	27 Aug 1882	D73	SALTER, A	30 Oct 1904	D177
RICHARDS, J	10 Nov 1888	D132	SALTER, A	24 Jun 1972	F54
RICHARDS, J	15 Aug 1925	E120	SALTER, A I	29 Dec 1963	N51
RICHARDS, J C	14 Sep 1944	F68	SALTER, E	10 Nov 1949	F54
RICHARDS, J F	4 Mar 1849	D73	SALTER, J	19 Jun 1895	D177
RICHARDS, M A	28 Apr 1949	F69	*SAUNDERS, L*	*21 Feb 1970*	*N253*
RICHARDS, S	1 Jun 1862	D73	SANDFORD, G C	6 Jan 1940	F137
RICHARDS, S	6 Mar 1908	D73	SANDFORD, M A	27 Aug 1975	F137
RICHARDS, S	[1914-1919] T35	p183	SAUNDERS, B	21 Nov 1962	E62
RICHARDS, S	11 Nov 1915	D132	SAUNDERS, J B	9 Sep 1929	E62
RICHARDS, S	17 Mar 1928	E144	SCOTT, L M	15 Dec 1967	N91
RICHARDS, S L	24 Feb 1853	D77	SCOTT, W G	4 Nov 1975	N91
RICHARDS, T	7 Sep 1857	D73	*SCULPHER, L*	*B/10 Feb 1982*	*N175*
RICHARDS, T	13 Oct 1892	D153	SEAMAN, E	16 Aug 1946	F35
RICHARDS, T	18 Sep 1920	E120	SEARLE, L	15 Oct 1979	F2
RICHARDS, W	27 Mar 1919	E144	SEDGBEER, A	2 Feb 1947	F10
RIDGWAY, S	*11 Dec 1962*	*N35*	SEDGBEER, C	7 Sep 1950	F10
RISDON, E	13 Aug 1924	E28	SEDGBEER, D M	1999	N289
ROACH, G & E	-	F38	SEDGBEER, L A	1967	F4
ROALS, H	5 Aug 1825	p165	SEDGBEER, S R	1999	N289
ROALS, J	27 Jun 1857	p165	SEDGBEER, V A	1950	F4
ROBBINS, M	5 Nov 1891	D41	SELLICK, C W	19 Apr 1976	C16
ROBBINS, S	23 Mar 1879	p167	SELLICK, E	21 Sep 1952	E81
ROBBINS, T	14 Apr 1894	p167	SELLICK, E J	17 Aug 1979	N211
ROBINSON, A A	24 Nov 1908	E70	SELLICK, H C	19 Jan 1981	N224
ROCKETT, E	15 Dec 1859	B5	SELLICK, M H	20 Nov 1939	F118
ROCKETT, F	27 Mar 1945	F174	SELLICK, O E	24 Oct 1974	N224
ROCKETT, J H A	21 Nov 1942	F174	SELLICK, R	27 Aug 1930	E55
ROGERS, A	10 Aug 1864	A33	SELLICK, S A	8 Jun 1934	E55
ROGERS, E	22 Nov 1824	V/F	SELLICK, T	21 Dec 1929	E81
ROGERS, E	8 Feb 1835	p167	SELLICK, V E	12 Dec 1959	F5
ROGERS, E	1 Dec 1865	p167	SEWELL, W	30 Aug 1983	N143
ROGERS, H	11 Aug 1888	D50	*SHEPHERD, A*	*11 Feb 1960*	*F8a*
ROGERS, J	29 Sep 1835?	p167	*SHEPHERD, A J*	*3 Apr 1960*	*F8a*
ROGERS, J	2 Feb 1868	A33	SHOPLAND, A	12 Jan 1981	F78
ROGERS, J	28 Nov 1882	D50	SHOPLAND, E	29 Jul 1982	F142
ROGERS, J	23 Jun 1911	E88	SHOPLAND, H	[1914-1919] T36	p183
ROGERS, P	11 Mar 1875	D5	SHOPLAND, J H	23 Jun 1952	F142
ROGERS, S	6 Sep 1814	V/F	SHOPLAND, S J	19 Apr 1953	F78
ROGERS, W	4 Aug 1843	A33	SIBLEY, L		N29
ROKER, D G	*6 Feb 1973*	*N234*	SILVESTER, E	4 Jan 1877	p165
ROSS, A W	4 Sep 1955	D36	SILVESTER, J	18 Nov 1877	p165
ROSS, J	3 Aug 1897	D36	SIMONS, E	10 Apr 1898	D39
ROSS, M R E	21 Jan 1951	D36	SIMONS, E	21 Feb 1956	F91
ROSS, W R	30 Sep 1995	W31	SIMONS, J	28 May 1894	D39
ROWE, R G	7 Mar 1997	N278	SIMONS, L	29 Jul 1958	F91
ROWLES, E C	21 Jul 1862	T2	SIMPSON, J	26 Jan 1963	N38
ROWLEY, W	*18 Jan 1965*	*N61*	SKINNER, C	2 Jan 1910	D49
RUSSELL, M L	6 Feb 1867	D71	SKINNER, H	3 May 1867	D49
			SLOCOMBE, A	7 Aug 1919	E151
			SLOCOMBE, C L	20 Sep 1960	N2
S			SLOCOMBE, E	19 Jul 1940	E151
S.	-	W8	SLOCOMBE, F G	1989	F109
C. S.	1908	C35	SLOCOMBE, G	2 Jul 1872	D149
D. S.	1890	D76	SLOCOMBE, G A	4 Dec 1957	F109
SAFFIN, G J	18 Jun 1983	N140	SLOCOMBE, M	15 Jan 1890	D149
SAFFIN, W H	*4 Sep 1970*	*N251*	SLOCOMBE, M	1993	F146

SLOCOMBE, S W	7 Jan 1957	F146	STONE, G	10 Apr 1997	F18	
SLOMAN, H	24 Feb 1890	A1	STONE, J	[1914-1919] T35	p183	
SLOMAN, J	27 Jul 1869	A1	STONE, J	20 Mar 1928	E131	
SMITH, A	1945	F65	STONE, J	28 Jun 1960	E152	
SMITH, A E	26 Jul 1981	N171	STONE, K	17 Jan 1923	A20	
SMITH, A R	14 Jul 1986	D212	STONE, K J	3 Jan 1986	N132	
SMITH, B G	15 Oct 1980	C21	STONE, L	14 Jul 1955	F27	
SMITH, C	20 Sep 1986	N118	*STONE, L M*	*25 Mar 1963*	*N41*	
SMITH, E	1964	F65	STONE, M	6 Sep 1858	D221	
SMITH, F E	*11 Sep 1968*	*N98*	STONE, M	8 Mar 1926	D40	
SMITH, F A	8 Oct 1994	N263	STONE, M A	21 Oct 1939	D35	
SMITH, F I	7 Oct 1990	N217	STONE, R	3 Apr 1864	D221	
SMITH, G J	27 Dec 1985	N131	STONE, R	4 Jul 1921	E131	
SMITH, H	31 Jan 1990	C21	STONE, R	4 Jul 1921	p168	
SMITH, J M P	*B/19 Jun 1975*	*N221*	STONE, R	3 May 1930	E6	
SMITH, M	23 Jan 1988	N131	STONE, R J	18 Mar 1914	D40	
SMITH, N E	15 Feb 1999	N118	STONE, S	5 Sep 1966	F18	
SMITH, P M	30 Nov 1944	F15	STONE, W	12 May 1915	B13	
SMITH, W	17 Feb 1974	N228	STONEFROST, A	7 May 1903	D70	
SNAPE, A	27 Mar 1895	D55	STONEFROST, D	6 Oct 1890	D70	
SNOWDEN, M	22 Feb 1931	E112	STOWELL, E	16 Feb 1950	F175	
SOMERS, P	4 Sep 1987	E135	STREETEN, H C	16 Nov 1921	E47	
SOUTHCOMBE, M	10 Jun 1935	E85	STREETEN, S	30 Apr 1947	E47	
SPARKS, H G	1992	W25	STRICKLAND, E	29 Apr 1994	W28	
STACEY, A S	17 Dec 1946	F177	STRICKLAND, W	[1914-1919] T35	p184	
STACEY, C E	4 Nov 1893	D155	STRICKLAND, W	30 Jan 1985	F143	
STACEY, E H	4 Nov 1893	D155	STRONG, E J E	18 Jun 1957	F42	
STACEY, E K	4 Nov 1893	D155	STRONG, J B	23 Sep 1967	F42	
STACEY, J H	5 Dec 1947	D155	SULLY, A	24 Mar 1885	D89	
STACEY, L B	18 Aug 1906	D155	SULLY, A	21 Apr 1898	D114	
STEARS, A M	30 Oct 1972	N59	SULLY, G	11 May 1857	D89	
STEARS, H L	23 Aug 1964	N59	SULLY, L	Sep 1880	T30	
STEEL, J T	24 Sep 1984	C23	SULLY, R	10 Nov 1841	D220	
STENNER, E	18 Aug 1954	D123	SULLY, W	2 Oct 1885	D114	
STENNER, J	8 Jan 1922	D123	SULLY, Y J	17 May 1973	N245	
STENNER, M	1998	N281	SUMMERS, J	25 Feb 1919	D44	
STEPHENSON, M	1 Sep 1620	T44	SUMMERS, M	25 Mar 1935	D44	
STEVENS, A M	25 Oct 1974	N219	SUTTON, F	12 Apr 1915	D215	
STEVENS, B	14 May 1955	F57	SWEETING, L L	13 Sep 1992	N142	
STEVENS, C T	5 Jun 1976	N219	SWEETING, M N	10 Feb 1987	N136	
STEVENS, E F	20 Sep 1996	C27	SWEETING, R A	19 Aug 1983	N142	
STEVENS, E W	19 Nov 1969	C27	SYMONS, A G	4 Aug 1976	N209	
STEVENS, E W	1981	T64	SYMONS, C	24 Jun 1937	E129	
STEVENS, H F	[1914-1919] T35	p183	SYMONS, R A	29 May 1941	E129	
STEVENS, M O	25 Apr 1991	W7				
STEVENS, T	-	C35				
STONE, A	21 May 1931	E7	**T**			
STONE, A	5 Sep 1961	N17	TAKLE, A	2 Aug 1905	E33	
STONE, A C	16 Jul 1948	F66	TAKLE, A	19 Apr 1952	E33	
STONE, A L	Mar 1949	F18	TAKLE, C	19 Mar 1956	E33	
STONE, B J	16 Mar 1953	E9	TAPP, G E	7 Dec 1994	W29	
STONE, D A	8 May 1992	F18	TARR, A W	4 Oct 1993	N257	
STONE E	1 Sep 1935	E9	*TARR, R M*	*8 Jan 2001*	*N257*	
STONE, E J	[1939-1945] B4	p185	TAYLOR, E	27 Oct 1949	C46	
STONE, E M	23 Feb 1921	E152	TAYLOR, I B	28 Sep 1985	N129	
STONE, E M	20 Sep 1953	E6	TAYLOUR, E W M	22 Oct 1928	T54	
STONE, F G	*31 Jan 1968*	*N41*	TEALE, H P	[1939-1945] B4	p186	
STONE, G	19 Dec 1915	A20	TENNANT, M W	7 Aug 1967	N87	

TENNANT, S M	27 Nov 1982	N87	TREBLE, E	27 Apr 1901	E137
TESTER, A L	1959	F166	TREBLE, E	3 Sep 1904	E137
TESTER, M	1989	F166	TREBLE, J	26 Jul 1871	E137
THOMAS, A	24 Dec 1827	A35	TREBLE, W	12 Jun 1876	A30
THOMAS, A J	3 Sep 1956	F129	TRELIVING, A A	19 Oct 1958	D185
THOMAS, E	14 Jan 1944	F119	TRELIVING, H	7 Feb 1919	D185
THOMAS, F	28 Apr 1982	N156	TRICKEY, A	11 Dec 1936	E56
THOMAS, F D	22 Aug 1951	F80	TRICKEY, M J	18 Jan 1937	E56
THOMAS, J	8 Mar 1822	A35	TROAKE, J	[1914-1919]	T36 p184
THOMAS, J	4 Jan 1844	A35	TUCKER, W G	[1914-1919]	T36 p184
THOMAS, J	10 Mar 1855	A35	*TUCKFIELD, B V A*	*20 Jan 1968*	*N93*
THOMAS, J	9 Nov 1856	A35	TUCKFIELD, E	8 Feb 1891	D23
THOMAS, J	25 Jan 1875	A34	TUCKFIELD, H J	19 Nov 1872	D23
THOMAS, V	26 Nov 1993	F129	TUCKFIELD, J	21 Apr 1885	D21
THOMAS, W	15 Mar 1865	A35	TUCKFIELD, M	19 Jan 1894	D21
THOMAS, W H T	14 Jan 1941	F119	TUCKFIELD, U R	27 Dec 1902	D6/D23
THOMPSON, S P	18 Oct 1968	F3	TUDBALL, A B G	31 Jan 1943	F120
THORNE, A E	15 Mar 1935	E39	TUDBALL, C G	29 Feb 1980	N182
THORNE, A K	28 Mar 1895	p167	TUDBALL, E	Dec 1957	V/I
THORNE, E	13 Jun 1866	p167	TUDBALL, E M	22 Nov 1914	B1
THORNE, E	7 Jan 1907	A13	TUDBALL, J	6 Aug 1937	E59
THORNE, E	29 Nov 1984	N148	TUDBALL, J E	5 May 1961	F43
THORNE, E A	17 Sep 1936	p166	TUDBALL, J G	30 Nov 1958	F43
THORNE, E J	18 Dec 1918	p167	TUDBALL, L G	19 Dec 1933	E61
THORNE, F	16 Dec 1926	p166	TUDBALL, M A	6 Mar 1969	E59
THORNE, G	-	A14	TUDBALL, P	15 Jan 1982	N182a
THORNE, G R	21 Mar 1914	A13	TUDBALL, P	*[15 Jan]* 1982	T56
THORNE, I	18 Jan 1960	F163	TUDBALL, W	18 Apr 1829	V/B
THORNE, J	6 Sep 1902	p167	TURNER, A E	19 Feb 1965	N62
THORNE, J E	14 Oct 1962	N32	TURNER, D J	7 Apr 1996	N272
THORNE, M	21 May 1958	F163	TURNER, E	10 Nov 1929	D214
THORNE, M A	22 Jun 1900	p164	TURNER, E M	2 Apr 1908	D214
THORNE, M A	22 Jun 1900	p165	TURNER, G D	10 Oct 1999	N272
THORNE, M N	17 May 1933	p165	TURNER, J	30 Mar 1883	D214
THORNE, T	6 Oct 1944	p165	TURNER, R	25 Mar 1895	D214
THORNE, T C	3 Jun 1883	p167	TURNER, S F	28 Dec 1915	D214
THORNE, W T	28 Mar 1985	N148	TURNER, V S	3 Dec 1987	N62
THRESHER, A	12 Oct 1863	A45	TURNER, W	25 Sep 1920	D214
THRESHER, I M	12 Feb 1892	D108	TWENEY, A S	4 Apr 1985	E116
THRESHER, T	8 Sep 1877	A45	TWENEY, J	18 Dec 1988	E115
THURTELL, J	-	C32	TWENEY, L M	4 Apr 1985	E116
THURTELL, M	-	C32	TWIGGER, G E	29 Dec 1977	C17
TICE, H	11 Feb 1861	D200	TYLER, A	3 Oct 1831	D95
TIDBOALD, C B	20 Nov 1961	E76	TYLER, A	26 Nov 1862	A49
TIDBOALD, J	14 Nov 1941	E76	TYLER, B	27 Jul 1794	D95
TIDBOALD, J R	17 Aug 1998	N282	TYLER, B	1837	V/E
TIER, D	1994	W21	TYLER, E	18 Dec 1849	D95
TIMEWELL, C	29 Jul 1859	A51	TYLER, E	6 Oct 1867	A50
TIMEWELL, J	3 Jan 1857	A51	TYLER, F G	13 Jan 1935	E30
TIMEWELL, J C	12 Jul 1866	A51	TYLER, H A	20 Nov 1939	E30
TIMEWELL, M	27 Dec 1888	C2	TYLER, I C	1 Feb 1915	E30
TOVEY, E M	28 Nov 1985	N130	TYLER, J	1833	V/E
TOWERS, A M L	*30 Oct 2000*	*N293*	TYLER, J	15 Aug 1865	D96
TOWERS, A M L	*14 Feb 2001*	*N297*	TYLER, M S M	25 Nov 1916	E30
TOWLER, S M	*B/17 May 2000*	*W37*	*TYLER, P P*	*25 Mar 1965*	*N64*
TRAINER, M	2 Feb 1888	B7	TYLER, T	30 Jun 1793	D95
TREBILCOCK, E	8 Feb 1967	E170	TYLER, T	6 Dec 1861	A50
TREBILCOCK, J H	28 Jan 1935	E170			

U			
UPHAM, E M	21 Mar 1949	E159	
UPHAM, J	1937	p161	
UPHAM, S W	11 Apr 1929	E159	
V			
VALLANCE, C	[1914-1919] T35	p184	
VALLANCE, W	[1914-1919] T35	p184	
VALUKS, P	1 Jun 1990	W6	
VARNEY, A	28 Dec 1923	E153	
VAULTER, B	15 May 1971	N247	
VAULTER, C	13 Feb 1975	F144	
VAULTER, C	30 Sep 1996	N247	
VAULTER, H	9 Jun 1992	W12	
VAULTER, H	9 Sep 1993	W12	
VAULTER, M	28 Nov 1961	N20	
VAULTER, S	19 Sep 1967	N20	
VERYARD?, J	6 Dec 18--?	B10	
VICARY, E	15 Dec 1922	E19	
VICARY, E	6 Aug 1925	E16	
VICARY, F J	2 Oct 1927	E21	
VICARY, J	22 Sep 1937	E19	
VICARY, M	12 Dec 1953	F57	
VICKERY, A	[1914-1919] T35	p184	
VICKERY, A	11 May 1957	F22	
VICKERY, A A	18 Jun 1971	F156	
VICKERY, C	9 Dec 1876	D94	
VICKERY, D A	8 Sep 1995	N266	
VICKERY, E J	9 Jun 1978	N198	
VICKERY, E W	9 Jun 1999	N285	
VICKERY, F B	31 Jan 1979	N198	
VICKERY, G	*[9 Dec 1876]*	D94	
VICKERY, H	4 Mar 1947	F156	
VICKERY, H W	27 Oct 1966	N76	
VICKERY, K M	16 Sep 1999	N290	
VICKERY, K T M	8 Jul 1968	N95	
VICKERY, W J	13 Mar 1972	F22	
VICKERY, W L	[1914-1919] T35	p184	
VINING, G J	3 Feb 1939	F51	
VINING, M	14 May 1959	F51	
W			
E. W.	1863	D138	
J. W.	1863	D139	
M. W	1878	D148	
M. J. W.	1859	D140	
W. W.	1820	D148	
W. W.	1884	D126	
W. W.	1890	D67	
WALDRON, E	19 Jan 1861	T12	
WALDRON, E C	7 Nov 1989	N200	
WALDRON, J	16 May 1862	T12	
WALDRON, J	4 Apr 1908	E108	
WALDRON, J	17 Apr 1978	N200	
WALDRON, L	24 Feb 1905	E108	
WALDRON, L	21 Nov 1911	E110	

WALDRON, W	7 Jan 1909	E110	
WALKER, A G	[1914-1919] T35	p184	
WALKER, A G	17 May 1915	T50	
WALKER, C A	2 Oct 1842	T1	
WALKER, E	14 Jan 1832	A42	
WALKER, E	14 Jan 1832	T1	
WALKER, F	7 May 1955	E23	
WALKER, T	6 Jun 1932	E23	
WALKER, W E	21 Jan 1997	N277	
WALSH, R	[1939-1945] B4	p186	
WALSH, R H	(1939-1945)	p168	
WALSH, R H	(1939-1945)	p174	
WAMBEY, M L F	8 Aug 1863	A58	
WARREN, A	31 Oct 1885	D68	
WARREN, A J	31 Dec 1969	F145	
WARREN, C	1 Nov 1969	N104	
WARREN, E E	30 Nov 1986	F115	
WARREN, E M	9 Apr 1958	F145	
WARREN, E S	30 Sep 1953	F50	
WARREN, H A	23 Oct 1970	F124	
WARREN, H J	8 May 1965	F115	
WARREN, H T	6 May 1892	D62	
WARREN, J	25 Apr 1940	F50	
WARREN, K	1980	N184	
WARREN, L E	21 Oct 1943	F175	
WARREN, L K	3 Mar 1954	F50	
WARREN, M	5 Jun 1882	D66	
WARREN, M	26 Jan 1942	F115	
WARREN, N F	5 Aug 1964	N58	
WARREN, S E	29 Jun 1973	N104	
WARREN, S G J	30 Jun 1958	F50	
WARREN, T	30 Jun 1882	D66	
WARREN, T	28 Sep 1928	D62	
WARREN, V A	[1914-1919] T36	p184	
WARREN, V A	7 Jun 1917	D32	
WARREN, W	4 Feb 1890	D66	
WARREN, W R	30 Jan 1970	F124	
WASOWICZ, F J	1984	N147	
WATERMAN, A	18 Sep 1903	E49	
WATERMAN, B	16 Aug 1919	E49	
WATERMAN, M	25 Aug 1921	E49	
WATERMAN, R	23 Jul 1903	E49	
WATTERS, E T	24 Aug 1996	N275	
WAYGOOD, W G	1994	N262	
WEALE, P	1996	F168	
WEBER, W	-	D207	
WEBBER, A J	7 Jun 1980	N42	
WEBBER, C H	20 Jan 1907	E102	
WEBBER, E	[1914-1919] T35	p184	
WEBBER, E	*B/4 Dec 1979*	*N181*	
WEBBER, E A	13 Jan 1922	D157	
WEBBER, F C	14 Feb 1941	F136	
WEBBER, G	12 Jun 1952	F95	
WEBBER, G T	5 Dec 1970	F95	
WEBBER, I S	5 Oct 1951	F106	
WEBBER, L	19 Jan 1968	F106	
WEBBER, L	27 Jan 1990	F136	
WEBBER, M	17 Jun 1860	A47	

WEBBER, M	17 Jun 1860	A47	WILSON, W	15 Oct 1960		F127
WEBBER, M	13 Oct 1995	N267	WILSON, W E	13 Mar 1964		F127
WEBBER, M A	17 Apr 1930	E102	WILSON-SMITH, N A	1996		C18
WEBBER, R	25 Jun 1843	A47	WINDHAM, H	29 May 1622		T45/46
WEBBER, W	6 May 1983	N42	WINDHAM, M	1 Sep 1620		T45/46
WEBBER, W J	[1914-1919] T35	p184	WINDSOR, E	3 Mar 1906		E104
WEILANDT, G M	13 May 1963	N42	WINDSOR, I	3 Feb 1910		E104
WERE, E	16 Dec 1869	D112	WINDSOR, L	29 Sep 1948		E97
WERE, J	12 Apr 1894	D136	WINDSOR, T	22 Jan 1931		E97
WERE, M	5 Nov 1878	D148	WINSLADE, R	24 Mar 1959		F76
WERE, S	20 Jul 1893	D136	*WINTER, J*	*16 Apr 2001*		*W42*
WERE, W	9 Oct 1820	D148	WINTER, S H	5 Dec 1895		D11
WESTALL, C E	*2 Dec 1967*	*N89*	WOOD, A E	1991		N152
WESTCOTT, S	18 Jan 1880	A12	WOOD, W W	21 Aug 1966		C44
WESTERN, L R	22 Aug 1993	W14	WOOD, W W	2 Oct 1974		C45
WESTERN, P D	12 Apr 1998	W14	WOODBURY, A	18 Dec 1957		F126
WHEBBY, T J	28 Jun 1933	E44	*WOODBURY, C*	*20 Aug 1975*		*F126*
WHELDON, R	[1939-1945] B4	p186	*WOODBURY, E C*	*B/26 Feb 1927*		*E166*
WHITE, A	*10 Feb 1971*	*N248*	WOODGATE, S J	7 Jan 1963		N37
WHITE, A L	-	*F117*	WOODGATE, W	5 Apr 1975		N37
WHITE, A T	*29 Oct 1960*	*N5*	WOODHOUSE, N C	9 Jan 1902		p168
WHITE, D	29 May 1976	N236a	WOODLAND, M	13 Jan 1950		F158
WHITE, D L M	1990	F79	WOOLAWAY, A R	20 Dec 1912		D28
WHITE, E G	1952	F79	WOOLAWAY, E	3 Oct 1941		F155
WHITE, F J	24 Apr 1956	F96	WOOLAWAY, E	14 Sep 1948		F155
WHITE, G	7 Jul 1906	E85	WOOLAWAY, R	11 Sep 1909		D28
WHITE, G	*B/2 Jul 1955*	*F117*	WRIGHT, E W	24 Jan 1952		F73
WHITE, J T	*23 Feb 1961*	*N13*	WRIGHT, F M	1977		F73
WHITE, K	29 May 1976	N236a	WRING, A H	26 Jun 1950		F72
WHITE, M A	21 Feb 1948	F96	WYATT, K	19 Feb 1981		N168
WHITE, M S	10 Jun 1935	E85	WYATT, M A	15 Jun 1886		D42
WHITE, P	29 May 1976	N236a	WYATT, R J	12 Mar 1946		F97
WHITE, V	1 Oct 1940	F86	WYATT, S	24 Jun 1956		F97
WHITE, W	25 May 1940	F86				
WHITFIELD, J	20 Dec 1905	E52				
WIGNEY, M R	28 May 1970	N252	**Y**			
WILDMAN, J	4 Dec 1876	D54	YANDLE, C	12 Feb 1893		D218
WILKES, I B	28 Apr 1907	E52	YANDLE, J	21 Oct 1887		D218
WILKES, J W	20 Dec 1905	E52	YEA, G	2 Oct 1811		T11
WILLIAMS, A	27 Aug 1916	E67	YEA, L	15 Jan 1811		T11
WILLIAMS, A H	9 Jan 1962	N25	YEA, W	18 Nov 1806		T11
WILLIAMS, C	8 Dec 1900	E68	YEANDLE, E	7 Sep 1965	N68	p168
WILLIAMS, G M	6 May 1978	N25	YEANDLE, S	12 Jun 1965	N68	p168
WILLIAMS, J	7 Apr 1853	p163	YOUNG, A	29 Jan 1866		p162
WILLIAMS, J	17 May 1919	E139	YOUNG, A J	14 Nov 1851		p162
WILLIAMS, M	27 Feb 1855	p163	YOUNG, A R	1 Feb 1871		p162
WILLIAMS, M A	21 May 1916	E67	YOUNG, E A	27 Sep 1901		p162
WILLIAMS, R F	17 Feb 1983	N160	YOUNG, J	26 Nov 1862		p162
WILLOUGHBY, C	2000	p162	YOUNG, M A	3 Nov 1902		p162
WILMOTT, F E	13 Dec 1967	N90	YOUNG, M H	28 Oct 1868		p162
WILMOTT, H T	9 May 1970	N90	YOUNG, R	-		p162
WILMOTT, L S R	21 Aug 1993	N125				
WILSON, A	*27 Mar 1967*	*N83*				
WILSON, A G	16 Mar 1998	N280				
WILSON, B H	1990	C19				
WILSON, G W M	1981	C19				
WILSON, I	22 Aug 1959	F108				
WILSON, J D	1985	N128				

Index